STATIUS
ACHILLEID

STATIUS
ACHILLEID

EDITED WITH INTRODUCTION,
APPARATUS CRITICUS AND NOTES
by
O.A.W. Dilke

New Introduction and Bibliography
by
Robert Cowan

BRISTOL
PHOENIX
PRESS

Cover illustration: based on a wall painting from Pompeii,
showing Oysseus and Diomedes unmasking Achilles on Scyros,
said to be after the Greek painter Athenion

Originally published in 1954 by
Cambridge University Press

New edition published in 2005 by
Bristol Phoenix Press
an imprint of The Exeter Press
Reed Hall, Streatham Drive,
Exeter, Devon, EX4 4QR
UK

Reprinted 2007

www.exeterpress.co.uk

This reprint is published with the permission of the
Syndicate of the Press of the University of Cambridge, Cambridge, England

British Library Cataloguing in Publication Data
A catalogue record for this book is available
from the British Library.

ISBN 978-1-904675-11-2

Printed in Great Britain by Booksprint

CONTENTS

INTRODUCTION

This introduction aims to explore some of the issues which it is important to consider when reading the *Achilleid*. The reader will, however, find few, if any, of them raised in Dilke's commentary. The concerns of Dilke, as of most commentators of his era, were primarily linguistic and philological. The immense scholarship and outstanding Latinity to be found in his annotations will help the reader to understand the language of the poem, to recognise points of its style and to see which other passages of Latin literature it resembles. His formidable *apparatus criticus* will show what alternatives to the printed text are contained in manuscripts and the conjectures of scholars. It is my hope that, given the diverse approaches of his commentary and of this new introduction, readers will find that each complements the other and both help them towards as full as possible an appreciation – and enjoyment – of this remarkable poem.

Statius and the *Achilleid*: why Achilles?

It might seem odd to write an epic poem about Achilles at the end of the first century CE. After all, there was already such a poem in existence, a poem which stood at the head of the Graeco-Roman epic, poetic, and even entire literary tradition – Homer's *Iliad,* whose subject matter was the wrath of Achilles. Yet this is exactly what the Roman poet Statius undertook to do when he began his *Achilleid*, a poem which would not just describe, as Homer had, the struggle with Hector but the hero's whole life, from his youth to his death at Troy.

He began but never completed it, so that all that has been handed down is one book and the first hundred and sixty odd lines of a second. This fragment, however, is one of the most enjoyable, interesting and innovative poems which have survived from antiquity. Statius describes the attempts of the sea-goddess Thetis to save her son from his predestined glorious death at Troy by concealing him on the island of Scyros disguised as a young girl. While there he falls in love with and seduces the daughter of King Lycomedes, Deidamia, before revealing his identity and his true self when Ulysses tempts him with weapons of war. As he sails to Troy with Ulysses and Diomedes, telling the story of his early life, the poem breaks off, presumably owing to Statius' death. All of this is described in vivid, ornate language, full of references to other texts. Three of the most striking characteristics of the poem are represented by three overlapping themes which this introduction sets out to explore in greater depth: the questions of gender, of genre and of intertextuality. However, it may be helpful at the outset to see just how the poem fits into Statius' poetic career.

Most of what we know of Statius' life comes from autobiographical details in his occasional poems, the *Silvae*. He was the son of a Neapolitan schoolmaster and poet. As a young man he cultivated patronage at Rome and reached the zenith of his career when he won, in about 90 CE, a prize at Domitian's Alban games for his poem on the emperor's German war. He failed, however, in the Capitoline games about four years later and appears to have taken the defeat badly. He retired to Naples and died at some point before the assassination of Domitian in 96.

Apart from the lost *Bellum Germanicum* and a pantomime script, *Agave*, his poetic works consisted of the epic *Thebaid*, five books of *Silvae* and the unfinished *Achilleid*. The *Silvae* are 'occasional' poems, written in a variety of metres, addressed to various wealthy patrons and dealing with varied subject matter: a statue of the emperor, a new road, descriptions of villas, animals and art-works, birthday and wedding poems, consolations on the deaths of loved ones and even a Pythonesque dead parrot![1] The *Thebaid* is an epic in twelve books describing the expedition of the Seven against Thebes and the fratricidal war between the sons of Oedipus, Polynices and Eteocles.[2] Despite its mythological subject matter and its grotesque, often fantastical narrative, its concerns are very contemporary and very Roman. Civil war was as much a recurrent feature of Roman history as it was of Theban mythology: it had recurred as recently as the 'year of four emperors' in 69 CE. The *furor* or frenzy, which drives the poem forward and its protagonists to destruction and crime, is the same as that which Lucan had depicted thirty years earlier in his epic on the Roman Civil War (*Bellum Civile*). Moreover, many have seen the depiction of the tyrannical Eteocles as a coded attack on either Domitian himself or on the principate in general. In any case, the *Thebaid* has a contemporary, political relevance, which few would see in the fragmentary *Achilleid*.

Although they have, as one might expect, many common features of style, the *Thebaid* and the *Achilleid* are very different poems. In the latter, at least in the part that was completed, there is none of that grimness which is the keynote of his earlier epic. This is not merely a change of direction but a self-conscious shift, a deliberate and explicit attempt to forge something different, not merely from the *Thebaid*, but from what one might tendentiously call the mainstream epic tradition. This writing of an epic which seems unlike epic is closely analogous to its portrayal of an Achilles who seems very unlike Achilles, a feminised, almost feminine figure whose presentation explores the limits of gender as the poem does those of genre.

Gender: why can't a man be more like a woman?

Gender does not simply correspond to biological sex. It depends, rather, on a number of criteria such as what one says and does, how one presents oneself. It is a product not of nature but of culture. If this thesis is widely accepted in many circles today, it can also be clearly shown to have been how the Romans thought about gender. Certain actions were manly, masculine, whether performed by a man or a woman; others womanly or feminine, regardless of their perpetrator. This negotiability of gender, the idea that its bounds might not be fixed, gave rise to a number of texts exploring those limits. In the Roman tradition it is Ovid who most frequently plays with ideas of gender and transgender. One thinks of the cross-dressing Hercules and Omphale in the *Fasti*; of the figures in the *Metamorphoses* who change from one gender to another – and sometimes back again – such as Iphis, Caeneus and Tiresias; or of the blending of Hermaphroditus and Salmacis into a being which is at once both genders and neither.[4] Such concerns are clearly important also in the *Achilleid*.

Achilles is the archetypal epic hero and that often means the same thing as being the archetypal masculine figure. His usual representation is as a warrior, a killing machine, whose natural habitat was on the battlefield. The Achilles with whom we are presented by Statius is a youth and specifically a mother's son. Long before we meet him in person, we see him through the worried eyes of Thetis, so that he is focalised as a child to be protected – not the heroic Achilles whom we might have expected.

Even when we eventually meet him, there is something of a surprise:

ille aderat multo sudore et pulvere maior,
et tamen arma inter festinatosque labores
dulcis adhuc visu: niveo natat ignis in ore
purpureus fulvoque nitet coma gratior auro.
necdum prima nova lanugine vertitur aetas,
tranquillaeque faces oculis et plurima vultu
mater inest: (1.159-65)

Despite the external masculine embellishments of dust, sweat and weapons, the boy beneath is described in very feminine terms, sweet with a snow white face, innocent of down, and hair more graceful than gold. Most tellingly – and both surprise and emphasis are provided by the enjambment – there is a lot of his mother in his appearance. This is the classic picture of the sexually ambiguous moment between childhood and adulthood. Achilles is neither man nor boy; he resembles a girl as much as a youth. That this is a specific moment in a trajectory of maturity is important. Though he is doomed to die, Achilles will grow into the masculine figure which the reader will recognise. In this respect, he differs from one of his closest intertexts,[6] Parthenopaeus.

Parthenopaeus is the youngest of the Seven who attack Thebes in the *Thebaid*. He too has an anxious mother, Atalanta, who knows that going to war will mean his death; he too is at that ambiguous age where his beauty is both masculine and feminine.[7] Behind both of them lies a further intertext, Virgil's warrior maiden, Camilla, who is also of ambiguous gender, a masculine Amazon, but one whose downfall is brought about by a 'womanly desire for plunder'.[8] By alluding to Camilla in his depiction of Parthenopaeus and to both in his depiction of Achilles, Statius further underlines the way in which each blurs the boundary between masculine and feminine. Camilla and Parthenopaeus, however, are cut off in their prime, virgins deflowered only by death.[9] Statius perhaps offers a commentary on these ephebes, these figures between childhood and adulthood, who never get the chance to pass beyond their *ephebeia*. He does this by showing us someone who does – Achilles.

Before he attains this maturity, before he moves from the tutelage of the centaur, Chiron,[10] and the protection of his mother, the ambiguity of his gender will be demonstrated yet further. When Thetis takes him to Scyros so that he may avoid being enlisted for the Trojan War, she persuades him to disguise himself as a woman, citing, in the classic Roman rhetorical style, *exempla* or paradigms of others who did likewise: Hercules at the court of Omphale; Bacchus in a trailing cloak of gold; Jupiter disguised as Diana for his rape of Callisto; the warrior Caeneus, who changed from man to woman and back again (1.260-4). It is not, however, her persuasion which wins him over but rather the sight of Deidamia (1.283-317). Thus it is masculine love for a woman which convinces him to compromise his masculinity. The complexity does not end there, for Deidamia and her sisters are themselves at the same ambiguous turning point from youth to maturity (1.290-2). They are, moreover, celebrating the rites of that most masculine of goddesses, Pallas Athene. Deidamia herself is compared both to the unambiguously feminine, erotic goddess Venus and to the virginal, androgynous Diana (1.293-6).[11] Both the watching lover and the desired object are problematised, as is the nature of desire.

Won over, Achilles allows his mother to dress him and turn him into a maiden. She softens (*mollit*, 326) his tough neck – an action which has overtones, not only of the change from masculine to feminine, but of the change from epic to elegy, of which more later.[12] She teaches him how to walk and moulds him like a sculptor moulding wax, a simile which seems to suggest that gender and even identity are not innate but can be moulded by external forces (1.330-4). Yet she need expend little effort; for there *is* something innately feminine, or at least innately ambiguous, about Achilles:

> *superest nam plurimus illi*
> *invita virtute decor, fallitque tuentes*
> *ambiguus tenuique latens discrimine sexus.*
> (1.335-7)

The tension between beauty and manliness – *virtus*, the Latin word for courage and valour derives from *vir* (man) – is maintained at this point; but it cannot be indefinitely maintained.

Two things conspire to disambiguate Achilles' gender: love and war. Deidamia discovers his secret, the hidden *vir* in Achilles, when he reveals his identity and his passion by raping her (1.560-674). Attitudes to rape in antiquity, especially within the expectations of mythological narrative, must be distinguished from contemporary ones.[13] It would probably be going too far to say that Achilles' action would have been regarded as entirely acceptable, though it would certainly not have attracted the condemnation it would today. The rape, violent though it is, is described and meant to be read as a result of his love for Deidamia. Statius at least does not go as far as Ovid who, in describing the scene in the *Ars Amatoria*, uses it as an *exemplum* for the justification of force as something desired by certain women.[14] However, the violence involved in the act is an important part of the revelation of Achilles' masculinity. He has intercourse with Deidamia because he is a man; and he does so with violence because he is a man.

Achilles' violence, of course, is key to the other factor which reveals (or determines) his true identity – war. The Trojan war re-enters the poem with appropriate violence as the whole of Greece makes ready for it (1.397-466). The seer Calchas has a confused vision of Achilles' hiding place (1.514-35). Ulysses and Diomedes are despatched to fetch him (1.538-59). The means which they employ are two-fold. First they sing the praises of war and glory to the assembled Scyrians, eliciting the desired reaction from Achilles, whose male passion for war reveals itself in his rapt attention while the other women turn their eyes away in fear. Indeed, he would have revealed himself then had not Deidamia – a protective lover in succession to a protective mother – dragged him away in a tight embrace (1.733-805). The second test is decisive: when the Greeks offer gifts to the maidens, all the daughters of Lycomedes choose wands, tambourines and girdles, to which 'the natural peacefulness of their sex led them'.[15] Achilles, by contrast, bellows, rolls his eyes and gazes at spear and shield (1.851-7). He is like a lion which forgets its domestication and reverts to nature (1.858-63). Achilles' gender, his masculinity, the poem seems to suggest, is a product of nature, not culture. In a masterly image, Statius has Achilles see, not his reflection, but himself (*se*) in the armour (1.864-6). It seems to reveal his true identity.

Achilles thus emerges from the sexually ambiguous phase between childhood and maturity; if this question of gender may also be read as one of genre, the poem emerges from generic ambiguity as a true epic. Achilles leaves behind both the childhood dependence on his mother and the elegiac devotion to his beloved; Troy, war and epic fill his heart (1.856-7). However, whether this apparent reassertion of the masculine, epic norm is sufficiently convincing to explain and nullify all the ambiguities of both gender and genre which have gone before must remain, at the very least, doubtful.

Genre: when is an epic not an epic?

The *Achilleid* is an epic poem.[16] The question of genre was one of immense importance to Roman literary theory.[17] Different genres were expected to have – or at least played with the expectation of having – certain more or less stereotypical characteristics: elegy would deal with love or mourning; satire would attack contemporary vices and follies in a low style; pastoral would evoke the loves and song-contest of shepherds; and so on. In terms of style, metre, language and subject matter, each genre had its own characteristic features. Epic, above all, was stereotyped as a martial, heroic, masculine genre, written in lofty, elevated style; it was the polar opposite of anything to do with love or the feminine. Horace characterised it as describing 'grim wars and the deeds of kings and generals', Virgil as being about 'kings and battles'.[18]

However, if we look at the poetic context in which Virgil gives this definition, we find that this rigid view of epic serves a specific rhetorical purpose. The poet tells how he was about to write an epic, about 'kings and battles', when Apollo tweaked his ear and forbade him (*Ecl.* 6.3-4). This example of the *recusatio* or polite refusal to write epic, alludes to the prologue of Callimachus' *Aetia,* where he too is prevented from writing epic. On both aesthetic and political grounds, miniaturist Callimacheans and ambivalent Augustans characterise – almost caricature – epic as an ossified, stereotyped genre whose only possible form was the sprawling, bloated 'big book', its only possible content endless battles. This characterisation of epic as a means of self-definition, of asserting what one's own genre is not, features strongly in genres such as elegy and satire. We need only read Juvenal's first satire or any of a multitude of Ovid's elegies to witness their self-construction as, respectively, relevant cutting-edge social comment and small-scale personal love poetry, both in polar opposition to a monolithic picture of epic.

Such an austere, battle-filled, men-only epic never, of course, existed. If we turn to the *Odyssey* at the head of the classical epic tradition, we find a poem which has few battles and whose central character, king though he is, fights for the very personal domestic aims of returning home and re-establishing his household. The *Aeneid* refutes both Juvenal and Ovid by dealing with contemporary Augustan politics and by devoting considerable space to the love story of Dido and Aeneas. Only the *Iliad*, complex though it is, could be with any justice characterised in the sort of stereotyped terms which we have seen. Significantly, it is the *Iliad* with which the *Achilleid*, like many other epics, engages, compares and contrasts itself. For it is not only other genres that create a phantom of the classic martial epic against which to react. Epic poets themselves revel in self-consciously pushing the bounds of what is acceptable in their chosen genre. Half way through his epic, Apollonius of Rhodes invokes a different muse to help him describe the 'un-epic' love story of Jason and Medea (*Argonautica* 3.1-5). Virgil in the *Aeneid* plays with various modes, the elegiac, the tragic, the pastoral and others, which counterpoint the poem's onward march, its epic teleology; arguably the most extreme example is Ovid's *Metamorphoses*, whose style and subject matter have led many to question whether it is an epic at all.[19]

The reasons for this generic play are various. Epic has been called a totalising genre,[20] one which attempts to subsume all other genres – indeed all of human (and divine) life – within its own capacious bounds. As such, it can safely contain these apparently 'un-epic' features within itself, since, if epic is everything, then everything is epic. More generally, all genres find a dynamic vitality by stretching and questioning their boundaries. Only by running the risk of being un-epic can one explore what it is to be epic. Moreover, genre is not simply a technical literary category; it carries with it ideological significance. For the Roman love poets, to write elegy rather than epic was to subscribe to a counter-cultural lifestyle which privileged the personal over the political, the private over the public, love over war. The epic mode within epic can be made to stand for the onward march of history, the history of the winners; any generic opposition to this epic mode opposes also that ideology.[21] All of these issues are at play in the *Achilleid*.

The poem has a number of straightforwardly epic characteristics: it is written in dactylic hexameters, the metre of epic since Homer, and of Roman epic since Ennius; its lofty style contains many of the features which mark out epic from 'lower' genres – elevated diction, elaborate similes, grand patronymics and periphrases; its subject matter appears on the surface to be in the grand tradition of Homer, Apollonius, Virgil and Statius' own *Thebaid* – war, heroes and gods who intervene in human affairs.[22] Of course, to subvert a genre and explore its limits, it is essential to be inside that genre. A poem which shared no features whatsoever with the epic tradition would be in no position to examine and question that tradition and its own place within it. How, then, does the *Achilleid* play with its epic and un-epic qualities? As so often with almost all works of literature, especially classical ones, it is useful to examine how the poem begins, how it sets out its generic stall.

The proem, in true epic style, declares the subject of the poem. Like the *Odyssey* and the *Aeneid*, it is to be about a man, one who is 'great-hearted', heroic, epic, and one who is referred to not by name but by a grand, epic patronymic – 'grandson of Aeacus'. The inspiration is to come from the epic Muse (1.3).[23] The poet then steps into his own poem to justify his choice of subject and to place it in generic context. He knows that Homer has already made Achilles famous; however, there is much more still to be sung – Statius will give us the *whole* Achilles. This work is to be an improvement on the *Iliad* and a sequel to his own *Thebaid*, which, he prays to Apollo, has not used up his sources of epic inspiration. Moreover, Achilles himself is arguably the quintessential epic hero – warlike, masculine, possessing all the qualities not merely of the epic hero but of epic itself. Yet there are already elements here which might question the epic quality of Statius' undertaking. The use of the word *amor* (1.5), albeit to describe the desire to sing of Achilles' exploits, jars in the context and hints at an unexpectedly erotic tone. More significantly, the poet's desire to 'lead the youth through the whole tale of Troy' uses the word *deducere*, a metaphor from spinning, but one adopted by the Callimacheans as the essence of fine, distilled, un-epic poetry. It is a *deductum ... carmen* which Apollo commands Virgil to sing instead of epic in the *Eclogue* 6 passage cited above, while Ovid's project in the proem to his *Metamorphoses* is to lead down (*deducere*) his poem to his own times. Already the *Achilleid*'s epic nature is problematised and its affiliation to Callimachean and especially Ovidian poetics suggested.

Certainly the subject matter of the completed part of the poem is far from the stereotype of 'conventional' epic. Instead of Achilles the man – the *vir* whose exploits Homer sang, analogous to the *Aeneid*'s *virum*, and the *andra* of the *Odyssey* – we have Achilles the boy, the youth on the verge of manhood. Instead of Achilles waging war at Troy, we have him hiding on Scyros. Instead of the masculine, epic Achilles, we have a feminised, almost transgendered Achilles, who all too easily passes as a girl among the masculinised, Pallas-worshipping females at the court of Lycomedes. The principal theme of the first book and the surviving fifth of the second is not war but love, the subject matter not of epic but of elegy.

The poem is not merely un-epic. It actively strives against being epic. Thetis in particular acts as a delaying, diverting force, attempting to derail the narrative from its destined epic track towards Achilles' glory and death. In this respect, she has much in common with other figures in the Roman epic tradition who work to retard the narrative, to stop the poem from reaching its *telos*, its epic goal. Pompey in Lucan's epic *Bellum Civile* may be read similarly; for the narrator has him ceaselessly delaying and trying to prevent the poem's march to the horrific *telos* of civil war and the end of the republic.[24] Even more closely related is the Juno of the *Aeneid*, whom Thetis specifically fails to imitate; for she cannot persuade Neptune to brew a storm as her forebear had Aeolus (1.30-94; cf. *Aen.* 1.34-123). The queen of the gods repeatedly attempts to delay the epic *telos* of her hated Trojans' arrival in Italy and Aeneas' establishment of the Roman people. Thetis, however, does not merely attempt to stop or delay the epic narrative. She attempts to divert it into another genre, to save her son from a martial, epic death at Troy by hiding him in a peaceful, almost pastoral idyll on Scyros, by feminising Achilles, by elegising the *Achilleid*.

We can only speculate as to how the *Achilleid* would have continued, whether the erotic tone would have persisted, or whether the martial norm (which seems to be reasserted through the intervention of Ulysses and Diomedes) would have retained its generic dominance. However, the conventional alignment of epic with war and the masculine in opposition to elegy with its erotic, feminine qualities might hint at the latter. We have seen that the text explores the issue of gender as Achilles moves through the ambiguous, ephebic phase between childhood and adulthood, but that the end appears to be a reassertion of the norm, of – if you will – 'nature', as it is constructed in the text; for he throws off his feminine disguise in favour of the weapons of war and abandons marital love with Deidamia for martial glory at Troy. Were we to push the text hard and adopt a 'strong' reading of the *Achilleid*'s engagement with the question of genre, it would be possible to read Achilles as an embodiment of epic (or of 'the epic'), as hero, text and genre explore, in their youth, their sexual and generic ambiguity as a step on the path to personal and poetic maturity. As Hinds says of the few certainties about what the rest of the poem would have been like, 'the *idea* of an essentially epic epic would have emerged stronger, not weaker, at the end of the *Achilleid*'s innovative negotiations with the genre.'[25] Unlike the other genres which define themselves in opposition to an externalised stereotype of epic, epic itself can only achieve a similar sort of self-definition by internalising generic conflict and leaving its readers to draw their own conclusions.

Intertextuality: haven't I read you before somewhere?

It is not only in the broad field of generic affiliation that the *Achilleid* is problematic and demanding of interpretation. It also demands to be read in relationship with other specific texts, a practice commonly known as intertextuality.

All texts are intertextual.[26] The very language in which they are written, the events and characters which they describe, all trigger connections and comparisons with other texts, written earlier or later. The classical tradition, however, tended to revel in its own intertextuality. Almost all Roman literature was derived in some way or other from Greek forebears; within the Roman tradition itself texts echo, evoke and allude to their predecessors. This practice has sometimes been interpreted as a sterile exercise in little more than glorified plagiarism; at best some would see it as an erudite game in which author and reader collude in creating and identifying obscure allusions to more or less obscure texts. The epic poets of the Flavian era, Statius and his contemporaries, Valerius Flaccus and Silius Italicus, have in the past been vilified for servile imitation of their epic predecessors, most notably Virgil.

More recently, however, intertextuality has been seen as a creative process.[27] It is a way of generating meaning by positioning oneself in relationship with other texts, at the same time commenting on and interpreting those earlier texts. Thus, when reading Thetis' request in the *Achilleid* that Neptune rouse a storm to stop Paris, the reader thinks both of Juno entreating Aeolus in *Aeneid* 1 and of Thetis herself asking Zeus to give Achilles glory in *Iliad* 1. This relationship, this intertextuality contributes to our reading of Thetis' action, in comparison and in contrast with the earlier episodes. Furthermore, we think differently about the Virgilian and Homeric intertexts precisely *because* Statius alludes to them and especially because he alludes to them both at the same time.[28] It might even be argued that Statius draws attention to his own allusion, to his own place in the epic tradition as he 'self-consciously signals a moment of belatedness – with Neptune playing the rôle of *secundi ... Iovis* to the "original" Jove of the *Iliad*.'[29] The effect of intertextuality is, of course, complex, unpredictable and personal. Different readers will respond in different ways to intertextual relationships, just as they will to any other feature of a text. *How* we compare Thetis with her Homeric equivalent and with Virgil's Juno cannot be fixed or predicted.

It is not surprising to find such self-conscious and even advertised intertextuality in a Statian epic. His *Thebaid* is not only full of allusions to a myriad of texts, most importantly the *Aeneid*, the *Metamorphoses*, the *Bellum Civile*, and Attic and Senecan tragedy; but on two occasions it specifically cites the *Aeneid* as a model, one which it disingenuously refuses to challenge. Statius' young, doomed heroes, Hopleus and Dymas, are offered the possibility of immortal glory alongside their Virgilian models, Nisus and Euryalus (*Thebaid* 10.445-8; cf. *Aen.* 9.446-9). That this allusion is literary rather than mythical may be confirmed by the fact that, in mythological chronology, the expedition of the Seven against Thebes was in the generation before the Trojan War; indeed one of the *Thebaid*'s main characters, Tydeus, is Diomedes' father. The 'real' Nisus and Euryalus have therefore not yet been born, though in the literary tradition they have existed for over a century. At the very end of the work, there is a unique coda in which the poet addresses his own poem and urges it not to try to rival the 'divine *Aeneid*' but to follow at a distance (*Thebaid* 12.816-7). Although this modesty is disingenuous and part of a strategy of self-fashioning, it prepares us fully for the direct and explicit engagement in the *Achilleid* proem with Homer's *Iliad*. Statius is aware of what had gone before and he is going to do something different, bigger and better. We the readers are meant to recognise this self-positioning and read the *Achilleid* 'against' the *Iliad* and its other intertexts.

Homer and Virgil are privileged intertexts. They stand as the canonical epic poets of the Greek and Roman tradition. As such, they represent that epic tradition and it is in relationship with them that the *Achilleid* fashions itself both in generic terms, as we have already seen, and more generally within the literary tradition. The language of the *Aeneid* pervades the poem and echoes, allusions, what you will, are duly noted – albeit without comment – in Dilke's scholarly commentary. The belated epic foreshadows and predicts events which are described or looked back on in the earlier poems. The prophecies of Proteus (reported by Thetis, 1.32-8) and Neptune (1.81-94) both relate episodes in the Trojan War and its aftermath. Neptune in particular, though refusing to raise a storm now, looks forward to the time when he, in his Homeric guise of Poseidon, will persecute the eponymous hero of the *Odyssey* :

> *dabo tollere fluctus,*
> *cum reduces Danai nocturnaque signa Caphereus*
> *exseret et dirum pariter quaeremus Ulixen.*

(1.92-4)

The future tenses playfully acknowledge that these events are in the mythological future, although they were related by Homer centuries before.

An alternative model of epic is offered by Ovid.[30] His *Metamorphoses* also deals with ambiguities of gender and identity, with love and its complications; it also represents an exploration of the limits of the epic genre. Numerous points of intertextuality between it and the *Achilleid*, especially their depictions of ambiguous gender, serve to align Statius' poem with an Ovidian model of epic.[31] Intertextuality here colours the whole poetic world of the *Achilleid*. It is not only Ovid's epic with which Statius engages. The earlier poet, himself preoccupied with questions of genre, described Achilles' stay on Scyros not only at *Met.* 13.162-70 but also in his elegiac, didactic poem on the art of love, the *Ars Amatoria* (1.681-704). Statius' comparatively oblique description of Achilles' rape of Deidamia demands to be read against the latter account. The flexibility of intertextuality means that the reader can either contrast Ovid's harsh violence with Statius' subtlety or take the allusion to the *Ars* as a signal to read in all the brutality which the *Achilleid* leaves unstated.

Various other texts might be considered privileged intertexts or, in less dynamic terms, sources. As so often with the largely lost literature of the classical world, many are no longer extant: Sophocles and Euripides each wrote a tragedy on the subject called *The Scyrians*; a fragmentary idyll by the Hellenistic poet, Bion, mentions Achilles' concealment. A surviving tragedy by Seneca, the *Troades*, refers to the episode and Fantham has convincingly argued that the *Achilleid* alludes to other parts of that play, most notably to Andromache's attempted concealment of her son Astyanax from the Greeks.[32]

One other text which demands particular attention, however, is Catullus 64.[33] This *epyllion* or short epic[34] describes the wedding of Achilles' parents, Peleus and Thetis, though much of it consists of a lengthy *ecphrasis* or description of a coverlet depicting the story of Ariadne and Theseus, followed by the song of the *Parcae* or Fates, predicting the Trojan War and the career of Achilles. That Statius should allude to it is, therefore, far from surprising. In terms of subject-matter, it deals with the early life of Achilles and in terms of style, it is another exploration of the limits of epic, an un-epic epic. There are various close verbal echoes to which Dilke draws attention in his commentary.[35] The most striking of these include the re-use of the *Parcae*'s own prophecy, first by Neptune, then by Achilles himself, and finally in the last line of the first book, which follows the young hero's sworn promise to return to Deidamia: *inrita ventosae rapiebant verba procellae* (1.961). This is a very clear allusion to Theseus' promises to Ariadne in Catullus: *irrita ventosae linquens promissa procellae* (64.59). Once again, the reader is invited to choose from a range of possibilities: does the allusion mean that Achilles will callously abandon Deidamia as Theseus did Ariadne? Does the implication – that she will be abandoned and Achilles' vows prove vain – suggest that the erotic tone would have persisted in the unwritten parts of the poem, perhaps with Briseis as a rival for Achilles' affections?[36] Does the slight alteration in sense suggest Achilles' poignant lack of control and of foreknowledge of his own fate in *contrast* with Theseus? It is the nature of intertextuality to leave the choice to the reader.

Robert Cowan
University of Bristol
2004

NOTES

1. Good introductions to the *Silvae* include: Hardie, A. *Statius and the* Silvae: *Poets, Patrons and Epideixis in the Graeco-Roman World* (Francis Cairns, Liverpool, 1983); the introduction to the edition and commentary by Coleman, K.M. on *Silvae IV* (Oxford University Press, 1988; repr. Bristol Classical Press, 2000); Newlands, C.E. *Statius'* Silvae *and the Poetics of Empire* (Cambridge University Press, 2002).

2. There is now a range of excellent criticism on the *Thebaid*, among which good starting points are: Vessey, D.W.T.C. *Statius and the Thebaid* (Cambridge University Press, 1973); Feeney, D.C. *The Gods in Epic. Poets and Critics of the Classical Tradition* (Oxford University Press, 1990); Hardie (1993).

3. The exception is Benker (1987) who reads the *Achilleid* as a critique of Domitian.

4. Hercules: *Fasti* 2.305-58; Iphis: *Met.* 9.666-797; Caeneus: *Met.* 12.168-209 and 459-535; Tiresias: *Met.* 3.316-38; Hermaphroditus: *Met.* 4.285-88.

5. On the motif of Thetis' anxiety, see especially Mendelsohn (1990).

6. For intertextuality in the *Achilleid*, see xvii-xx below.

7. His name is Greek for 'face of a maiden'. The young hero and his mother's concern for him are introduced at *Thebaid* 4.246-344; omens of his death on the battlefield and their fulfilment at 9.570-907. For further comparison of Achilles and Parthenopaeus, as well as other ephebic young men in the works of Statius, see La Penna (1996).

8. Virgil, *Aen.* 11.782. Camilla is introduced at the end of the catalogue of Latin allies at 7.803-17 and her *aristeia* occupies most of 11.498-867.

9. On this motif in the *Aeneid*, see Fowler, D. 'Vergil on Killing Virgins' in Michael Whitby, P. Hardie and Mary Whitby (eds) *Homo Viator. Classical Essays for John Bramble* (Bristol Classical Press, 1987).

10. On the rôle of Chiron and parallels with father figures in the *Silvae*, see Fantham (1999).

11. It may well be significant that the description of Achilles at 1.159-65, quoted above, is followed by a simile comparing him to the androgynous twin of Diana, Apollo. It is as Achilles' sister, that Thetis presents him to Lycomedes at 1.350.

12. On the generic implications of *mollis/durus*, see Kennedy, D. *The Arts of Love: Five Studies in the Discourse of Roman Love Elegy* (Cambridge University Press, 1993) 32-3.

13. For a forceful argument against accepting the historicising view of rape in Latin poetry, see Richlin, A. 'Reading Ovid's Rapes' in *Pornography and Representation in Greece and Rome* (Oxford University Press, 1991).

14. Ovid *Ars Amatoria* 1.681-704. See further below.

15. *quas sexus iners naturaque ducit*, 1.848. I translate the phrase as a hendiadys, though it is just as potent taken as 'nature *and* their sex'.

16. On the *Achilleid*'s generic play, see especially: Koster (1979); Barchiesi (1996); Hinds (2000).

17. Key studies are: Cairns, F. *Generic Composition in Greek and Roman Poetry* (Edinburgh University Press, 1972); Conte, G.B. *The Rhetoric of Imitation: Genre and Poetic Memory in Virgil and Other Latin Poets*, tr. Charles Segal (Ithaca, NY, 1986).

18. *res gestae regumque ducumque et tristia bella*: Horace *Ars Poetica* 73; *reges et proelia*: Virgil *Eclogues* 6.3.

19. See Hinds (1998) 135-42 for an argument that the *Achilleid* '*is* an epic: a markedly *Ovidian*, markedly *metamorphic* epic' (136-7).

20. Hardie (1993) 3.

21. The argument is crudely put to make the point. For more sophistication, see Quint, D. *Epic and Empire: Politics and Generic Form from Virgil to Milton* (Princeton University Press, 1993).

22. Lucan's *Bellum Civile* is the principal exception to the epic use of the 'divine apparatus' but the shocking nature of that omission makes it clear that it is very much the exception which proves the rule.

23. *diva, refer.* Again the epic tradition is almost unvarying from Homer to Silius Italicus in its invocation of the muse or muses. The exception once more is Lucan, who slyly comments that only Nero is suitable to inspire him to sing his epic of civil war (*Bellum Civile* 1.66).

24. On the Pompeian aspect to the narrative voice of *Bellum Civile*, see Masters, J. *Poetry and Civil War in Lucan's* Bellum Civile. (Cambridge University Press, 1992).

25. Hinds (2000) 244.

26. Of the vast bibliography on intertextuality in Roman poetry, particularly to be recommended are: Conte (see n. 17 above); Hinds (1998); Fowler, D. 'On the Shoulders of Giants: Intertextuality and Classical Studies' *MD* 39 (1997) 13-34, repr. in *Roman Constructions: Readings in Postmodern Latin* (Oxford University Press, 2000).

27. For the creative intertextuality of the Flavian epicists, see especially Hardie (1993).

28. On allusion as commentary and combinatory intertextuality in particular, see Hardie, P. 'Flavian Epicists on Virgil's Epic Technique' *Ramus* 18 (1989) 2-30.

29. Hinds (1998) 96, referring to 1.48-9.

30. See especially Rosati, *Momenti* (1994); Hinds (1998) 135-44.

31. See Hinds (1998) for references.

32. Fantham (1979).

33. See especially: Lauletta (1993); Hinds (1998) 124-9.

34. The short epic does not seem to have been considered a generic category in antiquity and the word *epyllion* did not then exist in that sense. However, enough features are shared by a number of Hellenistic and Neoteric poems for it to remain a useful term with which to discuss them.

35. See Dilke's notes, especially at 1.85, 1.86 f., 1.960 and 2.111.

36. A possibility suggested by Rosati, *Achilleide* (1994) 54-7.

SELECT BIBLIOGRAPHY

Commentaries since Dilke

Stace, *Achilléide*. texte établi & trad. par J. Méheust (Les Belles Lettres, Paris, 1971).

Stazio, *Achilleide*. introduzione, traduzione e note di Gianpiero Rosati (Biblioteca Universale Rizzoli, Milano, 1994).

Books and articles

Aricò, G. 'L'*Achilleide* di Stazio: Tradizione litteraria e invenzione narrativa' *ANRW* II.32.5 (1986) 2925-64.

——'Rileggendo l'*Achilleide*' in F. Delarue, S. Georgacopoulou, P. Laurens and A-M. Taisne (eds) *Epicedion: Homage à Publius Papinius Statius*. La Licorne 96 (Poitiers, 1996) 185-99.

Barchiesi, A. 'La guerra di Troia non avrà luogo: il proemio dell'*Achilleide* di Stazio' *AION* (*filol*) 18 (1996) 45-62.

Benker, M. *Achill und Domitian, Herrscherkritik in der* Achilleis *des Statius* (Erlangen-Nürnberg, 1987).

Burck, E. 'Die *Achilleis* des Statius' in E. Burck (ed.) *Das römische Epos* (Darmstadt, 1979) 300-58.

Dilke, O.A.W. '*Magnus Achilles* and Statian Baroque' *Latomus* 22 (1963) 498-503.

Fantham E. 'Statius' Achilles and his Trojan model' *CQ* 29 (1979) 457-62.

——'*Chironis exemplum*: on teachers and surrogate fathers in Achilleid and Siluae' *Hermathena* 167 (1999) 59-70.

Hardie, P. *The Epic Successors of Virgil: A Study in the Dynamics of a Tradition* (Cambridge University Press, 1993).

Hinds, S. *Allusion and Intertext: Dynamics of Appropriation in Roman Poetry* (Cambridge University Press, 1998).

——'Essential Epic: Genre and Gender from Macer to Statius' in M. Depew and D.D. Obbink (eds) *Matrices of Genre: Authors, Canons, and Society* (Harvard University Press, Cambridge, Mass., 2000) 221-44.

Johnson, W. R. 'Information and Form: Homer, Achilles and Statius' in S.M. Oherhelman, V. Kelly and R.J. Golsan (eds) *Epic and*

Epoch: Essays on the Interpretation and History of a Genre. (Lubbock, Texas, 1994) 25-39.

Juhnke, H., *Homerisches in römischer Epik flavischer Zeit. Untersuchungen zu Szenennachbildungen und Strukturentsprechungen in Statius'* Thebais *und* Achilleis *und in Silius'* Punica (Beck, Munich, 1972).

Koster, S. 'Liebe und Krieg in der *Achilleis* des Statius' *WJA* 5 (1979) 189-208.

La Penna, A. 'Modelli efebici nella poesia di Stazio' in F. Delarue, S. Georgacopoulou, P. Laurens and A-M. Taisne (eds) *Epicedion. Homage à Publius Papinius Statius.* La Licorne 96 (Poitiers, 1996) 161-84.

Lauletta, M. 'L'imitazione di Catulló e l'ironia nell'*Achilleide* di Stazio' *Latomus* 52 (1993) 84-97.

Mendelsohn, D. 'Empty Nest, Abandoned Cave: Maternal Anxiety in *Achilleid* 1' *ClAnt* 9 (1990) 295-308.

Rosati, G. 'L'*Achilleide* di Stazio: un'epica dell'ambiguità' *Maia* 44 (1992) 233-66; repr. with minor alterations as the introduction to his edn (1994).

——'Momenti e forme della fortuna antica di Ovidio: l'*Achilleide* di Stazio' in M. Picone and B. Zimmermann (eds) *Ovidius redivivus: von Ovid zu Dante* (M & P, Stuttgart, 1994) 43-62.

PREFACE

An annotated edition of Statius' *Achilleid* needs no apology, since none such exists in English and those published during this century are in many respects far from satisfactory. Whereas it is clear that in the Middle Ages the epic works of Statius were read and admired, modern readers too often limit their knowledge of the poet to the *Silvae*, a type of poem in which, as Quintilian observed, the defects of hasty composition are still visible even after a process of polishing. Only some 1125 lines of the projected epic on the life of Achilles, evidently all that Statius wrote, remain to us; but the Scyros story, which occupies the major part of this fragment, possesses a freshness and vividness of language only rarely encountered in the twelve books of the *Thebaid*.

My thanks are due in the first place to C. J. Fordyce, R. D. Williams and G. P. Goold, who by their suggestions and queries have helped me very considerably, and secondly to those in charge of the manuscripts at the Bibliothèque Nationale, Paris, and the libraries at Eton, Munich and Wolfenbüttel, where I was able to make a full collation of the principal manuscripts. Some microfilms of manuscripts were kindly lent to me by Mr Williams.

O. A. W. D.

GLASGOW 1953

INTRODUCTION

1. LIFE OF STATIUS

PUBLIUS PAPINIUS STATIUS[1] was born at Naples about the middle of the first century A.D.[2] His father,[3] a freeborn citizen, but of an impoverished family,[4] had moved there from Velia (Elea or Hyele). In Naples he opened a school attended by pupils coming from regions as far away as Lucania and Apulia; Statius enumerates the Greek poets whose works were taught there, and praises his prose renderings of Homer. He became known as a poet and rhetorician, and won prizes for poetry at the Augustalia in Naples.[5] He wrote a poem on the burning of the Capitol in the Civil War of A.D. 69, and intended writing one on the eruption of Vesuvius (A.D. 79).

The son thus grew up in a poetic and rhetorical atmosphere, evidently receiving his schooling and poetic training entirely from his father. He was taught to regard Virgil as the great master, who should be imitated but could not be rivalled;[6] and he may often, like Silius Italicus,[7] have visited Virgil's tomb outside Naples.[8] His early poetic efforts were crowned with success at the Neapolitan Augustalia[9] in or before A.D. 78.

The earlier years of Statius' life are not easy to follow. It appears from *Silv.* v, 3, 203 ff., 215 ff. that his father recited in Rome in A.D. 69 his poem on the Capitol, and that Statius himself gave readings of his poetry there in the presence of his father; but at what date he

---

[1] The name Sursulus (or from the tenth century Surculus) found in the Middle Ages arose from a confusion with the rhetorician of Toulouse, L. Statius Ursulus (*fl.* A.D. 56).

[2] Various dates between A.D. 45 and 61 have been conjectured; about A.D. 50 is the plausible conjecture of G. Giri, *Riv. Fil.* XXXV (1907), 440.

[3] Our information about the poet's father comes from *Silv.* v, 3.

[4] The assumption that he had equestrian status is not supported by *Silv.* v, 3, 116–20 (see *Proc. Class. Assoc.* L (1953), 'Communications'); but that passage implies a certain respectability and local standing.

[5] It does not necessarily follow from *Silv.* v, 3, 141 ff. that Statius' father visited Greece and won prizes at the Pythian, Nemean and Isthmian games, and H. Frère (*Silvae*, ed. Budé, 198 n. 6) denies this.

[6] *Th.* XII, 816 f.; cf. Dante, *Purg.* XXI, 97 f.   [7] Pliny, *Ep.* III, 7, 8.

[8] We may dismiss as improbable the attempts which have been made to account for 'the popular belief enshrined in Dante's *Purgatorio* that Statius was a convert to Christianity' (*Silvae*, tr. D. A. Slater, p. 13) by supposing that he met St Paul at Virgil's tomb.

[9] *Silv.* v, 3, 225 ff.

3

ceased to live in Naples is not clear. Either he or his father acquired, before A.D. 80, the small estate at Alba to which he refers in *Silv.* IV, 5, 1 f.; III, 1, 61 ff. He was still 'in the prime of his life'[1] when he married Claudia, a widow who had evidently lived mostly in Rome;[2] her previous husband, by whom she had one daughter, was a 'minstrel'.[3] As an aspiring and impecunious[4] poet, Statius found it in his interests to cultivate the friendship of wealthy patrons, though he did not attach himself to any one particular *patronus*: those whom he addresses in the *Silvae* were his friends at the later period when the poems were written, but some may have helped him rise to fame.

In about A.D. 80 Statius' father, who had helped him start the *Thebaid*, died at the age of sixty-five or just over.[5] This epic took Statius twelve years to complete,[6] and was probably finished in A.D. 91–2;[7] but from time to time during this period he gave readings from it. We may date to before A.D. 83, when the actor Paris was put to death, the famous lines of Juvenal:[8]

> curritur ad vocem iucundam et carmen amicae
> Thebaidos, laetam cum fecit Statius urbem
> promisitque diem: tanta dulcedine captos
> adficit ille animos tantaque libidine volgi
> auditur; sed cum fregit subsellia versu,
> esurit, intactam Paridi nisi vendit Agaven.

These show the struggling poet writing a mime called 'Agave' on the theme covered by Euripides' *Bacchae*, and, with his pleasant voice, attracting good and appreciative audiences by his recitations of the *Thebaid*.

It may have been in A.D. 90 that he won a prize at the Alban contest introduced by Domitian, his poem being a panegyric on the

---

[1] *Florentibus annis* (*Silv.* III, 5, 23)—perhaps about the age of thirty.

[2] In *Silv.* V, 1 epist. she is a friend of Priscilla, wife of Abascantus; in III, 5 she needs much persuasion to come to Naples, which she does not know.

[3] *Silv.* III, 5, 52 f. *canori coniugis*, 54 ff.

[4] Cf. Juv. VII, 82 ff., quoted below.

[5] *Silv.* V, 3, 233 f., 253 f.   [6] *Th.* XII, 811 f.

[7] It is true that in *Silv.* IV, 4, 87 ff. (A.D. 95) he writes as if the *Thebaid* had only just been completed; but the words in *Silv.* I epist. *adhuc pro Thebaide mea, quamvis me reliquerit, timeo*, together with the evidence of *Th.* I, 17 ff. (cf. Frère, pref. to *Silvae*, pp. xiv ff.), clearly point to an earlier date.

[8] Juv. VII, 82 ff.; cf. Dante, *Purg.* XXI, 88 ff.

German and Dacian expeditions of the emperor.[1] Domitian also gave Statius land at Alba on which there was a stream.[2] With such distinguished patronage from one who flattered himself as a poet,[3] Statius was able to attract attention; and while never committing himself to any long poem on Domitian, he constantly addresses him with the adulation common at this period.[4]

The *Silvae*, five books of occasional poems, mostly in hexameters, but three in hendecasyllables and (less successfully) one each in alcaics and sapphics, were written between A.D. 89 and the poet's death. It is from them that almost all our details of Statius' life come: during the Middle Ages, and until the rediscovery of the *Silvae* by Poggio in 1417, virtually nothing biographical was known. In the period covered by the *Silvae*, Statius has reached the position of an established poet. He once has the privilege of dining with the emperor;[5] he can count among his friends or patrons such distinguished names as the wealthy freedman Claudius Etruscus; the praetor Vitorius Marcellus; C. Vibius Maximus, prefect of Egypt in A.D. 104, who evidently helped him with the publication of the *Thebaid*;[6] Domitian's secretary Flavius Abascantus; and a young friend Crispinus, son of Vettius Bolanus, governor of Asia under Vespasian. In the literary world his contacts were evidently scantier. He was on friendly terms with Lucan's widow Polla Argentaria, and writes a poem in honour of the anniversary of Lucan's birthday;[7] Vibius Maximus, mentioned above, was a historian;[8] but whereas Statius and Martial had a number of friends in common, and often write on similar themes, it appears from the silence of each about the other that they were not on speaking terms.

It is clear from *Silv.* III, 5 that Statius' married life was a happy one. He had no children, but laments bitterly the death of a favourite house-slave whom he had freed.[9] A more lasting source of worry,

---

[1] *Silv.* III, 5, 28 ff., reading *tu* (Politian) for *ter*; IV, 2, 65 ff.; IV, 5, 22 ff.; V, 3, 227 ff.

[2] *Silv.* III, 1, 62 f. Alternatively this may mean that he had land at Alba, on to which Domitian allowed him to draw water from an aqueduct.

[3] See note on *Ach.* I, 14 ff.

[4] *Th.* I, 22 ff.; *Silv.* I epist. 'a Iove principium'; I, 1, 94 ff.; II epist. *sacratissimo Imperatori*; IV, 1; IV, 2, 57 ff.; IV, 3, 128 ff.; *Ach.* I, 14 ff. Cf. F. Sauter, *Röm. Kaiserkult bei Martial u. St.* (1934), 54; K. Scott, *Imperial Cult under the Flavians* (1936), 133; Lily R. Taylor, *Divinity of the Roman Emperor* (1931).   [5] *Silv.* IV, 2 (A.D. 94–5).

[6] *Silv.* IV epist.   [7] *Silv.* II, 7.   [8] *Silv.* IV, 7, 53 ff.   [9] *Silv.* V, 5.

however, was his failure in the Agon Capitolinus,[1] probably in summer 94. It may have been partly this and partly a serious illness[2] that made him decide in 94–5 to move from Rome to Naples. But a compromise may have been reached between his plans and Claudia's desire to stay in Rome; for in Books IV and V of the *Silvae* he appears sometimes to be writing from Rome, sometimes from Naples.[3] His death must have occurred about winter 95–6, certainly before Domitian's death in September 96.

2. DATE OF COMPOSITION
OF THE *ACHILLEID*

In *Silv.* IV, 7, 23, Statius, writing in spring or summer 95, laments that without his friend C. Vibius Maximus his Muse is sluggish, *et primis meus ecce metis haeret Achilles*. In *Silv.* IV, 4, 93 f. (summer 95) he writes:

> nunc vacuos crines alio subit infula nexu:
> Troia quidem magnusque mihi temptatur Achilles;

though he continues by wondering if he should not compose an epic on the exploits of Domitian (cf. *Ach.* I, 14 ff.). In *Silv.* V, 2, 162 f. and V, 5, 36 f. (A.D. 95–6) he refers to recitations of the *Achilleid*, i.e. of a portion of it, and to *novum Aeaciden*.

In addition, the *Silvae* are full of references to the story of Achilles, many of which deal with the theme covered by the completed portion of the *Achilleid*; e.g. *Silv.* I, 2, 216f. *cum Thetin Haemoniis Chiron accedere terris erecto prospexit equo* (almost the same phrase as *Ach.* I, 235); II, 1, 88f. *tenero sic blandus Achilli semifer Haemonium vincebat Pelea Chiron*; II, 6, 30f. *qualem nec bella caventem* (*canentem* codd. dett.) *litore virgineo Thetis occultavit Achillem*; V, 3, 193f. *quique tubas acres lituosque audire volentem Aeaciden alio frangebat carmine Chiron*; while in II, 6, 54 *Haemonium Pyladen* must refer to Patroclus (cf. *Ach.* I, 174f., 632f.). These, together with phrases like *senior*

---

[1] A four-yearly contest instituted by Domitian in summer 86. *Silv.* III, 5, 31 ff.; V, 3, 231 ff.
[2] *Silv.* III, 5, 37ff. and perhaps V, 4.
[3] See L. Legras, *Revue des Études Anciennes* IX (1907), 347; Frère, introd. to *Silvae*, pp. xixf.

Peleus (*Silv.* II, 1, 90; *Ach.* 1, 440), show that the subject of the *Achilleid* was in Statius' mind some time before he started writing the epic.

Jannaccone (p. 19) cannot believe that after finishing the *Thebaid* about A.D. 92 Statius wrote nothing but occasional poems for three years, and would argue that he started the *Achilleid* before 95. But while admitting that he may have sketched out a rough draft of the theme of the proposed epic earlier, we can hardly set aside the evidence given above; nor does it seem unlikely that after twelve years' work on the *Thebaid* he was content to rest from epic for a while.

Statius' death may not only have cut short the *Achilleid*, but prevented any thorough revision of the completed portion. It is important to bear this in mind when deciding whether the MS. tradition, in certain passages where it is not divided, can be considered sound. Editors, for example, have objected to the repetition *nova, novos* in I, 753 f.; but there are other repetitions almost as awkward, e.g. I, 666, 668 *premat, premit* in different senses; 226, 228 *pectoris, pectore*.[1] Similarly I, 663–4 have been suspected on the grounds that they are weak and unpoetic; but we can find even greater weaknesses, e.g. II, 91 *multumque faventibus*. Some scholars have tried to eliminate the awkwardness inherent in I, 927–9 by postulating a lacuna; but these lines too may merely indicate lack of revision. Whether we can go further and allow hiatus in II, 93 is much more doubtful.

3. THEME OF THE *ACHILLEID*

As originally planned, the *Achilleid* was intended to cover the entire life of Achilles. In *Ach.* 1, 3 ff. Statius tells us that, whereas Homer has dealt with the hero's career at Troy up to the death of Hector, he will sing of the concealment of Achilles in Scyros and his discovery by the Greeks, and also the whole of the Trojan War.

Of the completed portion, Book I deals mostly with Achilles in Scyros, while Book II, 1–167 deals with the voyage to Troy and

---

[1] Even in the *Thebaid* there are examples of such repetition: see Heuvel on *Th.* I, 74.

gives brief descriptions of the causes of the Trojan War and a boastful account by Achilles of his childhood in Thessaly (see synopsis below). The entire life of Achilles would thus have occupied at least twelve books, perhaps considerably more. Whether these would have equalled the level of composition of Book I is very doubtful: already in Book II graphic diction has given place to description based on set speeches. The Scyros story forms a pretty epyllion, far more skilfully managed than the story of Hypsipyle in Book V of the *Thebaid*, whereas the projected epic would have been even more episodic than the *Thebaid*. Statius was not alone among Roman poets in rejecting Aristotle's advice:[1] in addition to Juvenal's complaint about hoarse Codrus's recitations of his *Theseid*,[2] we hear of an epic on Theseus by Albinovanus Pedo;[3] a *Diomedia* in twelve books by Jullus Antonius, son of the triumvir M. Antonius;[4] a *Thebaid*, no doubt modelled like Statius' on that of Antimachus, by one Ponticus[5] (cf. what Prop. II, 34, 37 ff. says of 'Lynceus'); and numerous epics or epyllia on themes from Homer and the Cyclic poets.

4. SYNOPSIS

BOOK I

1–13. An introduction giving the scope of the proposed epic, which was intended not to stop, as the *Iliad* had stopped, with the killing of Hector, but to continue down to the death of Achilles.

14–19. Dedication to Domitian, with an apology for not yet writing an epic on the emperor.

20–94. Thetis, foreseeing danger for Achilles, is worried at the passing of Paris's ships on their return to Troy,[6] and appeals to Neptune to rouse a storm, but Neptune refuses.

---

[1] *Poetics* 1451 a διὸ πάντες ἐοίκασιν ἁμαρτάνειν ὅσοι τῶν ποιητῶν Ἡρακληίδα Θησηίδα καὶ τὰ τοιαῦτα ποιήματα πεποιήκασιν· οἴονται γάρ, ἐπεὶ εἷς ἦν ὁ Ἡρακλῆς, ἕνα καὶ τὸν μῦθον εἶναι προσήκειν.

[2] Juv. I, 2.   [3] Ovid, *ex Pont.* IV, 10, 71 ff.   [4] Ps.-Acro on Hor. *Od.* IV, 2, 33.

[5] Prop. I, 7, 1 ff.; I, 9, 9 f.; cf. Ovid, *Trist.* IV, 10, 47.

[6] Following the usual epic technique, Statius postpones the earlier background, Achilles' childhood and the origins of the Trojan War, making his characters narrate these in Book II.

95–197. Thetis visits the Centaur Chiron, Achilles' tutor, at his cave in Thessaly, and by pretending that she needs to perform magic rites induces Chiron to hand him over to her. Achilles appears, fresh from a lion-hunt, and sings to the accompaniment of a lyre.

198–282. Thetis decides to hide Achilles at the court of Lycomedes king of Scyros, conveys him there on dolphins as he sleeps, and asks him to dress as a girl.

283–396. Lycomedes' daughters, among whom Deidamia is outstanding, are dancing at a festival of Pallas, and Achilles immediately falls in love with Deidamia. Thetis persuades him to adopt her plan, transforms and beautifies him, teaches him how to act his part and leaves him in the custody of Lycomedes.

397–466. Greek preparations for the Trojan War.

467–559. The Greeks at Aulis clamour for Achilles, and Calchas during a trance reveals where Thetis has hidden him. Ulysses and Diomede resolve to search him out, and sail towards Scyros.

560–674. Achilles falls more than ever in love with Deidamia. He uses the occasion of a Bacchic festival to force his love upon her; she tells no one except her nurse.

675–818. Ulysses and Diomede reach Scyros and are entertained by Lycomedes.

819–926. After a dancing display Ulysses and Diomede produce their presents. Achilles is detected because he chooses armour while the king's daughters choose more feminine gifts, and suddenly reveals his true self. Meanwhile Deidamia has given birth to a son by him, and Achilles persuades Lycomedes to sanction the marriage.

927–60. Deidamia weeps at Achilles' impending departure.

BOOK II

1–22. Achilles, Ulysses and Diomede set sail.

23–48. Ulysses distracts Achilles' thoughts from Deidamia.

49–85. Ulysses recounts the origins of the Trojan War.

86–167. Achilles, in reply to Diomede's request, gives an account of his childhood years.

The story in the completed portion of the *Achilleid* thus divides itself into three sections: (1) Achilles' life in Thessaly (I, 95–197;

II, 86–167); (2) the origins of and preparations for the Trojan War, and the activities of Ulysses and Diomede outside Scyros (I, 20–94, 397–559; II, 1–85); (3) the Scyros episode (I, 198–396, 560–960).

5. SOURCES

Whereas in writing the *Thebaid* Statius had had not only Antimachus but one or more Roman predecessors who had covered the theme of the epic, in the *Achilleid*, if (as can perhaps be thought likely *ex silentio*) no poet had written a complete life of Achilles, he was bound, if not to be original, at least to draw from various sources.[1] Of the three sections of the plot mentioned above, section 2 is the least interesting and most mechanical: we feel that the poet is weary of recounting wars, and many of the descriptions are little more than variations on similar descriptions in the *Thebaid*. The historical narrative is a brief outline (though not so brief as in Ovid's *Metamorphoses*) built round the story of Achilles; and the question of its sources is of little importance.[2]

For the early life of Achilles,[3] Statius does not follow Homer, who, although he mentions that Chiron taught Achilles medicine,[4] says the boy was educated at Phthia by Phoenix[5] and sent to Troy with the consent of Thetis, although she foresaw his fate;[6] and on arrival in the Troad he was put under the care of Ulysses and Nestor.[7] Pindar[8] is the first extant poet who assigns Achilles to the guardianship of Chiron. In Ap. Rh. IV, 865–77 (cf. Paus. III, 18, 12) Peleus sends him to Chiron; but Statius entirely omits reference to Peleus as bringing up Achilles, and says that Thetis sent him.[9]

[1] K. Weitzmann, *Gk. Mythology in Byzantine Art* (Princeton, 1951), argues that the wide distribution throughout the eastern Mediterranean of pictorial representations of Achilles' childhood indicates as their source not Statius but a single Greek original. This would have included the birth of Achilles, which although it is not treated by Statius occurs in art.

[2] The conflicting traditions with regard to the events leading to Thetis' marriage are discussed in the note to I, 1 f.

[3] For the dipping of Achilles into the Styx see note to I, 133 f.

[4] *Il.* XI, 832. [5] *Il.* XVIII, 436 ff., etc. [6] *Il.* XVIII, 439 ff.

[7] *Il.* XI, 769 ff.; cf. VII, 125 ff., IX, 252 ff.

[8] *Pyth.* VI, 21 ff.; *Nem.* III, 43 ff.; cf. note to *Ach.* II, 98 ff.

[9] Kürschner, *P.P.S. quibus...fontibus*, p. 26, notes that Thetis is also the agent in *Orph. Arg.* 387 and on the *puteal Capitolinum* (Baumeister, I, p. 4), which gives a series of scenes from the life of Achilles.

The connection of Achilles with Scyros is only a passing one in Homer, who mentions that on his way to Troy he captured twelve cities, including 'lofty Scyros, city of Enyeus',[1] where his son Neoptolemus was brought up.[2] The *Little Iliad*[3] said that he was shipwrecked on Scyros and met Deidamia there; the scholiast on *Il.* XIX, 326 comments ἡ ἱστορία παρὰ τοῖς κυκλικοῖς. During the fifth century Polygnotus painted Achilles among the maidens at Scyros,[4] and later Athenion of Maroneia painted the recognition scene;[5] the latter was a favourite theme among the Pompeii fresco-painters,[6] who depict Ulysses, Diomede, Agyrtes, Achilles in female dress with spear and shield, Lycomedes bewildered, Deidamia frightened, fleeing or clasping Achilles' knees. The plays entitled Σκύριοι by Sophocles and Euripides dealt with the story, and Euripides' play may have inspired Alexandrian writers. Of particular interest is the mutilated idyll attributed to Bion,[7] which briefly mentions the origins of the Trojan War, and relates how Achilles hid among the daughters of Lycomedes, learning about wool-making instead of weapons and resembling the king's daughters in the colour of his cheeks, his gait and his hair. After telling how Achilles was a constant companion to Deidamia, it breaks off in the middle of a speech by him σπεύδων κοινὸν ἐς ὕπνον.

Among Roman writers Horace[8] has one reference and one allusion to the Scyros story; Ovid has more detailed descriptions in *Met.* XIII, 162–70, 179; *A.A.* I, 681–704, a passage whose brutality Statius is careful to avoid, although he imitates much of its language; and Seneca refers to the episode in *Tro.* 213f., 339ff. Ovid may also be thinking of it when he mentions the tragedian *mollem qui fecit Achillem*.[9]

[1] *Il.* IX, 667f. [2] *Il.* XIX, 326ff. (327 probably corrupt); *Od.* XI, 506ff.
[3] Fr. 3 Monro. [4] Paus. I, 22, 6. [5] Pliny, *N.H.* XXXV, 134.
[6] E.g. P. Herrmann, *Denkmäler der Malerei*, Farbendruck IV (Naples, Museo Nazionale; a small reproduction in M. H. Swindler, *Ancient Painting*, fig. 456); L. Curtius, *Die Wandmalerei Pompejis*, pl. II; W. Helbig, *Wandgemälde*, etc., nos. 1296–7, 1299–1302. Most of these represent the moment when Ulysses detects Achilles, and are probably copied from the painting by Athenion mentioned above. M. H. Swindler (*op. cit.* p. 284) thinks that Polygnotus' painting too represented this subject, but it may simply have portrayed Achilles among the maidens.
[7] Bion XV (incert. idyll. 6 Ahrens), 5ff.
[8] *Od.* I, 8, 13ff.; II, 5, 21ff., quoted in note to *Ach.* I, 336f.
[9] *Trist.* II, 409ff., which, however, Owen refers to the Ἀχιλλέως ἐρασταί of Sophocles. Livius Andronicus, Ennius and Accius each wrote a play called 'Achilles', but whether these included the Scyros story we do not know.

Philostratus, *Hero.* XIX, 3 (vol. II, p. 198 in Kayser's 1870–1 ed.), dismisses the concealment of Achilles among Lycomedes' daughters as unfitting to his character, and makes Peleus send him to Scyros to punish Lycomedes for having killed Theseus (see n. on 1, 207 ff.). When Lycomedes protests that he killed him in defence of his kingdom, Achilles acquits him and marries Deidamia. From Scyros he is taken by Thetis to Phthia, and then joins the Greeks at Aulis.

Of the mythographers, ps.-Apollodorus [1] merges the various earlier and later versions of the story. The scholiast on Hom. *Il.* XIX, 326 diverges from Statius' version by stating (*a*) that Peleus took Achilles to Scyros; and (*b*) that Lycomedes knew of the trick, and himself dressed the boy in girl's clothes and hid him among his daughters. Hyginus (96) derives his account mainly from Statius.

6. LANGUAGE AND STYLE

Statius has in several places borrowed from Catullus' *Marriage of Peleus and Thetis* epyllion (Cat. LXIV), e.g. 1, 85 from Cat. l. 350; 1, 86f. from l. 345; 1, 960 from l. 59; II, 111 from l. 342. But the two chief works which inspired him and helped him to mould his language in the *Achilleid* were the *Aeneid* and Ovid's *Metamorphoses*.[2] The former he uses especially in the construction and wording of his speeches (see, for example, notes to 1, 43, 135 ff.), while the influence of the *Metamorphoses* can be seen in constant *loci similes*. But this is not to say that the *Achilleid* is lacking in originality. It has been observed [3] that the outstanding quality of the *Achilleid* is the poet's ability to draw vivid and detailed pictures of the scenes in Thessaly and Scyros. The portrait of the young hero in 1, 159 ff. (cf. note on 1, 162), the dance in honour of Pallas in 1, 285 ff., above all the recognition scene in 1, 841 ff., these and many others seem, by their powers of description, to be implanting a pictorial representation into the mind of the listener or reader.

[1] III, 13, 8; for the earlier life of Achilles III, 13, 6.

[2] The affinity with Lucan is not pronounced in the *Achilleid*. Some reminiscences of Valerius Flaccus can be observed.

[3] See especially T. S. Duncan, 'The Influence of Art on Description in the Poetry of P.P.S.' (who would have added more force to his arguments by adducing the information available from Greek and Roman art); cf. Simcox, *Lat. Lit.* II, 57.

Criticisms can certainly be made. The details of the mythological descriptions are apt to strike the modern reader as grotesque; e.g. *gradu totiens obstante* (II, 148); *centumque dei numerare catenas* (I, 210). In several places the wording is too lengthy: at I, 198 ff. Thetis takes a long time deciding where to hide Achilles; the arming of the Greeks at I, 412–37 is tedious and too reminiscent of the similar description in the *Thebaid* (see note to 423 ff.); and at I, 831 ff. and II, 131 ff. we have displays of erudition in the style of Callimachus. Statius' knowledge of the geography of Greece and the Aegean is questionable and, certainly in places, borrowed from other poets (see notes to I, 201, 410 f., 677 ff.).

The speeches, descriptions and similes have their merits and demerits. The shorter speeches, such as that of Ulysses to Lycomedes in I, 728 ff., are on the whole more effective than the longer ones. The descriptions are enlivened by unusual words and phrases (cf. summary below), and the shorter parentheses, such as *o quantum gaudia formae adiciunt* (I, 167 f.), or *qui pueris sopor* (I, 229), are very pointed.

SIMILES. There are twenty similes in Book I, none in Book II; of these, nine each are drawn from mythology and animal life, two from human activities.[1] Mythology: I, 165 ff., 180 f., 344 ff., 484 ff., 588 ff., 615 ff., 758 ff., 824 ff., 839 f. Animal life: I, 212 ff., 277 ff., 313 ff., 372 ff., 459 ff., 555 ff., 704 ff., 746 ff., 858 ff. Human activities: I, 307 f., 332 ff.

METAPHORS. The majority of the metaphors in the *Achilleid* are not of original inspiration. The most frequent are from fire (transferred usually to love, but in I, 399 to anger), from drinking and from athletics. There are, however, some striking metaphors which occur once or twice only in the poem.

From fire: I, 161 *natat ignis in ore*, 277 *igne iuventae*, 303 *bibit ossibus ignem*, 636 *virginis ignem*; II, 40 *quos suppresserat ignes*; I, 164 *tranquillae...faces oculis*, 304 *fax vibrata medullis*, 637 *aequaevam...facem*, 399 *flammata* (see context).

From drinking, etc.: I, 303 *bibit ossibus ignem*, 433 *(ferrum quod) vulnera...bibat*, 8 f. *si veterem digno deplevimus haustu, da fontes mihi*,

---

[1] For a brief classification see L. Legras, *Revue des Études Anciennes* X (1908), 60 ff.; his total is nineteen, since he does not mention I, 180 f.

Phoebe, novos, 667 *hausurum poenas,* 794 *aure trahentem*; cf. also 521f. *caligine sacra pascitur.*

From athletics: 1, 17f. *hoc sudare...pulvere* (cf. 16 *laurus*), 258 *extremis admota pericula metis,* 673 *plenis...metis* (of childbirth), 793 (*non umquam*) *campo maiore exercita virtus.*

Other notable metaphors: 1, 10 *Aonium nemus...pulso,* 188 *laudum semina* (and II, 89 *laudum...semina pandere*), 1, 265 *nubem...malignam* (and 646 *nube soporis*), 400f. *facinus...asperat,* 403 *iura...calcata rapina,* 410f. *gentes...alligat unda,* 425 *Mars efferat aurum,* 433 *conspirante veneno,* 435 *pigris...addunt mucronibus iras* (cf. Sil. VII, 344), 451 *latratum pelago,* 457f. *moles in corpus vultumque coit,* 513 *si magnum Danais pro te dependis Achillem* (the reading is doubtful; if as given, cf. 945 *patriam pensare toris*), 625f. *primum...florem animi,* 762 *perlibrat visu,* 790 *fretum longa velorum obtexitur umbra,* 932 *tuos dignabere portus* (so PEBKQR: see note).

ALLITERATION. For the most part Statius' use of alliteration is moderate, amounting merely to the juxtaposition of two words with the same initial letter, or to the frequent occurrence of one or more consonants in a line. Extensions of the first of these are lines such as 1, 727 *ostensa pacem praefatus oliva,* or successive lines repeating the same initial letter, e.g. 872f. (*perfida palleat* followed by *patrem pudeatque*). More outstanding examples of alliteration are: 1, 166 *permutat plectra pharetris,* 211 *timidae tellus tutissima matri,* 849f. *aut teretes thyrsos aut respondentia temptant/tympana, gemmatis aut nectunt tempora limbis.*

COMPOUND PHRASING. Legras, *loc. cit.,* remarks that Statius is fond of phrases consisting of a verb and its object, instead of a single verb, to make the expression more vivid. Achilles' embraces of Deidamia while the love-affair is still innocent are expressed by the phrase *ligat amplexus* (1, 576); but 1, 642f. *veros admovet amplexus* shows the power behind his later love. Some other examples are 1, 918f. *effert...gradum,* 930 *lacrimas... solvit,* II, 155 *liquidam nodare palen et spargere caestus*; and see note on 1, 68.

EXAGGERATION. Poetic exaggeration is a feature found in epic poetry from Homer onwards, and in 1, 471 *aequum moenibus orbem,* of Ajax's shield, Statius is imitating the Homeric description, though in the previous lines *septem...armenti reges* carries the exaggeration a stage further. We may note also the exaggerated description in I, 101–3 of the reception given to Thetis by the mountains of Thessaly, Chiron's cave and Spercheus; I, 445 f. *ipsum iam puppibus aequor deficit et totos consumunt carbasa ventos*; 933 f. *capta reportans Pergama* and the similar phrases in 958 f., II, 65; II, 154 *in nubila condere discos*. Akin to this type of exaggeration is the use of verbs which treat apparent actions as if they were real: I, 462, 678 (but not in the same sense; see notes to these lines), 679 *crescere* (*ante oculos crescente Samo*), II, 22 *discedere* (*longo Scyros discedere ponto*), I, 332 *vivere* (*victurae... cerae*; cf. *Silv.* III, 1, 95 *viventes...ceras*).

ORIGINALITY IN WORDING. As in the *Thebaid* and the *Silvae*, we find a number of words which are rare either in themselves or in their meaning:

(*a*) ἅπαξ εἰρημένα: I, 383 *abnato*, 395 *interfuro*, 821 *Scyreides*.

(*b*) Words found only in the *Achilleid* and in later writers: I, 406 *degrassor*, 231 *effulguro*, 373 *grego*, II, 131 *rotatus* (subst.), I, 601 *temerator*.

(*c*) Uncommon compounds: I, 110 *accubitus*, 8 *depleo*, II, 67 *inexcitus*, I, 791 *irrevocatus*, 450 *montivagus*, 208 *personus*.

(*d*) Greek words: I, 186 *chelys* (a favourite word with Statius), 828 *entheus*, 358 *gymnas*, 609, 716 *nebris*, II, 155 *pale*, I, 595 *trieteris*. See also note on I, 950 *thyrsa* heterocl. pl.

(*e*) Unusual meaning or construction. The following are some of the more outstanding examples: I, 629 *desertor* adj., 479 *linea* (lineage), 833 *pecten* (a dance), 762 *perlibro* (*vultus ac pectora Ulixes perlibrat visu*). See also p. 16, and note on I, 212 *vicino*.

7. GRAMMAR AND SYNTAX

The following summaries are not intended to present a complete survey of the grammar and syntax of the *Achilleid*, but to outline some of the more characteristic features. For comparison with the *Thebaid* and *Silvae* and with other writers, reference should be made to the notes on the passages cited.

INFINITIVE. The freedom with which the infinitive is used after verbs is particularly noticeable:

(a) After verbs of will, resolution, desire, refusal: I, 785 ff. *quis enim non visere gentes...ardeat?*, 352 f. *arma...petebat ferre*, 348 *tumet* (conj. Gronovius) *conponere crines*, 281 f. *fremit...inire imperia*, 199 f. *quibus abdere terris destinet*, 917 *nec...abnuerit...se iungere.*

(b) After verbs of permission: I, 74 *da pellere luctus*, 92 *dabo tollere fluctus.*

(c) After verbs of command, persuasion, prohibition: I, 693 f. *sociisque resumere pontum imperat*, 707 f. *ne...cura canum...moneat vigilare magistros* (=*ut vigilent*), 685 f. *iussa Thetin...vertere leges arcebant.*

(d) After verbs of possessing or imparting skill: I, 581 *tenuare... lanas demonstrat* (cf. the normal prose constr. 635 f. *tenuare...scio*), and perhaps II, 51 *electus...certamina solvere.*

(e) Infinitive of purpose after verbs of motion: I, 133 f. *natum... fero mergere*, 209 f. *Aegaeona...missa sequi*, 288 *exierant dare veris opes*, 735 f. *imus explorare aditus*, 821 f. *ibant ostentare choros*; II, 31 *adgressus flectere.*

(f) Infinitive after verbs of statement or emotion: I, 16 *dolet altera vinci*, 282 *alios miratur discere cursus*, 483 *vinci...fatetur.*

CHANGE OF TENSE. Present and past tenses are very freely mixed, e.g.: I, 51 f. *dixit...aspicit*, 100 *reppulit...feriunt*, 122 f. *erumpit...crepuit*, 251 *occupat...adfata* (*est*), 325 f. *aspicit...iniecit*, 426 f. *sidunt...viderunt*, 466 *cogitur...contempsit*, 559 *poscit...sēdēre*, 566 ff. *elegit...admovet*, 622 f. *consedere...tacent*, 645 ff. *replevit... putant...tollitur...vibrabat*, 692 ff. *emisit...imperat*, 695 f. *accedunt... erat*, 726 f. *dixerat...cernit...praefatus* (*est*), 827 ff. *movent...dedit... pulsant...lēgēre*, 878 f. *cecidere...consumitur*; II, 20 f. *insiluit...abripitur*, 30 f. *sentit...adgressus* (*est*), 132 ff. *citent...tenderet*, 161 f. *claudat...cederet.*

ACCUSATIVE OF DIRECT OBJECT. The following are noteworthy: I, 14 *stupeo* with direct obj. (also in Virgil; cf. 499 *fremo*, if *fremant* is the correct reading), 87 *undo* with direct obj., 18 f. *molior* with personal obj., 475 *loquor* with personal obj. and predicate.

RETAINED ACCUSATIVE after passive verb: I, 853 *caelatum pugnas.*

ACCUSATIVE OF RESPECT, ADVERBIAL ACCUSATIVE. (1) The poetic 'accusative of the part affected' is found (*a*) with past participles: I, 53, 77, 95, 302, 764; II, 5; (*b*) with a passive finite verb or infinitive: I, 300, 859; (*c*) with an adj., I, 351 *torva genas*. (2) Statius is fond of neuter accusatives, sing. and pl., with adverbial force. *Multum* occurs frequently, sometimes unexpectedly: I, 3, 145, 201, 379, 449, 664, 800; II, 91; also I, 686 *multa*, 838 *plurima*. We likewise find I, 323 *laetum*, 373 *longum*, 660 and II, 9 *omnia*, I, 832 *obvia*.

GENITIVE WITH ADJECTIVES. Note I, 233 *securus pelagi*, 311 *turbae securus*, 911 *blandus...precum*.

OBJECTIVE GENITIVE, other than direct object. I, 63 *terrarum crimina*, 636 *virginis ignem*.

DATIVE OF PURPOSE. I, 421 *iaculis rarescitis umbrae*, 428 f. *caeduntur robora classi, silva minor remis*; see also note to I, 531.

ABLATIVE OF PLACE with verbs of motion. I, 43 f. *gurgite nostro Rhoeteae cecidere trabes*, II, 16 *spumante salo iaciens...exta*, I, 329 *sua dilecta cervice monilia transfert*.

INSTRUMENTAL ABLATIVE of person. I, 219 *an (natum) magno Tritone ferat*.

PREPOSITIONS. Note the following:

I, 59 *a pectore*, 256 f. *praeclusaque leti tantum a matre via est*, 623 *solus ab agmine*.

I, 593 f. *lucus...sublimis ad orgia...stabat*.

I, 473 *omnis in absentem belli manus ardet Achillem*, 485 f. (*cum*) *Gradivus in hastam surgeret*, 800 *steriles damnatus in annos*.

I, 41 *patria iam se metitur in hasta*, 559 *in remis...sedere*, 672 *aegros in pondere menses*.

I, 223 *pelagi sub valle*, 476 *Haemoniis sub vallibus*, 713 *ambiguo sub pectore*, 817 *tranquilla sub pace*, 953 *hunc...sub corde tene* (and II, 29 *sub corde*), II, 13 *fluctu...sub ipso*.

ADVERBS. See notes on I, 141 *magis*, 176 *longe*, 186 *extremo*. Statius does not avoid placing adverbs at the end of the hexameter, even when unemphatic, as I, 768 *semper*.

TRANSFERRED EPITHET. The poetic construction by which an epithet is transferred from one expressed substantive to another is represented by I, 192 *Minoia bracchia tauri*, II, 157 f.

APOSIOPESIS. This device is employed not infrequently in the *Achilleid*: I, 47, 140, 157, 657, 780, II, 42, and probably I, 502, 737.

ZEUGMA. I, 279 *campis fluviisque et honore superbo*; 627 *agitare* in different senses governing *tela* and *feras*.

OXYMORON. I, 21 *blande populatus*, 398 f. *dulcibus armorum furiis*.

COMPARATIO COMPENDIARIA. I, 111 f. *(stabula) non aequa nefandis fratribus*; cf. 809, an interesting variation on comparatio compendiaria, *(natas) divarum vultibus aequas*.

ANASTROPHE. I, 129, 269, 319, 654; II, 78. Cf. also the transpositions, not necessitated by the metre, I, 734 *metuam quid enim*, 748 *videat donec*.

8. CHARACTER-DRAWING[1]

It is difficult to summarise character-drawing in an uncompleted epic. Achilles at Scyros is an attractive blend of masculine and feminine traits; but from the short glimpse of his heroic characteristics in Book II we may doubt if we should have liked the warrior equally well in the continuation of the epic. Thetis combines the foreknowledge and cunning of a goddess with the frailty of a human mother. Lycomedes is simply *placidissimus* and for the most part indulgent *ingenio parentis* (I, 363). Deidamia stands out more as a personality after the birth of Pyrrhus; her farewell speech at I, 931 ff. and the pathetic scene on the tower at II, 23-6 show her in tragic circumstances which appealed to the great admirer of Statius, Dante.[2] Of the other characters the most colourful is the crafty Ulysses, the Sherlock Holmes who has Diomede as his Dr Watson.

9. INFLUENCE OF STATIUS

Apart from Juvenal we hear nothing of Statius from contemporary sources, and until the last days of the Roman Empire there are only passing references.[3] But Ausonius, Claudian and Apollinaris Sidonius

---

[1] See Elizabeth C. Evans, *Harvard Stud. in Class. Philol.* LVIII–LIX (1948), 214–17.

[2] *Inf.* XXVI, 61 f.; he also mentions her and her sisters in *Purg.* XXII, 114.

[3] See Schanz-Hosius, *Röm. Lit.* II, p. 544; the reference to Gordian I is misleading, since the writer (A.D. ? 362–3) merely means that Gordian wrote an epic called *Antoninias* on the life of the Antonines, just as the *Achilleis* sets out to be a life of Achilles.

have read his works thoroughly, and Claudian's *Rape of Proserpine* is to a large extent modelled on the *Achilleid*. The eighty-nine poor hexameters entitled 'Verba Achillis in parthenone, cum tubam Diomedis audisset'[1] also owe much to Statius. In the Middle Ages, while the *Silvae* were almost unknown, manuscripts of the *Thebaid* and *Achilleid* were frequently copied; the library at York possessed a Statius in the eighth century.[2] From the tenth century onwards there is evidence of the use of these poems in schools;[3] and a manuscript of Gonville and Caius College, Cambridge,[4] which gives a reading-list probably originating in the last quarter of the twelfth century, includes both the *Thebaid* and the *Achilleid*, the latter with the words: *Statius Achilleidos* (sic) *etiam a viris mult⟨a⟩e gravitatis probatur* (!). Dante, Chaucer and others[5] evidently had access to these poems in the original.

10. MANUSCRIPTS

1. P = Puteaneus[6] (Parisinus 8051), ninth century: *Thebaid* and *Achilleid*. This is not only the earliest MS. of the *Achilleid* but the only extant representative of a class which never underwent very serious corruptions. It has been shown by Klotz[7] and others that it is derived from a MS. which (i) abounded in missing or illegible words or letters, especially at the ends of lines; these are normally omitted by P with no attempt to make good the deficit; (ii) had letters *n* and *r*, *c* and *g*, and endings -*us* and -*ur*, looking very similar; (iii) had some similarity between *a* and *u*: P often writes *a* so as to look like *u*, *ic* or *ci*. These confusions can only mean that the immediate predecessor of P was a minuscule MS., which cannot therefore be earlier than the eighth century. At the end of Book IV of the *Thebaid*,

---

[1] *Poet. Lat. Min.* ed. Baehrens, IV, 322.

[2] Alcuin, *Versus de sanctis Eborac. eccl.* l. 1553. It seems likely, as thought by O. Müller, *Quaest. Stat.* pp. 6ff., that the *Achilleid* was included in this; but Kohlmann, pref. to *Ach.* p. vi, rightly dismisses attempts to link it up with our MS. tradition. Cf. Klotz, pref. to *Ach.*

[3] M. Manitius, *Geschichte d. lat. Lit. d. M.-A.* I, 634; II, 11; Kohlmann, pref. to *Ach.* p. vi.

[4] C. H. Haskins in *Harvard Stud. in Class. Philol.* XX (1902), 91.

[5] Among British admirers of Statius in the Middle Ages we may mention Josephus Iscanus, who in his epic *De Bello Troiano* has several reminiscences of the *Achilleid*. A more recent work inspired by the *Achilleid* is the drama *Achille in Sciro* of Metastasio (1698–1782).

[6] So called from its owner Claude Dupuy (d. 1594). Earlier it belonged to the monastery of Corbie in Picardy, and it may have originated there (O. Müller, *Electa Statiana*, p. 12).

[7] Prefaces to *Achilleid* and *Thebaid*. Cf. A. Souter, *CQ*, I (1907), 80.

however, a reference is made in P to the '*Codex Iuliani V.C.*', and *V.C.* (*vir clarissimus*) is a semi-official title not likely to be later than the sixth century. These words must therefore have been copied from P's predecessor, and must refer to an earlier MS.

The readings of P frequently differ from all or most of the other MSS. Where, in such cases, P's reading is not an obvious error, it is usually to be preferred to the alternative reading or readings; but care has to be exercised, especially where the alternatives are very similar, and modern editors have perhaps been apt to accept too often P's unsupported text.

2. The group consisting of E and R.

(i) E = Etonensis 150 (M. R. James's catalogue),[1] eleventh century, containing (1) Theodulus; (2) Maximian, *Elegies*; (3) Statius, *Achilleid* only; (4) Ovid, *Remedium Amoris*; (5) Ovid, *Heroides* I, 7–VII, 157;[2] (6) Arator, *Hist. Apost.* The *Achilleid* was first collated, very incompletely, by C. Schenkl, *Wiener Studien* IV (1882), 96; a fuller, but still incomplete, collation was made by H. W. Garrod for the Oxford text; corrections and additions will be found in my article in *CQ* XLIII (1949), 45. The ignorance of the scribe is clear from the numerous misspellings.[3]

(ii) R = Monacensis 14557 (Ratisponensis), containing (1) Walter of Châtillon, *Alexandreis*; (2) Ovid, *Fasti* (extracts); (3) Statius, *Achilleid* only (fourteenth century); (4) a treatise on Macrobius, *Somn. Scip.* Only twenty-one readings from this MS. have previously been published,[4] by F. V. Gustafsson in *Festschr. J. Vahlen*, 493. In spite of its late date, it can be considered as valuable as E, to which it bears a strong affinity, though clearly not descended from E.

Apart from the cleavage, already mentioned, between P and the other MSS., there is a frequent cleavage between PER and the rest; see, for example, app. cr. to I, 86, 121, 247, 316, 468, 521, 744, 747, 779, 806, 911; II, 42, 131; and in these places the former are probably

[1] Facsimile of beginning and palaeographical comment in *New Palaeog. Soc.* I, pl. 110.

[2] Cf. Ov. *Her.* ed. Palmer, p. xxxv.

[3] Minor misspellings have not been recorded in the app. cr. (the spelling of Greek names by the scribe of E is particularly poor); thus at I, 20 E's *eualio* for *Oebalio* is not recorded, as being on a par with many other misspellings.

[4] No letter has therefore been assigned to it by editors. The letter M is unsuitable, having been used to denote a group of *codd. dett.*

in every case to be preferred.[1] Nevertheless where P has obvious mistakes, as a rule neither ER nor the other MSS. follow it. At I, 908 ER have *prostravit*, correctly; P *prostavit*; BKQC *proiecit*. At II, 17, where the MSS. differ, the reading *iuberes* given by E and the second hand of R is to be preferred. Sometimes the cleavage is PE, PR or PEBR against the other MSS. Often ER have the same false reading, sometimes with an affinity to the *codd. dett.* From II, 43 to the end, the affinity of E with P is almost negligible, but R continues its affinity: see app. cr. to II, 46, 68, 98, 100, 115, 116, 121–2, 137, 149. Thus either (*a*) as assumed in the conjectural stemma below (p. 25), E and R are independently conflated from two MSS., which may be the same two in each case, or (*b*) both are derived from a conflated MS. which had many alternative readings. Since alternative readings are very rare in MSS. of the *Achilleid*, (*a*) is more likely.

3. The ω group.

(i) Q = Parisinus 10317, tenth century: *Thebaid* and *Achilleid*. Lines 529–661 of Book I and 150–67 of Book II are missing in the first hand and supplied in a later hand; lines 881–2 of Book I are missing in the first and supplied by the second hand.

(ii) K = Gudianus 54 (Herzog August Bibliothek, Wolfenbüttel), eleventh century: *Thebaid* and *Achilleid*. Lines 521–661, 881–2 of Book I are missing in the first and supplied by the second hand.

(iii) C = Bruxellensis 5338, eleventh century. This MS. forms part of the same book as Brux. 5337, which contains the *Thebaid*; but whereas Brux. 5337 is a particularly good MS., having affinities with N (Cheltoniensis), Brux. 5338, which is in a different hand, is a poor representative of the ω class. Garrod dismisses it altogether, and would even consider it as possibly derived from a MS. copied from Q; but as it does not follow Q in more than a small number of the latter's mistakes, we should rather call it a 'nephew' of Q. Even so, its value is slight.[2] Lines 529–660, 662 of Book I are

---

[1] See note to I, 806.

[2] The following are addenda and corrigenda to the readings of C in Klotz's edition, which were collated for him by Vollmer: I, **44** Hẹthẹẹ (Rẹthẹẹ *sup. lin.*)   **84** illic *ex* illuc   **131** Nanque C[1]: Iamque C[2]   **143** Iussa C[1]   **152** Thessaliaeve *ex* -que   **189** timidae (u *supra* i *prius*)   **205** Cyclades   **259** immitte C[1]   **269** stigis (o *supra* i *alt.*)   **292** timentes (u *supra* i)   **298** auro *ex* -um C[3]   **306** impulsas C[2] (s *alt. in ras.*)   **326** tum   **383** Innatat

supplied by the second hand at the end of the work; lines 881-2 of Book I are missing.

The chief characteristic of the ω group is its omission of the lines mentioned above. Evidently in its hyparchetype a sheet of four pages, each of about thirty-three lines, had dropped out. As is to be expected, the readings of Q, K and C are extremely similar.

4. B = Bernensis 156, eleventh century; *Thebaid* (b in Klotz) and *Achilleid*. Lines 881-2 of Book I are missing in the first hand, but 529-661 are not missing. The readings of B are usually those of ω, whether or not these agree with P; but in a substantial minority of cases we find PEBR against ω or Pω against EBR. At I, 123 PB, together with two *codd. dett.*, have *Notaque*, others *Motaque*; at I, 693 PB *sociisque*, others *sociosque*. At I, 265 B appears to have changed *Has* to *Hac*, a reading which Postgate had already conjectured. In general, however, B is of little help towards the establishment of the text.

5. The *codices deteriores* can be divided into two classes:

(i) Those which Kohlmann designated as M, namely: t (Trevirensis), p (Parisinus 8052), G (Gudianus 52), H (Helmstadiensis), D (Dommerichianus). These have the division between Books I and II (see below) after I, 674.[1]

(ii) Inferior MSS., the majority of which are of late date; many divide the *Achilleid* into five books and contain the spurious line *aura silet; puppis currens ad litora venit* at the end.

Editors since Kohlmann have rightly rejected the readings of both classes, since even where individual MSS. give the correct reading, it has probably been borrowed from P itself.[2] MSS. of the M class

---

385 timido] magno   **452** transnare   **505** abditus *ex* add-   **539** nec enim   **548** in castris ducere (ducere *in ras.*; dicere C⁴)   **549** negant   **554** Laxatur   **579** Laudat   **583** vocis   **611** ꝺsualentia (*sic*)   **653** celsi   **662** Obstupuit   **672** Urgentemque Cᴵ   **698** Aetholus (*om.* -que)   **735** imus   **751** pelasg//   **800** multes (*potius quam* -os)   **901** Dasne age nos voluisse videtur C²   II, **13** Aequoreis Cᴵ: Aequoribus (*om.* -que) C²   **55** ideo *ex* adeo   **65** captis illam tunc devehit argis Cᴵ   **70** aut] et   **75** Et generum et raptam sc.   **81** Quòd Cᴵ   **96** Sic orat teneris Cᴵ   **132** iesa rotent Cᴵ   **144** solutus *ex* -is   **146** qua] cum C²   **163** monitus sub sacrae (*cum signo transl.*; *om.* -que).

¹ Leidensis XVIII 136 K (thirteenth century), treated separately by Kohlmann since it divides the books correctly, has no particular merit except that it avoids some of the mistakes typical of the *codd. dett.*

² Corruptions occurring in all or most of M, but not in the first hand of PEBKQR, are: I, **19** praeludat (-det t)   **27** undisonis   **43** primum in   **61** Cui   **149** Olim ferre

are not quoted in the app. cr. unless there is otherwise only the evidence of P for the reading adopted; the readings of the M class as a group are given only where they agree with MSS. of the better class.[1]

DIVISION OF BOOKS

1. P, E, the first hand of B, the MSS. of the ω class and the Leidensis divide the two books so that Book I ends at l. 960.[2] Not only is this the best MS. tradition, but it represents the division known to Priscian (who quotes *Ach.* I, 794) and Eutyches (*Ach.* I, 898), and is used in all modern editions.

2. The MSS. of the M class divide the books into I, 1–674 (Book I), I, 675–II, 167 (Book II). This was no doubt an attempt to turn Book II into a completed book. As older editors followed this division, the old numbering is given in the left margin of the present text for comparison.

3. R divides the work into four books, ending at I, 396, 674, 960; II, 167.

4. Certain late MSS. go still further and try to make the work into a completed epic, by (*a*) a division into five books, ending at I, 197, 396, 674, 960 and II, 167; this is found also in the second hand of B; (*b*) the addition of the spurious line after II, 167 which also occurs in the Leidensis and in a late hand in EBR.

These four categories do not necessarily, as some scholars have assumed,[3] indicate the relative worth of MSS.; e.g. R is infinitely more valuable than the Leidensis.

---

155 Insidias **179** novavit **200** diversa **205** hinc **229** Quis **231** effulserat **319** Hosne **393** thiasos tantum nihil **394** Hic **413** Aere sonant (-at) **467** et *om.* **484** bellantes **508** Eia rumpe laxa **512** Sis felix **618** invasit (-dit) **710** portum **728** pridem vestras **791** ruit **853** qui forte **854** acclivem **860** rapi] ruit **939** arripitur **943** spectabunt **944** catenis] lacertis II, **22** scyros longe decrescere **46** feruntur **93** his armis primum intendisse lacertos, *vel similia metri gratia* **96** crescentibus (*cf. adn.*) **134** tortu] tractu.

[1] Where the words '*cum dett.*' occur in the app. cr. of this edition, they are to be taken as designating M or the majority of M. Where P alone is quoted for a reading, it may be assumed that M agree with the other MSS.

[2] The words 'Lib. 2' (arabic numeral) found in the margin of P at I, 675 are in a very late hand.

[3] It is perhaps owing to this that B and R have not previously been collated.

ANCIENT COMMENTARIES

The *Achilleid* is poorly provided with ancient commentaries and scholia. They may be subdivided as follows:

1. Lactantius Placidus.[1] The commentary of Lactantius Placidus (fifth–sixth century; not identical with the grammarian Placidus) on the *Thebaid* and *Achilleid* is preserved, as regards the *Achilleid*, in Cod. Monac. 19482, Cod. Univ. Brux. and (fragmentary) Cod. Vat. Urb. 361, and we have also readings of it from a lost Cod. Pithoeanus used by Lindenbrog (Tiliobroga). The commentator is dependent to a very large degree upon Servius. The notes on the *Achilleid* become more and more scanty as it progresses: on *Ach.* I, 1–200 there are notes on sixty-six lines; on I, 201–400, on twenty-seven lines; on I, 401–600, on ten lines; on I, 601–800, on five lines; on I, 801–960, on one line; on Book II, none. Neither as regards text nor exposition is much help obtained.

2. The scholia contained in Cod. Dresdensis D^c 157 (thirteenth century), fairly full on the beginning of Book I, but also diminishing towards the end of the book, have been published.[2] They appear to be of ancient origin, but are not connected at all with Lactantius. In places the scholia are unintelligible, and the help derived is again small.

3. A useful list of other MSS. containing scholia on the *Achilleid* is given by Jannaccone, introd. pp. 8 ff.[3] The great majority of these are of late date, and their scholia are of practically no value; apart from simple explanations of words they depend on Servius, and seem to originate from a different source from those on the *Thebaid*.[4] Of the MSS., other than *codd. dett.*, listed above, R and C contain scholia[5], E only a few.

4. Other scholiasts are quoted in Barth's commentary; but in view of his untrustworthiness in such respects[6] it is possible that he invented them.

---

[1] See *RE* s.v. Lactantius Placidus. [2] M. Manitius, *Rhein. Mus.* LIX (1904), 597.
[3] See also Schanz-Hosius, *Röm. Lit.* II, 539.
[4] Klotz, pref. to *Achilleid*, p. xxxviii.
[5] Not mentioned by Jannaccone; those of R are in the second hand.
[6] See A. S. Wilkins, *CR*, X (1896), 14; A. Klotz, *Rhein. Mus.* LIX (1904), 373 shows that Barth's MSS. did exist, but the same may not be true of the 'vet. schol.' whom Barth adduces.

STEMMA

With our defective knowledge, and when allowance is made for interplay among MSS., it is difficult to draw anything approaching an accurate stemma. P, which has scholia neither in the *Thebaid* nor the *Achilleid*, probably derived the text of the two from the same source; C certainly did not, and BKQ probably did not.[1] Thus the ω of the *Achilleid* has not necessarily a connection with the ω of the *Thebaid*. It seems almost certain, however, that Pω are descended in the *Achilleid*, as they unquestionably are in the *Thebaid*,[2] from a common archetype; e.g. at *Ach.* I, 222 all the MSS. have *thetis* for *Tethys*. The diagram attempts to explain the conflated nature of ER, the assumed double transmission being represented by dotted lines.

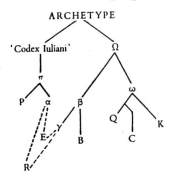

11. BIBLIOGRAPHY

SELECTED EDITIONS AND COMMENTARIES

J. BERNARTIUS, Antwerp, 1595.
F. LINDENBROG (Tiliobroga), Paris, 1600.
J. G. GEVARTIUS, Leiden, 1616.
J. F. GRONOVIUS, Amsterdam, 1653.
K. VON BARTH (commentary), Zwickau (Cygnea), 1664.
C. BERALDUS (whence ed. in usum Delph.), Paris, 1685.
J. E. AMAR and N. E. LEMAIRE, Paris, 1825–30.
N. PINDER, *Selections from the less known Latin poets*, 403 ff. (*Ach.* I, 816–84 only), Oxford, 1869.

[1] The lacunae of Q in Books VIII, X, XI of the *Thebaid* indicate a predecessor with thirty-line pages, whereas the lacuna in *Ach.* I, 529–661 indicates one with a larger page (see p. 22 above).
[2] See Klotz, pref. to *Thebaid*, pp. xl–xli.

P. KOHLMANN, *Specimen novae Achill. St. editionis* (I, 1–396 only), Emden, 1877.

P. KOHLMANN, Teubner ed., Leipzig, 1879.

A. S. WILKINS, *Corp. poet. Lat.* ed. J. P. Postgate (IV, 420), 1904.

H. W. GARROD, Oxf. Class. Text, *Thebaid* and *Achilleid*, 1906.[1]

M. R. J. BRINKGREVE, *Achilleid* only, Rotterdam, 1913.[2]

A. KLOTZ, Teubner ed., Leipzig, 2nd ed. 1926.[3]

SILVIA JANNACCONE, *Achilleid* only, Florence, 1950.[4]

LACTANTIUS

Ed. R. JAHNKE, Teubner, Leipzig, 1898.

TRANSLATIONS (whole of Statius)

J. M. N. D. NISARD, Collection des Auteurs Lat., Paris, 1850–3.

J. H. MOZLEY, Loeb ed., London, 1928.

CONCORDANCE (whole of Statius)

R. J. DEFERRARI and M. C. EAGAN, Brookland, D.C., 1943.[5]

GENERAL

L. LEHANNEUR, *De Statii vita et operibus*, Paris, 1878.

J. MIEDEL, *De anachronismo qui est in P.P.S. Theb. et Ach.*, progr. Passau, 1891–2.

W. HÄRTEL, *Studia Statiana*, diss. inaug. Leipzig, 1900, pp. 17 ff.

P. THOMAS, *Le poète Stace*, diss. inaug. Gand, 1904.

L. LEGRAS, 'Les dernières années de Stace', *REA*, x (1908), 34.

T. S. DUNCAN, *The Influence of Art on Description in the Poetry of P.P.S.*, diss. Baltimore, 1914.

C. BRAKMAN, 'Ad Statium', *Mnem.* 2nd ser. LVII (1929), 251.

D. S. ROBERTSON, 'The Food of Achilles', *CR*, LIV (1940), 177.

ELIZABETH C. EVANS. 'Portraiture in Ancient Epic', *Harvard Studies in Class. Philol.* LVIII–LIX (1948), 189, 214.

R. HELM, 'Papinius', *RE*, XVIII, 3, 984, 997 (1949).

K. WEITZMANN, *Gk. Mythology in Byzantine Art* (Princeton, 1951), pp. 19–21, 85–7, 165–8, 192–3; figs. 12–16, 205–11.

RELATIONSHIP WITH OTHER POETS[6]

R. BITSCHOFSKY, *De C. Sollii Apollinaris Sidonii studiis Statianis*, Vienna, 1881.

B. DEIPSER, *De P.P.S. Virgilii et Ovidii imitatore*, diss. phil. Argent. v (Strasbourg, 1881), 91.

---

[1] Criticisms by R. Helm, *Berl. Phil. Woch.* XXVII (1907), 590; A. Souter, *CQ*, I (1907), 80; P. H. Damsté, *Mnem.* 2nd ser. XXXV (1907), 130.

[2] Criticisms by R. Helm, *Berl. Phil. Woch.* XXXV (1915), 550; H. W. Garrod, *CR*, XXVIII (1914), 67.

[3] Criticism of first ed. by R. Helm, *Berl. Phil. Woch.* XXII (1902), 972.

[4] Criticism by L. Herrmann, *Latomus*, XI (1952), 222.

[5] Abounds in mistakes, but provides useful material.

[6] Several of these articles contain little or no reference to the *Achilleid*.

II. BIBLIOGRAPHY

W. Michler, *De P.P.S. M. Annaei Lucani imitatore*, diss. Breslau, 1914.

R. B. Steele, 'Interrelation of the Lat. poets under Domitian', *CPh*, xxv (1930), 328.

P. Ercole, 'Stazio e Giovenale', *Riv. indo-greco-ital.* xv (1931), 43.

J. H. Mozley, 'St. as an Imitator of Virgil and Ovid', *Cl. Weekly*, xxvii (1933), 33.

SOURCES

E. Eissfeldt, *Ueber Quellen u. Vorbilder des P.P.S.*, progr. Helmstadt, 1900.

H. Kürschner, *P.P.S. quibus in Achilleide componenda usus esse videatur fontibus*, diss. Marburg, 1907.

A. Körte, 'Euripides' Skyrier', *Hermes*, lxix (1934), 1; cf. R. Pfeiffer, 'Die Σκύριοι des Sophokles', *Philol.* lxxxviii (1933), 1.

K. Weitzmann (see 'General').

See also Roscher, *Lex. Mythol.*, and *RE*, both s.v. 'Achilleus', 'Lykomedes', etc.

MSS. AND SCHOLIA[1]

P. Kohlmann, 'Die Pariser Handschr. der Ach. des St.', *Philol.* xxxiv (1876), 474.

C. Schenkl, 'De Statii Ach. cod. Etonensi', *Wiener Stud.* iv (1882), 96.

K. Wotke, 'Handschr. Beitr. zu St.', *Zeitschr. f. d. österr. Gymn.* xlii (1891), 200.

H. Mayer, 'Ueber eine Berliner Handschr. der Ach. des St.', *Philol.* li (1892), 381.[2]

R. Förster, 'Handschr. der Zamoyski'schen Bibliothek', *Rhein. Mus.* lv (1900), 456.[3]

F. V. Gustafsson, 'De St. Ach. cod. Monacensi', *Festschr. J. Vahlen* (1900), 491.

L. Castiglioni, 'Analecta' (a codex Ambrosianus), *Studi ital.* xii (1904), 279.

A. Klotz, 'Die Bartschen Statiushandschr.', *Rhein. Mus.* lix (1904), 373.

M. Manitius, 'Dresdener Scholien zu St. Ach.', *ibid.* 597.

K. Hartmann, '2 Fragm. antiker Schriftsteller aus der Augsburger Stadtsbibl.', *Berl. Phil. Woch.* xxvii (1907), 733.[4]

New Palaeographical Society, *Facsimiles*, i, pl. 110; cf. E. Maunde Thompson, Introduction to Gk. and Lat. Palaeography, pp. 350, 352 (facs. 121).

H. Tranchant, 'Le codex Univ. Brux.', *L'Antiquité Cl.* iii (1934), 451, pl. XXVI.[5]

O. A. W. Dilke, 'The Cod. Etonensis of St. Ach.', *CQ*, xliii (1949), 45.

TEXTUAL CRITICISM (see also criticisms of editions)

F. A. Menke, *Obs. crit. in St. Ach.*, Göttingen, 1814.

O. Müller, *Rhein. Mus.* xviii (1863), 189.

H. A. Koch, *Coniectan. in poetas Lat. pars altera*, progr. Frankfurt, 1865.

H. Köstlin, *Philol.* xxxv (1876), 532; xxxvii (1877), 289.

E. Baehrens, *Bursians Jahresber.* x (1877), 52.

---

[1] For other publications of scholia see Schanz-Hosius, *Röm. Literaturgeschichte*, ii, 539.

[2] This MS. is of no value; its scholia are given in *Philol.* liii (1894), 194.

[3] Also a poor MS.; the influence of P is noticeable in the omission of *pulso* at 1, 10 (*thebe* later hand). [4] A thirteenth-century MS.

[5] A twelfth–thirteenth-century MS. similar to Brux. 5338, but much overrated by the writer, since his extract shows it to be very corrupt.

C. E. SANDSTRÖM, *Studia critica in Pap. St.*, Upsala, 1878.

H. BLÜMNER, *Königsberger wiss. Monatsbl.* VI (1878), 156.

J. J. CORNELISSEN, *Mnem.* 2nd ser. VII (1879), 308.

R. BITSCHOFSKY, *Fleckeisens neue Jahrb.* CXXI (1880), 499.

C. SCHENKL, *Wiener Stud.* IV (1882), 96.

O. MÜLLER, *Electa Statiana*, progr. Berlin, 1882.

L. HAVET, *Rev. de Phil.* VI (1882), 178; VII (1883), 102.

H. DEITER, *Philol.* XLIII (1884), 404.

M. C. P. SCHMIDT, *Woch. f. Phil.* IV (1885), 1099.

U. VON WILAMOWITZ-MÖLLENDORFF, *De tribus carminibus Lat.*, Göttingen, 1893–4.

F. VOLLMER, *Rhein. Mus.* LI (1896), 27.

H. DEITER, *Philol.* LVII (1898), 343.

F. V. GUSTAFSSON, *Festschr. J. Vahlen* (1900), 493.

A. KLOTZ, *Philol.* LXI (1902), 292.

P. H. DAMSTÉ, *Mnem.* 2nd ser. XXXV (1907), 130.

M. R. J. BRINKGREVE, *Mnem.* 2nd ser. XLII (1914), 108.

K. PRINZ, *Philol.* LXXIX (1924), 188.

W. MOREL, *CR*, LV (1941), 75.

D. S. ROBERTSON, *CR*, LVI (1942), 117.

R. D. WILLIAMS, *Proc. Camb. Philol. Soc.* n.s. I (1950–1), 17.

G. P. GOOLD, *CR*, n.s. I (1951), 71.

A. KER, *CQ*, n.s. III (1953), 10.

LANGUAGE, GRAMMAR, METRE, ETC.

O. MÜLLER, *Quaestiones Statianae*, Berlin, 1861.

J. AE. (EMIL) NAUKE, *Obs. crit. et gramm. in P.P.S.*, diss. Bratislava, 1863.

K. KRAUSE, *De P.P.S. comparationibus epicis*, Halle, 1871.

E. KRANICH, *Die Alliteration bei P.P.S.*, Mähr. Neustadt, 1886.

H. L. WILSON, *The Metaphor in the Epic Poems of P.P.S.*, Baltimore, 1898.

A. KLOTZ, 'Thyrsa, Neutr. plur.', *Archiv f. Lat. Lex.* XII (1900), 130.

M. SCHAMBERGER, *De P.P.S. verborum novatore*, diss. phil. Hall. XVII (1907), 231.

A. KLOTZ, 'Thyrsa, Neutr. plur.', *Archiv f. Lat. Lex.* XV (1908), 401.

P. H. DAMSTÉ, 'De verbi mutandi usu apud P.P.S.', *Sertum Nabericum* (Festschr. S. A. Naber), Leiden (1908), 79.

H. SCHUBERT, *De P.P.S. artis gramm. et metr. ratione*, diss. Greifswald, 1913.

R. LUNDERSTEDT, *De synecdochae apud P.P.S. usu*, diss. Jena, 1913.

O. A. W. DILKE, 'The Metrical Treatment of Proper Names in St.', *CR*, LXIII (1949), 50.[1]

R. D. WILLIAMS, 'The local Abl. in St.', *CQ*, n.s. I (1951), 143.

[1] For the word *Edonius* cf. P. Wessner, 'Lucan, Statius u. Juvenal bei den röm. Grammatikern', *Phil. Woch.* XLIX (1929), 334.

P. PAPINI STATI
ACHILLEIS

CODICES

P = codex Parisinus 8051 (Puteaneus) saec. ix.
E = codex Etonensis 150 saec. xi.
B = codex Bernensis 156 (Danielis) saec. xi.
K = codex Guelferbytanus (Gudianus 54) saec. xi (in supplementis k).
Q = codex Parisinus 10317 saec. x (in supplementis q).
R = codex Monacensis 14557 saec. xiv (Ratisponensis).
l = Lactantius.

LIBER PRIMUS

MAGNANIMUM Aeaciden formidatamque Tonanti
progeniem et patrio vetitam succedere caelo,
diva, refer. quamquam acta viri multum inclita cantu
Maeonio (sed plura vacant), nos ire per omnem—
sic amor est—heroa velis Scyroque latentem   5
Dulichia proferre tuba nec in Hectore tracto
sistere, sed tota iuvenem deducere Troia.
tu modo, si veterem digno deplevimus haustu,
da fontes mihi, Phoebe, novos ac fronde secunda
necte comas: neque enim Aonium nemus advena pulso   10
nec mea nunc primis augescunt tempora vittis.
scit Dircaeus ager meque inter prisca parentum
nomina cumque suo numerant Amphione Thebae.
   At tu, quem longe primum stupet Itala virtus
Graiaque, cui geminae florent vatumque ducumque   15
certatim laurus—olim dolet altera vinci—,
da veniam ac trepidum patere hoc sudare parumper
pulvere: te longo necdum fidente paratu
molimur magnusque tibi praeludit Achilles.
   Solverat Oebalio classem de litore pastor   20
Dardanus incautas blande populatus Amyclas
plenaque materni referens praesagia somni
culpatum relegebat iter, qua condita ponto
fluctibus invisis iam Nereis imperat Helle,

2 cęlo P² (*om.* P¹)   3 Diva re refer E   multū *ex* multa Q: multa *O. Müller*
canto E   4 vocant BK¹Q   per *om.* E   5 sic] hic *Menke* la/tentem E
8 veterem P: veteres EBR: vere *ex* veteres KQ   deplevimus *ex* defl- P hausta Q¹
9 Da mihi feve (o *add.* E² *sup. lin.*) novos fontes ER   10 annium E pulso *om.* P
11 albescunt B²K²R *cum dett.*: anguescunt *Bernartius*   13 suo numerant tuo
anphione E   14 primus P ital/a Q   15 florent *ex* floret Q ducemque P
17 sudare EQR: suadere P *cum dett.*: su/dere K: su/dare *ex* suadere B: sordere
Baehrens   18 nondum E paratu *ex* -um P: *ex* -o Q   21 clam depopulatus
Menke (*cf. Sid. Carm.* IX, 122)   22 somnii B²   24 nereis *om.* B¹, *add. in mg.*
man. rec.

cum Thetis Idaeos—heu numquam vana parentum   25
auguria!—expavit vitreo sub gurgite remos.
nec mora et undosis turba comitante sororum
prosiluit thalamis: fervent coeuntia Phrixi
litora et angustum dominas non explicat aequor.
Illa ubi discusso primum subit aëra ponto,   30
'Me petit haec, mihi classis' ait 'funesta minatur,
agnosco monitus et Protea vera locutum.
ecce novam Priamo facibus de puppe levatis
fert Bellona nurum: video iam mille carinis
Ionium Aegaeumque premi; nec sufficit, omnis   35
quod plaga Graiugenum tumidis coniurat Atridis:
iam pelago terrisque meus quaeretur Achilles,
et volet ipse sequi. quid enim cunabula parvo
Pelion et torvi commisimus antra magistri?
illic, ni fallor, Lapitharum proelia ludit   40
inprobus et patria iam se metitur in hasta.
o dolor, o seri materno in corde timores!
non potui infelix, cum primum gurgite nostro
Rhoeteae cecidere trabes, attollere magnum
aequor et incesti praedonis vela profunda   45
tempestate sequi cunctasque inferre sorores?
nunc quoque—sed tardum, iam plena iniuria raptae.
ibo tamen pelagique deos dextramque secundi,
quod superest, complexa Iovis per Tethyos annos
grandaevumque patrem supplex miseranda rogabo   50
unam hiemem.'
            Dixit magnumque in tempore regem
aspicit. Oceano veniebat ab hospite, mensis
laetus et aequoreo diffusus nectare vultus,

---

25 idaeis P   **30** ubi *om.* P   subiit B^1: petit E   **32** vera *ex* vana Q: *ex* verba K
33 nova E   faucibus de pupe E   **35** om/nis (*del.* i) E   **36** graiugerum E
38 ille R   **39** comissimus P: comisimus E   **40** ni BEKQR: nil P, *cod. Coll.*
Lincoln.   **42** o //seri (seri *ex* miseri) B   **44** Rhoetea P   **45** profana *Cornelissen*
47 tardum] tardum est R *cum dett.*: tarde est E   **48** secundam E   **49** super
est Q   amnes ER *et dett. quidam*   **50** miserando E   **51** dixit *om.* Q   tempore]
pectore Q: tēp E   rege *ex* reges P   **52** oceani *ex* -o Q   **53** aequoreos *Koch*
diffussus EB

unde hiemes ventique silent; cantuque quieto
armigeri Tritones eunt scopulosaque cete   55
Tyrrhenique greges circumque infraque rotantur
rege salutato; placidis ipse arduus undis
eminet et triplici telo iubet ire iugales;
illi spumiferos glomerant a pectore cursus,
pone natant delentque pedum vestigia cauda;   60
cum Thetis: 'O magni genitor rectorque profundi,
aspicis in qualis miserum patefeceris usus
aequor? eunt tutis terrarum crimina velis,
ex quo iura freti maiestatemque repostam
rupit Iasonia puppis Pagasaea rapina.   65
en aliud furto scelus et spolia hospita portans
navigat iniustae temerarius arbiter Idae,
eheu quos gemitus terris caeloque daturus,
quos mihi! sic Phrygiae pensamus gaudia palmae,
hi Veneris mores, hoc gratae munus alumnae.   70
has saltem—num semideos nostrumque reportant
Thesea?—si quis adhuc undis honor, obrue puppes,
aut permitte fretum! nulla inclementia: fas sit
pro nato timuisse mihi. da pellere luctus,
nec tibi de tantis placeat me fluctibus unum   75
litus et Iliaci scopulos habitare sepulcri.'
    Orabat laniata genas et pectore nudo

54 Unde PEBR: Undae (-ę) KQ hiemes PBR: ȳmes (e *post* y *add. sup. lin.*) E:
hilares KQ ventique] et venti E quieto] soluto ER[1]   55 Armigeri/ P scopulosaque *ex* -asaque P: scopolosaque K   56 circum (*om.* que) E   57 pladis//
(*del.* que; ci *sup. lin.*) E   58 triciplici E iuvet P   59 glomerantes *ex* glomerant
a Q cursus P: fluctus EBKQR   60 caudae *Weitingh*   61 Tum R   62 patefeceris *ex* -erit E   67 *om.* B[1] Na/vigat E   68 Eheu PQ: Heu E[1]R: Heu heu E[2]B
cum dett.: Eh heu K caeloque PEBR: pelagoque KQ *cum dett.* (pe- *in ras.* Q)
69 gaudia P: praemia EBKQR *cum dett.*   70 His E[2] mores veneris E   71 Hee
saltem R: Assaltim E num PB: numi E: n̄ *ex* num K: non R *cum dett.*: nunc (-nc
in ras.) Q nostrumve *Queck*   72 undis honor P, *Leid.*: honor undis ER: undis
honos BKQ   73 Haut P: et *Wakefield* nullum B[1]   74 tumuisse B[1] da pellere
luctus P: da tollere fluctus BKQR: adtolle (da tollere E[2]) fructus E   75 Ne R
de tantis] detentis *Brandes* me *ex* de Q fluctibus unum EBKQR: fluctibus
unam P: neptibus unam *Baehrens*: fluctibus imum *Havet*: fletibus udam O. *Müller*:
luctibus unum *Deiter*   76 iliacis oculos P   77 genas] comas R, *et* Q[2] *in ras.*

caeruleis obstabat equis. sed rector aquarum
invitat curru dictisque ita mulcet amicis:
'Ne pete Dardaniam frustra, Theti, mergere classem;   **80**
fata vetant: ratus ordo deis miscere cruentas
Europamque Asiamque manus, consultaque belli
Iuppiter et tristes edixit caedibus annos.
quem tu illic natum Sigeo in pulvere, quanta
aspicies victrix Phrygiarum funera matrum,   **85**
cum tuus Aeacides tepido modo sanguine Teucros
undabit campos, modo crassa exire vetabit
flumina et Hectoreo tardabit funere currus
inpelletque manu nostros, opera inrita, muros!
Pelea iam desiste queri thalamosque minores: **90**
crederis peperisse Iovi; nec inulta dolebis
cognatisque utere fretis: dabo tollere fluctus,
cum reduces Danai nocturnaque signa Caphereus
exseret et dirum pariter quaeremus Ulixem.'
Dixerat. illa gravi vultum demissa repulsa,   **95**
quae iam excire fretum et ratibus bellare parabat
Iliacis, alios animo commenta paratus,
tristis ad Haemonias detorquet bracchia terras.
ter conata manu, liquidum ter gressibus aequor
reppulit et niveas feriunt vada Thessala plantas.   **100**
laetantur montes et conubialia pandunt

---

78 aquis E sed P: tunc EBKQR rector P*l*: ductor EBKQR *cum dett.*
81 verant P; *cf. Th.* xII, 380 diis *ex* deas Q   **82** Europamque asiamque P:
Europeque asieque E: Europaeque asiaeque BKR *cum dett.*: Europae atque
asiaeque Q: Europen Asiamque *Menke* belli P: bella EBKQR   **83** edixit (e-
in ras.) tristes et (et K²) K indixit E   **84** natum in Sigeo *Lachmann ad Lucr.*
III, 374   **85** Aspicie E   **86** tepido PER: trepidos BKQ teucros PER: teucro
BKQ   **87** Undavit P: Undabit *ex* -vit E: mutabit *Damsté*; *v. adn.* vetabit *ex*
-vit E   **88** tardavit P*l*: tardabit (b *in ras.*) E pondere *l*; *v. adn.*   **89** manu
BKQR: ma(u *sup. lin.*) E: manus P operarii irrita E   **91** Crederis PR:
Cre//deris K: Credideris EBQ*l*   **92** Cognatisque P: Cognatis EBKQR
94 queramus K¹ ulixem EBKQ: ulixen P(R?) *et schol. Th.* IX, 307; *cf. Housman,*
Journ. Philol. xxxi (1910), 259–60   **95** dimissa EK: remissa R   **96** Quae iam *ex*
Qua&am (*i.e.* quaedam) P exiere R   **97** animo P: iterum EBQR: iterum/////
(*eras.* animo) K; *v. adn.*   **98** terra P   **99** aequor] iter E   **101** conubilia E

antra sinus lateque deae Sperchios abundat
obvius et dulci vestigia circuit unda.
illa nihil gavisa locis, sed coepta fatigat
pectore consilia et sollers pietate magistra 105
longaevum Chirona petit. domus ardua montem
perforat et longo suspendit Pelion arcu;
pars exhausta manu, partem sua ruperat aetas.
signa tamen divumque tori et quem quisque sacrarit
accubitu genioque locum monstrantur; at intra 110
Centauri stabula alta patent, non aequa nefandis
fratribus: hic hominum nullos experta cruores
spicula nec truncae bellis genialibus orni
aut consanguineos fracti crateres in hostes,
sed pharetrae insontes et inania terga ferarum. 115
haec quoque dum viridis; nam tunc labor unus inermi
nosse salutiferas dubiis animantibus herbas,
aut monstrare lyra veteres heroas alumno.
et tunc venatu rediturum in limine primo
opperiens properatque dapes largoque serenat 120
igne domum, cum visa procul de litore surgens
Nereis; erumpit silvis—dant gaudia vires—
notaque desueto crepuit senis ungula campo.
tunc blandus dextra atque imos demissus in armos
pauperibus tectis inducit et admonet antri. 125
    Iamdudum tacito lustrat Thetis omnia visu

102 Spercheos *Menke*; *v. adn.* obundat *Havet* 104 fatigant R 106–7 *om.* K¹,
suppl. K² *in mg.* 107 longa (o *supra* a) E pelion *ex* spelion E 108 exusta E
rupera P 109 Signa *ex* Signat P et que E: quem R sacrarit *Menke*: sacravit P:
sacrarat BEKR *cum dett.*: s/ararat (c *sup. lin.*) Q: sacrasset *Prisc.* 110 locum
PKR², *Prisc.*: locumque B: locus E: locus (?) *ex* locum Q: *om.* R¹: loci *Menke*
monstratur (*cum dett.*) *ex* -antur Q intus ER 112 hic] ac ER 113 belli E
genalibus E: gentilibus *Baehrens* ortu E 114 rateres *ex* gr- P 115 inavia E
116 viridis] iuvenis R *et sub lin.* K²: virididis E inertu E 117 duviis
animalibus E 119 *om.*, *add. in mg.* E tum K: cum B 121 surgens PER:
mater BKQ 122 erupit E *cum dett.* 123 Notaque PB: Motaque EKQR
senis *ex* senes E 124 Tu R atque imos] que himo (i *in ras.*) E demissus PR:
summissus EBQ: summissos K in armis R¹: intrans E 125 admonet P, *Trev.*:
admovet EBKQR antri P: antris EBKQR 126 Iamdum R omā P: omīa E

nec perpessa moras: 'Ubinam mea pignora, Chiron,
dic', ait, 'aut cur ulla puer iam tempora ducit
te sine? non merito trepidus sopor atraque matri
signa deum et magnos utinam mentita timores?   130
namque modo infensos utero mihi contuor enses,
nunc planctu livere manus, modo in ubera saevas
ire feras; saepe ipsa—nefas!—sub inania natum
Tartara et ad Stygios iterum fero mergere fontes.
hos abolere metus magici iubet ordine sacri   135
Carpathius vates puerumque sub axe peracto
secretis lustrare fretis, ubi litora summa
Oceani et genitor tepet inlabentibus astris
Pontus. ibi ignotis horrenda piacula divis
donaque—sed longum cuncta enumerare vetorque.   140
trade magis!' sic ficta parens: neque enim ille dedisset,
si molles habitus et tegmina foeda fateri
ausa seni. tunc ipse refert: 'Duc, optima, quaeso,
duc, genetrix, humilique deos infringe precatu.
nam superant tua vota modum placandaque multum   145
invidia est. non addo metum, sed vera fatebor:
nescio quid magnum—nec me patria omina fallunt—
vis festina parat tenuesque supervenit annos.
olim et ferre minas avideque audire solebat
imperia et nostris procul haut discedere ab antris;   150
nunc illum non Ossa capit, non Pelion ingens

---

127 chiro P   128 dic] Sic ER   iam] ia E   129 num merito B: num
inmerito K²: iam merito *Prinz*   130 dolores ER   131 namque: *v. adn.*
infensos BKQ, *Prisc., Eutych.*: infessos P: in ensiferos (-eros *cum ras.*) E: infestos
R contuor] tueor E   132 libere P manus] genas B ubera *ex* libera E
133 Inreferas E   134 ad *om.* P fere E   135 magici EBKQR: magni P iuvet P
136 vatis Q sub *om.* E pacto (*i.e.* peracto) P: probato EBKQR: reducto
Owen   137 secretis *ex* sacratis R   138 illaentibus E austris Q² *in ras.* (s *prius*
sup. lin.)   139 ibi P: ubi EBKQR ignotis (? -iis) *ex* ignotus E   141 ficta P:
fata EBKQ: fa/ta R enim *del.* Q² illa R¹   143 ipse P: ille EBKQR
144 instringe E   145 nam] non *Havet*; *v. adn.*   146 invia (di *sup. lin.*) E
147 Nescia Q nec *ex* non E paria BK²Q omnia P: omīa E   148 vis] Lus E
tenerosque R *cum dett.*   149 et ferre] effere P avideque audire P: et obire audita
EBKQR   150 discedere EBKQR²: desce/dere P: discere R¹

Pharsaliaeve nives. ipsi mihi saepe queruntur
Centauri raptasque domos abstractaque coram
armenta et semet campis fluviisque fugari,
insidiasque et bella parant tumideque minantur.   155
olim equidem, Argoos pinus cum Thessala reges
hac veheret, iuvenem Alciden et Thesea vidi—
sed taceo.'
    Figit gelidus Nereida pallor:
ille aderat multo sudore et pulvere maior,
et tamen arma inter festinatosque labores   160
dulcis adhuc visu: niveo natat ignis in ore
purpureus fulvoque nitet coma gratior auro.
necdum prima nova lanugine vertitur aetas,
tranquillaeque faces oculis et plurima vultu
mater inest: qualis Lycia venator Apollo   165
cum redit et saevis permutat plectra pharetris.
forte et laetus adest—o quantum gaudia formae
adiciunt!—: fetam Pholoes sub rupe leaenam
perculerat ferro vacuisque reliquerat antris
ipsam, sed catulos adportat et incitat ungues.   170
quos tamen, ut fido genetrix in limine visa est,
abicit exceptamque avidis circumligat ulnis,
iam gravis amplexu iamque aequus vertice matri.
insequitur magno iam tunc conexus amore
Patroclus tantisque extenditur aemulus actis,   175
par studiis aevique modis, sed robore longe,
et tamen aequali visurus Pergama fato.

---

152 Pharsaliaeve nives P: Thessaliaeve (Thesal-) nives BKQ: Thessalie nives R:
Thessaliae iuvenes E; *v. adn.*   **153** domos *ex* domus E   **154** fluvisque PE
155 timideque P: tumidique EBKQR: *alii* tumideque, timidique   **156** argoos
PE²BKQ (argo os P): arogos E¹: argivos R: argeos *Trev.*: argolicos (*ut conj.*
N. Heinsius) *Patav.* 233 puuis E   **156–7** pinus cum thesea vidi P¹, *verbis*
Thessala...et omissis: *corr.* P²; *v. adn.*   **158** frangit R   **160** arma *om.* Q
165 venatur R¹   **166** senis E   **169** vacuusque R   **170** asportat R   **172** ex-
ceptam abidis E   **174** tunc *om.* K   **175** accenditur *Bernartius*   **176** modo
B   nec robore longe *Sandström*: sed robora longe *Schrader*: sed robore
dispar (*ut conj. Colinaeus*) *cod. Coll. Lincoln.*   **177** Sed tamen Q²: et tandem
Sandström

Protinus ille subit rapido quae proxima saltu
flumina fumantisque genas crinemque novatur
fontibus: Eurotae qualis vada Castor anhelo   180
intrat equo fessumque sui iubar excitat astri.
miratur comitque senex, nunc pectora mulcens
nunc fortis umeros; angunt sua gaudia matrem.
tunc libare dapes Baccheaque munera Chiron
orat et attonitae varia oblectamina nectens   185
elicit extremo chelyn et solantia curas
fila movet leviterque expertas pollice chordas
dat puero. canit ille libens inmania laudum
semina: quot tumidae superarit iussa novercae
Amphitryoniades, crudum quo Bebryca caestu   190
obruerit Pollux, quanto circumdata nexu
ruperit Aegides Minoia bracchia tauri,
maternos in fine toros superisque gravatum
Pelion: hic victo risit Thetis anxia vultu.
nox trahit in somnos; saxo collabitur ingens   195
Centaurus blandusque umeris se innectit Achilles,
quamquam ibi fida parens, adsuetaque pectora mavult.
    At Thetis undisonis per noctem in rupibus astans,
quae nato secreta velit, quibus abdere terris
destinet, huc illuc divisa mente volutat.   200
proxima, sed studiis multum Mavortia, Thrace;

---

178 rapidoque pr. R   **179** fuscantesque *Cornelissen* crinesque ER: crimenque
K¹Q   **180** vaga P   **181** fessumque EBKQR: fessusque P astris E
183 gaudia *add.* E² *sup. lin.*   **185** attonitae varia obiectamina P: attonitam vario
(vari E) oblectamine EBKQR nectens PBK¹ (n- *in ras.* B): fallens K²: mulcens
Q: mulcet E *cum dett.*   **186** chelyn] citharam ER curas] verba B (curas *in mg.*)
187 experta/s Q: expertes K   **188** laudem Q¹   **189** quod (*i.q.* quot) PEBK¹:
quo *ex* quod Q: quae K²: quo modo R superaret Q: superavit R   **190** crudo
ER: *om.* B¹ quo *ex* quod K: quod PQ: quid B: que R: *om.* E (*et* bebricia)
192 minoia PB*l*: minoi/ KQ: minoi (-oi *in ras.* E) ER tari P   **193** gratum R
194 victo BKQ: huicto P: ficto ER *cum dett.*: iuncto *Gustafsson*   **196** blandum-
que EB: blandisque R se innectit P: innectit EBKQR achillem E   **198** hastans
P: adstans B   **199** abdere EBKQR (ab- *in ras.* Q): addere P *et dett. quidam*
telis P   **200** Destinat EQ   **201** sed] nec K² *et in mg.* B² (*om.* B¹ *spatio
relicto*)

nec Macetum gens dura placet laudumque daturi
Cecropidae stimulos; nimium opportuna carinis
Sestos Abydenique sinus. placet ire per artas
Cycladas; hic spretae Myconosque humilisque Seriphos   **205**
et Lemnos non aequa viris atque hospita Delos
gentibus. inbelli nuper Lycomedis ab aula
virgineos coetus et litora persona ludo
audierat, duros laxantem Aegaeona nexus
missa sequi centumque dei numerare catenas.   **210**
haec placet, haec timidae tellus tutissima matri.
qualis vicino volucris iam sedula partu
iamque timens, qua fronde domum suspendat inanem;
providet hic ventos, hic anxia cogitat angues,
hic homines: tandem dubiae placet umbra, novisque   **215**
vix stetit in ramis et protinus arbor amatur.
    Altera consilio superest tristemque fatigat
cura deam, natum ipsa sinu conplexa per undas
an magno Tritone ferat, ventosne volucres
advocet an pelago solitam Thaumantida pasci.   **220**
elicit inde fretis et murice frenat acuto
delphinas biiugos, quos illi maxima Tethys
gurgite Atlanteo pelagi sub valle sonora
nutrierat—nullis vada per Neptunia glaucae
tantus honos formae nandique potentia nec plus   **225**
pectoris humani—; iubet hos subsistere pleno
litore, ne nudae noceant contagia terrae.
ipsa dehinc toto resolutum pectore Achillem,

---

202 macedum Q² laudumve *Baehrens*   **203** Ciclopides R   **204** artas P: altas
EBKQR; *v. adn.*   **205** his Q myconos/ (*eras.* que) Q: myconos R *cum dett.*
humilesque K seristos EB: seristes R   **206** atque inhospita Q: et inospita E
207 inbellis R nicomedis E   **208** consona R   **209** dura E   **210** Iussa ER *et*
dett. quidam   **212** volucres P   **213** fronde *ex* fronte E suspendat EBKQR:
suspendit P   **214** hic...hic PBK¹Q: hinc...hinc K²R *cum dett.*: hinc *ex* hunc...
hinc E anxia] auxit E   **215** Hic PBK¹: Hinc R: Hinc *ex* Hic K²Q; *ex* Hunc E
dubiae] tiliae *Damsté*   **219** ventosve E   **220** solita E   **221** Elicit] -it *in ras.*
K¹ (*ex* -et), Q¹ frenat murice E   **222** Delphines ER biiugos PER: biiuges
BKQ thetis *codd.*   **224** Nutrigerat P   **225** honor E   **226** iuvet P   **227** nec R
228 corpore *Wakefield*

qui pueris sopor, Haemonii de rupibus antri
ad placidas deportat aquas et iussa tacere   **230**
litora; monstrat iter totoque effulgurat orbe
Cynthia. prosequitur divam celeresque recursus
securus pelagi Chiron rogat udaque celat
lumina et abreptos subito iamiamque latentes
erecto prospectat equo, qua cana parumper   **235**
spumant signa fugae et liquido perit orbita ponto.
illum non alias rediturum ad Thessala Tempe
iam tristis Pholoe, iam nubilus ingemit Othrys
et tenuior Sperchios aquis speluncaque docti
muta senis; quaerunt puerilia carmina Fauni   **240**
et sperata diu plorant conubia Nymphae.
Iam premit astra dies humilique ex aequore Titan
rorantes evolvit equos et ab aethere magno
sublatum curru pelagus cadit, at vada mater
Scyria iamdudum fluctus emensa tenebat,   **245**
exierantque iugo fessi delphines erili,
cum pueri tremefacta quies oculique patentes
infusum sensere diem. stupet aëre primo:
quae loca, qui fluctus, ubi Pelion? omnia versa
atque ignota videt dubitatque agnoscere matrem.   **250**
occupat illa manu blandeque adfata paventem:
'Si mihi, care puer, thalamos sors aequa tulisset,
quos dabat, aetheriis ego te conplexa tenerem
sidus grande plagis, magnique puerpera caeli

229 *om.* E, *add. in mg.* pueri E: pueri/ K   **230** At P adportat Q   **231** effulgurat
PEBR: effulgerat KQ (-serat Q *rec. man. cum dett.*)   **232** diva E   **233** rogat
EBKQR: rotat P: notat *Schenkl*   **234** ereptos (e *prius sup. lin.*) E: ereptus R[1]:
areptos R[2]   **235** Et (t *punctis not.*) recto E: Erepto R[1]   **239** tenuior *Postgate*:
senior P: tenuis EBKQR: segnior et *Gustafsson* spercheos P: sperchios BK:
sperchius EQR   **240** sevis E   **242** humilique P: humilisque BKQ: humidus-
que ER *et dett. quidam*   **244** in curru R at EBQ: ad P: ac R: ac *ex* ad K
245 emissa P   **247** patentes PER: iacentes BKQ: paventes *Baehrens*   **248** aera
R   **249** fluctus] *alterum* u *in ras.* P versa P *et cod. Barthii:* versat EBKQR
252 tulisset P: dedisset EBKQR   **253** ethereos B   **254a** Clato columba
iubat lachesis trahit atro poscat (=Clotho colum baiulat, Lachesis trahit, Atropos
occat) E: ·.· *in mg.* E[2]

nil humiles Parcas terrenaque fata vererer.   **255**
nunc inpar tibi, nate, genus, praeclusaque leti
tantum a matre via est; quin et metuenda propinquant
tempora et extremis admota pericula metis.
cedamus, paulumque animos submitte viriles
atque habitus dignare meos. si Lydia dura   **260**
pensa manu mollesque tulit Tirynthius hastas,
si decet aurata Bacchum vestigia palla
verrere, virgineos si Iuppiter induit artus,
nec magnum ambigui fregerunt Caenea sexus:
hac sine, quaeso, minas nubemque exire malignam.   **265**
mox iterum campos, iterum Centaurica reddam
lustra tibi: per ego hoc decus et ventura iuventae
gaudia, si terras humilemque experta maritum
te propter, si progenitum Stygos amne severo
armavi—totumque utinam!—, cape tuta parumper   **270**
tegmina nil nocitura animo. cur ora reducis
quidve parant oculi? pudet hoc mitescere cultu?
per te, care puer, cognata per aequora iuro,
nesciet hoc Chiron.' sic horrida pectora tractat
nequiquam mulcens; obstat genitorque roganti   **275**
nutritorque ingens et cruda exordia magnae
indolis. effrenae tumidum velut igne iuventae
si quis equum primis submittere temptet habenis:
ille diu campis fluviisque et honore superbo
gavisus non colla iugo, non aspera praebet   **280**

---

255 Nihil P   **256** praeclusaque *ex* -culs- Q: praeclausaque K   **257** a matre PE: matre BKQR   **259** submitte] depone B   **260** avitus P: habitas B¹ licia ER¹: ledia B   **261** -que *om.* R   **263** Verere E arcus P   **264** cena E¹: e *add. sup. lin.* E²   **265** Hac *ex* Has (*ut vid.*) B (hac *Postgate*): Hae P: Has EKR, (-s *in ras.*) Q nubemque...malignam P: numenque...malignum EBKQR   **267** Lusta P iubente P: Ivente E   **269** stagis R   **270** totumtumque P   **271** nihil P nocturna K¹ reduces P   **273** puer *om.* E¹, *add. sup. lin.* E²   **274** hęc (ę *in ras.*) Q   **275** Nec quiquam E mulcent E¹ obstant K   **276** -que *om.* K¹ magnae BKQR: magna E: manent P: manant *Klotz* (*quo recepto post* indolis effrenae *interpungit Gustafsson*)   **277** Indo//lis (*eras.* ci) P effreni R   **278** subminittere E tempet P: temptat K   **279** fluvisque P

ora lupis dominique fremit captivus inire
imperia atque alios miratur discere cursus.
　Quis deus attonitae fraudes astumque parenti
contulit? indocilem quae mens detraxit Achillem?
Palladi litoreae celebrabat Scyros honorum　　　　　　285
forte diem, placidoque satae Lycomede sorores
luce sacra patriis, quae rara licentia, muris
exierant dare veris opes divaeque severas
fronde ligare comas et spargere floribus hastam.
omnibus eximium formae decus, omnibus idem　　　　290
cultus et expleto teneri iam fine pudoris
virginitas matura toris annique tumentes.
sed quantum virides pelagi Venus addita Nymphas
obruit, aut umeris quantum Diana relinquit
Naidas, effulget tantum regina decori　　　　　　　295
Deidamia chori pulchrisque sororibus obstat.
illius et roseo flammatur purpura vultu
et gemmis lux maior inest et blandius aurum:
atque ipsi par forma deaest, si pectoris angues
ponat et exempta pacetur casside vultus.　　　　　　300
hanc ubi ducentem longe socia agmina vidit,
trux puer et nullo temeratus pectora motu
deriguit totisque novum bibit ossibus ignem.
nec latet haustus amor, sed fax vibrata medullis
in vultus atque ora redit lucemque genarum　　　　　305
tinguit et inpulsam tenui sudore pererrat.
lactea Massagetae veluti cum pocula fuscant

---

281 dominique *ex* domumque K　fremit P: gemit EBKQR *cum dett.*　　283 aus-
tumque R　　285 celerabat Q　scyros (sciros) EBKQR, *Prisc.*: scyrus P　honorem
Prisc.　　287 a patriis E　　288 versis P　severas *ex* sorores K²　　289 comas
ligare P　　291 et *om.* E　expleta QR　　292 animique B¹KQ　　293 pelagi
virides ER¹　inclita R　nympha P　　294 relinquat K: reliquit E
295–6 quantum R　decoro...choro ER　Deidamea P　　297 et] e *Gevartius* (?)　　298 gemis E　　299 deest P: deae EBKQR　　300 et excepta R:
excepta E　pacetur P: placetur EBKQR　capside P　　301 socia *om.* R
302 temerarius R　vultu (mo *supra* vul) P; *cf.* 297, 300　　303 Deriguit
BQ¹: Diriguit PEKQ²R　　305 redit] subit *Damsté*: ruit *Garrod*　　306 impulsum
edd. vett.　　307 fucant D. *Heinsius*

sanguine puniceo vel ebur corrumpitur ostro,
sic variis manifesta notis palletque rubetque
flamma repens. eat atque ultro ferus hospita sacra   310
disiciat turbae securus et inmemor aevi,
ni pudor et iunctae teneat reverentia matris.
ut pater armenti quondam ductorque futurus,
cui nondum toto peraguntur cornua gyro,
cum sociam pastus niveo candore iuvencam   315
aspicit, ardescunt animi primusque per ora
spumat amor, spectant hilares obstantque magistri.
   Occupat arrepto iam conscia tempore mater:
'Hasne inter simulare choros et bracchia ludo
nectere, nate, grave est? gelida quid tale sub Ossa   320
Peliacisque iugis? o si mihi iungere curas
atque alium portare sinu contingat Achillem!'
mulcetur laetumque rubet visusque protervos
obliquat vestesque manu leviore repellit.
aspicit ambiguum genetrix cogique volentem   325
iniecitque sinus; tum colla rigentia mollit
submittitque graves umeros et fortia laxat
bracchia et inpexos certo domat ordine crines
ac sua dilecta cervice monilia transfert;
et picturato cohibens vestigia limbo   330
incessum motumque docet fandique pudorem.
qualiter artifici victurae pollice cerae

308 vel] veluti P   **310** recens ER *cum dett.*   **311** Dissiciat P: Dissiciat *ex*
Disseciat K: Dissiceat BQ: Discutiat ER *cum dett.*   **313** armati K¹ ductorque
P: rectorque EBKQR   **315** pastu (*ex* -us Q) EQ   **316** ardescunt PER:
ardescuntque BKQ   **317** obstantque P, *Trev.*: obtantque B: optantque EKQR
318 tempore *ex* -a K tempore conscia R   **319** Hosne R² *cum dett.*: Has Q
320 gelido E *et dett. quidam*   **322** portare *ex* -ate E achillem EBKQR: achillen
P; *cf. ad* 94   **323** laetumque BKQ: laetu/que *ex* laetumque P: letusque ER *cum
dett.* visosque P: virusque K supervos E: superbos BR   **325** cogique *Heinsius:*
cogique (t *sup. lin.*) *Leid.*: cogitque *cett.* volantem K¹: nolentem R   **326** iniectat-
que *Brinkgreve* tum BKQ: tunc PER recentia P: rigenda E   **328** imp/exos
(-l-) K donat P   **329** dilecta sua *Damsté*: sua tractata (?) *l*   **330** pictorato P
cohibens PER: cohibet BKQ   **331** Incessus motusque R   **332** artifici PBKQ,
Prisc.: artificis ER *cum dett.*

accipiunt formas ignemque manumque sequuntur,
talis erat divae natum mutantis imago.
nec luctata diu; superest nam plurimus illi   335
invita virtute decor, fallitque tuentes
ambiguus tenuique latens discrimine sexus.
Procedunt, iterumque monens iterumque fatigans
blanda Thetis: 'Sic ergo gradum, sic ora manusque,
nate, feres comitesque modis imitabere fictis,   340
ne te suspectum molli non misceat aulae
rector et incepti pereant mendacia furti.'
dicit et admoto non cessat comere tactu.
sic ubi virgineis Hecate lassata Therapnis
ad patrem fratremque redit, comes haeret eunti   345
mater et ipsa umeros exsertaque bracchia velat;
ipsa arcum pharetrasque locat vestemque latentem
deducit sparsosque tumet conponere crines.
Protinus adgreditur regem atque ibi testibus aris
'Hanc tibi' ait 'nostri germanam, rector, Achillis—   350
nonne vides ut torva genas aequandaque fratri?—
tradimus. arma umeris arcumque animosa petebat
ferre et Amazonio conubia pellere ritu.
sed mihi curarum satis est pro stirpe virili;
haec calathos et sacra ferat, tu frange regendo   355
indocilem sexuque tene, dum nubilis aetas
solvendusque pudor; neve exercere protervas

---

333 ignemque] lignumque *Blümner*   **335** diu est R   **336** Invita P, *cod.*
Bentleii: Invicta EBKQR: iam victa *Damsté*   **338** monens...fatigans P: monet
...fatigat EKQR: monet rursusque fatigat B   **339** ergo manus sic ora
(sicoro E) gradumque ER   **340** imitavere P   **341** Ne *ex* Nec K: Nec R
342 incepti PER: incerti BKQ   **343** Dicit PBKQR: Dixit E *cum dett.* cessat
EBKQR: distat P; *v. adn.* tactu *ex* tacta E   **344** laxata R *et schol.* Th. III, 422
therapnis *schol. ibid.*: therapinis P: pharetris EBKQR   **345** fratrem patremque
reddit E   **346** levat E: vestit R (ves. br. *cum signo transl.*)   **347** pharetramque
R arcu pharetraque levat *Schrader* locat PKQ: gerit EBR vestemque latentem
P: vestesque latentes EBKQR   **348** tumet *Gronovius*: timet PEB: studet R,
sup. lin. K² (*om.* K¹), *in ras.* Q   **350** achillis EB²KR: achilles P: achilli B¹Q
351 cenas P   **353** ferre] *alterum* r *in ras.* E: *alt.* e *sup. lin.* P   **356** sexuque
PEBQ: sexumque KR *cum dett.*   **357** catervas P *et ante corr.* (?) B¹

gymnadas aut lustris nemorum concede vagari.
intus ale et similes inter seclude puellas;
litore praecipue portuque arcere memento.   360
vidisti modo vela Phrygum: iam mutua iura
fallere transmissae pelago didicere carinae.'
   Accedit dictis pater ingenioque parentis
occultum Aeaciden—quis divum fraudibus obstet?—
accipit; ultro etiam veneratur supplice dextra   ·365
et grates electus agit: nec turba piarum
Scyriadum cessat nimio defigere visu
virginis ora novae, quantum cervice comisque
emineat quantumque umeros ac pectora fundat.
dehinc sociare choros castisque accedere sacris   370
hortantur ceduntque loco et contingere gaudent.
qualiter Idaliae volucres, ubi mollia frangunt
nubila, iam longum caeloque domoque gregatae,
si iunxit pinnas diversoque hospita tractu
venit avis, cunctae primum mirantur et horrent;   375
mox propius propiusque volant, atque aëre in ipso
paulatim fecere suam plausuque secundo
circumeunt hilares et ad alta cubilia ducunt.
   Digreditur multum cunctata in limine mater,
dum repetit monitus arcanaque murmura figit   380
auribus et tacito dat verba novissima vultu.
tunc excepta freto longe cervice reflexa
abnatat et blandis adfatur litora votis:
'Cara mihi tellus, magnae cui pignora curae
depositumque ingens timido commisimus astu,   385

---

358 haut R²   359 Tectus ale R   363 parentis] patentes Q   365 etiam] et R
veneratus EK   366 erectus E   367 niveo P; *cf. Th.* VII, 275 *et secundum E. H.*
Alton (CQ 1923, 179) *Th.* IV, 130   visum E   370 Dehinc (n *sup. lin.* P) PR: Dein
EBKQ   choris R *cum dett.*   371 ceduntque locum R *et conj. Damsté:* clauduntque locum *Garrod*   374 pennas BK²Q: pennes R   diverso B: -que *in ras.* K²
hospita *ex* -e K   tactu R   376 propius *om.* PBKR   atque] sociam iamque B
377 fere R   suam plausuque *ex* suamque plausu E   378 et alta E¹: et ablata R
379 cuncta E¹   380 reperit K   fingit R¹   381 vultu PER: voto BKQ
383 Adnatat B   384 pignore R¹   385 tumido B¹   comisimus P: com-
missimus E   austu R¹

sis felix taceasque, precor, quo more tacebat
Creta Rheae; te longus honos aeternaque cingent
templa nec instabili fama superabere Delo,
et ventis et sacra fretis interque vadosas
Cycladas, Aegaeae frangunt ubi saxa procellae,   390
Nereidum tranquilla domus iurandaque nautis
insula; ne solum Danaas admitte carinas,
ne, precor! "Hic thiasi tantum et nihil utile bellis:"
hoc famam narrare doce, dumque arma parantur
Dorica et alternum Mavors interfurit orbem,—   395
cedo equidem—sit virgo pii Lycomedis Achilles.'
    Interea meritos ultrix Europa dolores
dulcibus armorum furiis et supplice regum
conquestu flammata movet; quippe ambit Atrides
ille magis, cui nupta domi, facinusque relatu   400
asperat Iliacum: captam sine Marte, sine armis
progeniem caeli Spartaeque potentis alumnam,
iura, fidem, superos una calcata rapina.
hoc foedus Phrygium, haec geminae commercia terrae?
quid maneat populos, ubi tanta iniuria primos   405
degrassata duces?—coeunt gens omnis et aetas:
nec tantum exciti, bimari quos Isthmia vallo
claustra nec undisonae quos circuit umbo Maleae,
sed procul, admotas Phrixi qua semita iungi
Europamque Asiamque vetat, quasque ordine gentes   410
litore Abydeno maris alligat unda superni.
fervet amor belli concussasque erigit urbes.
aera domat Temese, quatitur navalibus ora

---

387 te *om.* E[1]   honor BKQ   cingnt E: cingant Q   **388** superavere P
390 plangunt *N. Heinsius*   **391** domos Q   noctis P   **392** ne *ex* nec K:
nec R   **393** Ne precor PKQ[1]: Deprecor EBQ[2]R *cum dett.* thiasi *om.* R
394 narrare *om.* R[1]   **395** Docira P   intorserit Q   **396** Credo B[1]K[2] achillis
PQ   **397** ultrix EBKQ: ultris R: victrix P   *versum bis scripsit* E   **398** Ducibus B
400 domo P[1]   **401** raptam E   **403** iura] ? Ira E[1] una *om.* P[1]   **404** phrygiū
fedus Q[2] *in ras.*   phrigie (fr-) ER   **405** iniurimos E[1]   **407** istha P[1]
408 indosonae K[1]   circumit K   unda ER   **409** admotas PBK: ad motas Q:
amotas E: amotae *Gronovius*: amoti *dett., Kohlmann*   **410** *ante* 409 R   Europam
asiamque R   **412** conclusasque P   **413** domant R   hora E

Eubois, innumera resonant incude Mycenae,
Pisa novat currus, Nemee dat terga ferarum,   415
Cirrha sagittiferas certat stipare pharetras,
Lerna gravis clipeos caesis vestire iuvencis.
dat bello pedites Aetolus et asper Acarnan,
Argos agit turmas, vacuantur pascua ditis
Arcadiae, frenat celeres Epiros alumnos,   420
Phocis et Aoniae iaculis rarescitis umbrae,
murorum tormenta Pylos Messenaque tendunt.
nulla inmunis humus; velluntur postibus altis
arma olim dimissa patrum, flammisque liquescunt
dona deum; ereptum superis Mars efferat aurum.   425
nusquam umbrae veteres: minor Othrys et ardua sidunt
Taygeta, exuti viderunt aëra montes.
iam natat omne nemus; caeduntur robora classi,
silva minor remis. ferrum lassatur in usus
innumeros, quod rostra liget, quod muniat arma,   430
belligeros quod frenet equos, quod mille catenis
squalentis nectat tunicas, quod sanguine fumet
vulneraque alta bibat, quod conspirante veneno
inpellat mortes; tenuant umentia saxa
attritu et pigris addunt mucronibus iras.   435
nec modus aut arcus lentare aut fundere glandes
aut torrere sudes galeasque attollere conis.
hos inter motus pigram gemit una quietem
Thessalia et geminis incusat fata querellis,

---

415 Nisa movet R   nemea R   **416** sagitti/ E¹: fera *sup. lin.* E²   **417** iuventis
(c *supra* t) P   **418** acarnan P: acarnas EKR (aspera carnas), BQ   **420** epirus Q
422 messenaque PEBR: messanaque KQ   tradunt R   **425** Doma dn̄ E
ereptum P: et raptum EBKQR   superis P   efferat] asserit *Baehrens*   **426** arida B
sidunt PR: sidunt *ex* findunt KQ: findunt B: fiunt E   **428** omne *ex* omnem P
429 remis minor R   laxatur (s *sub* x) E: laxatur R *cum dett.*   in PER: ad BKQ
430–1 quod *ex* quid *passim* K: quid *passim* R   **431** frenat EBQ¹   **432** squa-
mantes *vel* squamatas *Menke*   **433** quot P   cum spirante B   **434** Innumeras
mortes R   tenuant umentia *Paris.* 7647, *Leid.* (hum-): tenuat umentia P: tenuantur
mitia EKQ: tenuantur mecia B: tenuantur grandia R   **435** pigris P: nigris EBKQR
436 modus est aut E   **437** galeas aut tollere (aut *in ras.*) Q   **438** una P: hora
ER: ora K²: ore BK¹Q   **439** Thessalia P: Thessalis (Thesalis, Tess-) EBKQR

quod senior Peleus nec adhuc maturus Achilles.   **440**
  Iam Pelopis terras Graiumque exhauserat orbem
praecipitans in transtra viros insanus equosque
Bellipotens. fervent portus et operta carinis
stagna suasque hiemes classis promota suosque
attollit fluctus; ipsum iam puppibus aequor   **445**
deficit et totos consumunt carbasa ventos.
Prima ratis Danaas Hecateia congregat Aulis,
rupibus expositis longique crepidine dorsi
Euboicum scandens Aulis mare, litora multum
montivagae dilecta deae, iuxtaque Caphereus   **450**
latratum pelago tollens caput. ille Pelasgas
ut vidit tranare rates, ter monte ter undis
intonuit saevaeque dedit praesagia noctis.
coetus ibi armorum Troiae fatalis, ibi ingens
iuratur bellum, donec sol annuus omnes   **455**
conficeret metas. tunc primum Graecia vires
contemplata suas; tunc sparsa ac dissona moles
in corpus vultumque coit et rege sub uno
disposita est. sic curva feras indago latentes
claudit et admotis paulatim cassibus artat.   **460**
illae ignem sonitumque pavent diffusaque linquunt
avia miranturque suum decrescere montem,
donec in angustam ceciderunt undique vallem;
inque vicem stupuere greges socioque timore
mansuescunt: simul hirtus aper, simul ursa lupusque   **465**
cogitur et captos contempsit cerva leones.
  Sed quamquam et gemini pariter sua bella capessant

---

440 negat huc P   **441** gratumque hauserat (ex *sup. lin.*) Q   **442** transa P: trastra E   **443** fervent *ex* -ens E et perta E   **444** permota B suasuasque P **445** iam / puppibus (*eras.* a) KQ   **447** Hecateia] hec atria E   **449** scindens *Menke*   **450** delicta K iustaque E   **451** Lustratum R pelasgans P **452** tranara (e *supra ult.* a) P: transnare BKQ: transire ER *cum dett.* monte *ex* -es E   **455** Iuratur *ex* -us K: Inflatur R amnes P   **456** Configeret E **458** cetumque E   **459** Disposita EBQR: Disposita *ex* Deposita K: Deposita P **460** Cludit KQ classibus PQ: c/assibus R   **461** Illę P: Ille EBKR diffisaque *Garrod*: diffussaque E linqunt PE   **462** Avita P   **466** contempnit *ex* –psit Q²   **467** lacessant *Menke*

Atridae famamque avida virtute paternam
Tydides Sthenelusque premant, nec cogitet annos
Antilochus septemque Aiax umbone coruscet   **470**
armenti reges atque aequum moenibus orbem,
consiliisque armisque vigil contendat Ulixes:
omnis in absentem belli manus ardet Achillem,
nomen Achillis amant et in Hectora solus Achilles
poscitur; illum unum Teucris Priamoque loquuntur   **475**
fatalem. quis enim Haemoniis sub vallibus alter
creverit effossa reptans nive? cuius adortus
cruda rudimenta et teneros formaverit annos
Centaurus? patrii propior cui linea caeli,
quemve alium Stygios tulerit secreta per amnes   **480**
Nereis et pulchros ferro praestruxerit artus?
haec Graiae castris iterant traduntque cohortes.
cedit turba ducum vincique haud maesta fatetur.
sic cum pallentes Phlegraea in castra coirent
caelicolae iamque Odrysiam Gradivus in hastam   **485**
surgeret et Libycos Tritonia tolleret angues
ingentemque manu curvaret Delius arcum,
stabat anhela metu solum Natura Tonantem
respiciens, quando ille hiemes tonitrusque vocaret
nubibus, igniferam quot fulmina posceret Aetnen.   **490**

468 Atrides Q² avida PER: avidi BK²Q: audi K¹: aucta *Damsté* paterna K
469 stelenusque (sthel-, stell-, thel-) EBKQR premant EBKQR: premat P
470 Antilochous P: Antilochos *Klotz* septeno B alax P   **471** aequo...orbe B²
aequo/ *ex* aequum K: equet R   **472** Consilii R *cum dett.*   **474** hectore R¹
475 unum *om.* E   **476** valibus P   **477** effo/sa (u *supra* o Q²) Q: effosa R¹
adortus PKR: ad ortus E: ab ortu (*cum dett.*) *ex* adortus Q: abortu B   **478** et
om. R   **479** patrum R: proprii B proprior PEBK¹R libera Q   **480** secretius
annos R   **481** Nerei P praestruxerit PKQ (r *alterum sup. lin.* P): praestrinxerit B:
pertrinxerit E: perstrinxerit R *cum dett.*   **483** vincique] umque (ci *sup. lin.*) E
hauit (?) P   **484** pallentes PEBKQR (l *prius sup. lin.* P): Pallenes *Wilamowitz*:
palantes *Aldus*: bellantes *dett.* flegera E quo irent R   **485** iamque] iam E
486 lybricos P   **488** metu EBKQR¹: metum R²: metu *ex* metus P *rec. man.*;
v. adn. sola P Natura] iam turba *Baehrens*   **490-1** *transp.* P   **490** Nubilus
EBKQ: Nubilius R¹ quot *in ras.* Brux. 5338 *rec. man.*, Leid. *pr. man.*: quod PK
(? Q¹): quo Q²: qui R: que// B: quae E *cum dett.* fulmen *ex* fulmina K posceret
ex -erat E aetnen P: ethnam ER²: ethnan *ex* -en K²: ęthnam Q: ennam BR¹

Atque ibi dum mixta vallati plebe suorum
et maris et belli consultant tempora reges,
increpitans magno vatem Calchanta tumultu
Protesilaus ait—namque huic bellare cupido
praecipua et primae iam tunc data gloria mortis—:   495
'O nimium Phoebi tripodumque oblite tuorum
Thestoride, quando ora deo possessa movebis
iustius aut quaenam Parcarum occulta recludes?
cernis ut ignotum cuncti stupeantque fremantque
Aeaciden? sordet volgo Calydonius heros   500
et magno genitus Telamone Aiaxque secundus;
nos quoque—sed Mavors et Troia arrepta probabunt.
illum neglectis—pudet heu!—ductoribus omnes
belligerum ceu numen amant. dic ocius: aut cur
serta comis et multus honos? quibus abditus oris   505
quave iubes tellure peti? nam fama nec antris
Chironis patria nec degere Peleos aula.
heia, inrumpe deos et fata latentia vexa,
laurigerosque ignes, si quando, avidissimus hauri!
arma horrenda tibi saevosque remisimus enses,   510
numquam has inbelles galea violabere vittas,
sed felix numeroque ducum praestantior omni,
si magnum Danais pro te dependis Achillem.'

491 ibi ex ubi K vallati ex velato K plebo P   492 consultantempora P¹ (corr. P²)
493 Increpans E¹ chalcanta ex -te E   494 ait EBKQR: agit P   495 primi...
martis cod. Bentleii   data gloria PER: data copia BKQ: rata gloria Damsté
497 Thestorides R   498 quaenam (que nam E) EKQ: q̄n̄ā B: quianam P: quo
nam R   499 cuncti EBR: cuncti/ K: cunctis PQ   fremantque ER: premantque
PKQ: petantque B   500 sordet EBKQR: sordent P   502 et PER: sed BKQ
arrepta BKQR: abrepta PE; cf. 784; II, 21 probabat Q²   503 neclectis P:
negletis E   doctoribus R   504 quur P   505 multus PER: mutus (l sup. lin. Q)
KQ: mitis B   506 Quave iubes BKQ: Quave (sic) iuves P: Qua iubeas ER:
quave iuvet Phillimore (in apographo suo)   507 aula] arma R¹   508 //rumpe R
vexa] r supra e P² (i.e. vera)   509 -que om. Q   511 galea violabere BKQR:
galea violavere (-re in ras.) E: galeare violare P   512 praestantior] -rae- in ras.
rec. man. P   513 Siġ P   pro te dependis (-e de- in ras.) P: pro te deprehendis
(cf. 518) E: pro te portendis (-ntis B) BKQ: per te portendis R, Brux. 5338 pr.
man.: promte portendis Baehrens (propere Deiter); v. adn.

Iamdudum trepido circumfert lumina motu
intrantemque deum primo pallore fatetur   515
Thestorides; mox igne genas et sanguine torquens
nec socios nec castra videt, sed caecus et absens
nunc superum magnos deprendit in aethere coetus,
nunc sagas adfatur aves, nunc dura sororum
licia, turiferas modo consulit anxius aras   520
flammarumque apicem rapit et caligine sacra
pascitur. exsiliunt crines rigidisque laborat
vitta comis, nec colla loco nec in ordine gressus.
tandem fessa tremens longis mugitibus ora
solvit, et oppositum vox eluctata furorem est: 525
'Quo rapis ingentem magni Chironis alumnum
femineis, Nerei, dolis? huc mitte: quid aufers?
non patiar: meus iste, meus. tu diva profundi?
et me Phoebus agit. latebris quibus abdere temptas
eversorem Asiae? video per Cycladas altas   530
attonitam et turpi quaerentem litora furto.
occidimus: placuit Lycomedis conscia tellus.
o scelus! en fluxae veniunt in pectora vestes.
scinde, puer, scinde et timidae ne cede parenti.
ei mihi raptus abit! quaenam haec procul inproba virgo?'   535
    Hic nutante gradu stetit amissisque furoris
viribus ante ipsas tremefactus conruit aras.
    tunc haerentem Ithacum Calydonius occupat heros:

514 motu *supra* voto Q   **515** deum *ex* dom Q   **516** torques E   **517** necastra
K¹QR¹ absens *ex* amens P: amens R *cum dett.*   **518** magno R deprehendit E:
deprendet KQ¹ in aethera P: in ordine E²R¹: in aere R²: ordine E¹ coetos P
519 sagax PB¹ dira R   **520** turicremas *Menke*   **521** apicem PER: apices
BKQ **521-2** et…crines *om.* R¹   **524** tremor R   **525** appositum vix
luctata (e *sup. lin.*) E est *om.* ER   **527** nereia Q² aufers EBKQR: audes
aufers P   **529-661** *om.* KQ; **529-660** *add. in mg.* K *alt. man.* (k; *multa non legere*
poteramus), **529-662** *folio inserto* Q *rec. man.* (q)   **529** at me *Sandström* addere P
temptes (a *supra alt.* e) E   **530** vide B cladas E: cidas cicladas q   **531** et *in*
ras. P   **532** pla//cuit (-ca-) q   **533** influxe (s *sub* x) E in] ad ER   **534** cede
Pq (? k): crede EBR *cum dett.*   **535** A mihi E: Heu mihi R procul hec quaenam
(hec *sup. lin.*) q procul *om.* B est procul inp. virgo est R   **536** amissis B:
annusisque E: emissisque *Barth*   **537** aras *ex* arat E

'Nos vocat iste labor: neque enim comes ire recusem,
si tua cura trahat. licet ille sonantibus antris   540
Tethyos aversae gremioque prematur aquosi
Nereos, invenies. tu tantum providus astu
tende animum vigilem fecundumque erige pectus:
non mihi quis vatum dubiis in casibus ausit
fata videre prior.' subicit gavisus Ulixes: 545
'Sic deus omnipotens firmet, sic adnuat illa
virgo paterna tibi! sed me spes lubrica tardat:
grande quidem armatum castris inducere Achillem,
sed si fata negent, quam foedum ac triste reverti!
vota tamen Danaum non intemptata relinquam.   550
iamque adeo aut aderit mecum Peleius heros,
aut verum penitus latet et sine Apolline Calchas.'
    Conclamant Danai stimulatque Agamemno volentes.
laxantur coetus resolutaque murmure laeto
agmina discedunt, quales iam nocte propinqua   555
e pastu referuntur aves, vel in antra reverti
melle novo gravidas mitis videt Hybla catervas.
nec mora, iam dextras Ithacesia carbasus auras
poscit, et in remis hilaris sedere iuventus.
    At procul occultum falsi sub imagine sexus   560
Aeaciden furto iam noverat una latenti
Deidamia virum; sed opertae conscia culpae
cuncta pavet tacitasque putat sentire sorores.
namque ut virgineo stetit in grege durus Achilles

---

539 vacat E   recusem P: recusen E: recuse' R: recuso Bkq (u *sup. lin.* q)   **540** Si
te E   trahit E[I]   **541** aversae PEq: a/verse B: adversae k: everse R   aquosi PEBq:
aquosae k: aquoso R   **543** facundumque BR   pecto P[I]   **544** Non PE: Nam
BkqR   te quis R: mi qui q   adsit *Schrader*   **546** omnipotens sic annuit illaque
firmet Bk (firmat k)   **547** sed spes me q   **548** Grande quidem EqR: Grande
equidem Bk: Grandem equidem P   est castris BqR (? k)   **549** negant B   **551** aut
om. P   **552** polline q   **553** -que *om.* E[I]   volentes *om.* q   **554** Laxatur E   -que
om. R   **555** qualis P   **556** aves PEBkR: apes q: oves *Baehrens*   **557** gravitas P
558 ithace/ia B: ithacus iam *rec. man.* Pq   **559** ad remos q: in transtris R   hilares
Pq; *cf.* 901   **560** Ad P: Haud Bk   occulta Bk   **561** noverant P   u/na (-a-) E
la/tenti E   **562** Deidamea P   **564** virgineos R[2]   greges R   durus PEBqR:
k *legere non potuimus*

exsolvitque rudem genetrix digressa pudorem,   565
protinus elegit comitem, quamquam omnis in illum
turba coit, blandeque novas nil tale timenti
admovet insidias: illam sequiturque premitque
improbus, illam oculis iterumque iterumque resumit.
nunc nimius lateri non evitantis inhaeret,   570
nunc levibus sertis, lapsis nunc sponte canistris,
nunc thyrso parcente ferit, modo dulcia notae
fila lyrae tenuesque modos et carmina monstrat
Chironis ducitque manum digitosque sonanti
infringit citharae, nunc occupat ora canentis   575
et ligat amplexus et mille per oscula laudat.
illa libens discit, quo vertice Pelion, et quis
Aeacides, puerique auditum nomen et actus
adsidue stupet et praesentem cantat Achillem.
ipsa quoque et validos proferre modestius artus   580
et tenuare rudes attrito pollice lanas
demonstrat reficitque colos et perdita dura
pensa manu; vocisque sonum pondusque tenentis,
quodque fugit comites, nimio quod lumine sese
figat et in verbis intempestivus anhelet,   585
miratur; iam iamque dolos aperire parantem
virginea levitate fugit prohibetque fateri.
sic sub matre Rhea iuvenis regnator Olympi
oscula securae dabat insidiosa sorori
frater adhuc, medii donec reverentia cessit   590
sanguinis et versos germana expavit amores.

565 genitix q   **567** blandęque (*i.e.* -aeque) P nihil P   **569** iterum iterumque B
revixi E: illa revisit R   **570** nimium R alteri E non] nunc q   **571** nunc
lapsis E   **572** motae *Heinsius*   **574** sonanti EBkqR: sonantis P   **575** cithara
Prinz nunc] n̄ q canentis PEqR: tenentis Bk   **576** Eligat R amplexu et
millena ER (mille *in mg.* ? E²)   **577** discit *ex* dicit P, *in ras.* R   **579** cantat]
n *sup. lin.* P: laudat Bk   **580** et valid' q   **581** attrite R   **582** colos PEkR:
colu' q: colus B perfida durat P   **583** vocique sonus E tenentes q: canentis R
584 fuget E nimioque lum. R se/se (-s-) P   **585** Figit Bkq *cum dett.* intem-
pestibus P   **586** iam iamque] /iamque P¹ (*corr.* P²) dolus P parentem R¹:
parenti ER²   **587** fugit (? -iit) *ex* fugut E   **588** regnare E¹   **589** dabat *ex*
stabat q   **591** veros *codd. dett.* amore P¹

[tandem detecti timidae Nereidos astus.]
　Lucus Agenorei sublimis ad orgia Bacchi
stabat et admissum caelo nemus; huius in umbra
alternam renovare piae trieterida matres　　　　　　595
consuerant scissumque pecus terraque revulsas
ferre trabes gratosque deo praestare furores.
lex procul ire mares; iterat praecepta verendus
ductor, inaccessumque viris edicitur antrum.
nec satis est: stat fine dato metuenda sacerdos　　　600
exploratque aditus, ne quis temerator oberret
agmine femineo: tacitus sibi risit Achilles.
illum virgineae ducentem signa catervae
magnaque difficili solventem bracchia motu—
et sexus pariter decet et mendacia matris—　　　　605
mirantur comites. nec iam pulcherrima turbae
Deidamia suae tantumque admota superbo
vincitur Aeacidae, quantum premit ipsa sorores.
ut vero e tereti demisit nebrida collo
errantesque sinus hedera collegit et alte　　　　　610
cinxit purpureis flaventia tempora vittis
vibravitque gravi redimitum missile dextra,
attonito stat turba metu sacrisque relictis
illum ambire libet pronosque attollere vultus.
talis, ubi ad Thebas vultumque animumque remisit　615
Euhius et patrio satiavit pectora luxu,
serta comis mitramque levat thyrsumque virentem
armat et hostiles invisit fortior Indos.

592 decreti R¹ *versum uncis inclusit Garrod (et vide ad 772)*; **592a** *habet* R *in mg.*
Producente novos partus de more lucina　　**594** uius *add.* E² *sup. lin. (om.* E¹*)*
umbra] ume P　　**595** Alternam P: Alternum Bkq: Alterne ER　renovare PER:
revocare Bq (? k)　triethyrida P: triaterica ER (? k): trietherica B: triateria q
596 spissumque P: sacrumque B: cesumque R　revulsis q　　**597** Terre P　deos R
598 Rex P　　**599** educitur P: indicitur R　　**600** satis stat est P　　**602** sibi risit
PR: subrisit EBkq　achillis P　　**604** bachia P¹　　**607** Deidamea P　amota R
608 aeacidae P: aeacide EBkqR　　**609** e tereti *cod. Helmstad.*: et tereti PBk: et
territi E: tereti (the-) qR　dimisit B *cum dett.* misit nebreida E　nebria q
611 flaventia] squalencia q　vitis (*corr. sup. lin.*) P　　**613** Attonita R　reclictis E
615 ubi athenas E　　**617** conis E

Scandebat roseo medii fastigia caeli
Luna iugo, totis ubi somnus inertior alis   620
defluit in terras mutumque amplectitur orbem.
consedere chori paulumque exercita pulsu
aera tacent, tenero cum solus ab agmine Achilles
haec secum: 'Quonam timidae commenta parentis
usque feras? primumque imbelli carcere perdes   625
florem animi? non tela licet Mavortia dextra,
non trepidas agitare feras? ubi campus et amnes
Haemonii? quaerisne meos, Sperchie, natatus
promissasque comas? an desertoris alumni
nullus honos, Stygiasque procul iam raptus ad umbras   630
dicor, et orbatus plangit mea funera Chiron?
tu nunc tela manu, nostros tu dirigis arcus
nutritosque mihi scandis, Patrocle, iugales:
ast ego pampineis diffundere bracchia thyrsis
et tenuare colus—pudet haec taedetque fateri—   635
iam scio. quin etiam dilectae virginis ignem
aequaevamque facem captus noctesque diesque
dissimulas. quonam usque premes urentia pectus
vulnera? teque marem—pudet heu!—nec amore probabis?'
  Sic ait et densa noctis gavisus in umbra   640
tempestiva suis torpere silentia furtis
vi potitur votis et toto pectore veros
admovet amplexus; vidit chorus omnis ab alto

619 roseo] niveo *Menke*   **620** totisque E   **621** Desilit E ad B   **622** pulsu]
cusu (r *sup. lin.*) P[1]: pulsu *add.* P[2]   **623** Aere P agmine] inguine q achillis P
624 Hoc R   **625** perdis P   **627** sagittare P: agitat q   **628** quaerisne (quer-)
BkqR: quaeresne P: querisve E sperchee q   **629** Promissamque (Promm-)
comam ER: Promissaque comas B an] at E   **630** Ullus E   **631** Ducor
EBkR[1]   **632** tu nunc] Tunc E manu] gradumanu P (vel *sup. lin.* P[2]) tu
nostros Bk   **634** e/go E thisis E   **635** colus PBkq: colos (cho-) ER piget E
haec P[1]: heu *cett.* (u *in ras.* E) -que *om.* P[1]   **636** virginis] iuvenis B (virginis
in mg.)   **637** Aequae namque q: Eque B   **638** usque EBkqR: ipse P;
cf. Th. IV, 568 premes urentia E: premes verentia R: presumerentia P: premes
urgentia B: premis urgentia (-cia) kq   **639** teque PEBR: meque kq nec
PEBR: sed kq probabis EBkq: probaris PR   **643** vidit P: risit EBqR *cum*
dett.: risu k: rubuit *Scriverius*: visit *Castiglioni* ablato E

astrorum et tenerae rubuerunt cornua Lunae.
illa quidem clamore nemus montemque replevit;   **645**
sed Bacchi comites, discussa nube soporis,
signa choris indicta putant; fragor undique notus
tollitur, et thyrsos iterum vibrabat Achilles,
ante tamen dubiam verbis solatus amicis:
'Ille ego—quid trepidas?—genitum quem caerula mater   **650**
paene Iovi silvis nivibusque inmisit alendum
Thessalicis. nec ego hos cultus aut foeda subissem
tegmina, ni primo te visa in litore: cessi
. te propter, tibi pensa manu, tibi mollia gesto
tympana. quid defles magno nurus addita ponto?   **655**
quid gemis ingentes caelo paritura nepotes?
"Sed pater—" ante igni ferroque excisa iacebit
Scyros et in tumidas ibunt haec versa procellas
moenia, quam saevo mea tu conubia pendas
funere: non adeo parebimus omnia matri.'   **660**
[vade sed ereptum celes taceasque pudorem.]
  Obstipuit tantis regina exterrita monstris,
quamquam olim suspecta fides, et comminus ipsum
horruit et facies multum mutata fatentis.
quid faciat? casusne suos ferat ipsa parenti   **665**
seque simul iuvenemque premat, fortassis acerbas
hausurum poenas? et adhuc in corde manebat
ille diu deceptus amor: silet aegra premitque
iam commune nefas; unam placet addere furtis

---

645 montesque R   **646** dimissa ER nube sororis (*ex* -es) k: nocte sorores Bq
648 vibrat P   **649** solatus P: solatur EBkqR   **650** quid EBkqR: qui P genitum
quem *ex* gemitum quem P: gemitum quem E: genuitque R   **651** paene Iovi
Gustafsson: Paene iovis P: Pineios B: Peneis kq: Penei E: Peneleis R: Paeoniis
Wilamowitz: Peliacis (*quod sibi arrogavit Jannaccone*) edd. *vett.* commisit q
652 fedas E   **653** Tecmina q: Tegm na E primo EBqR: e primo P: primum k
te vias P: tuivisa E **655** magno *ex* -nu E **656** gemes P ingentem...nepotem ER
(neptem E[1])   **657** sed pater ante] Ante sub atro E: Antque sub R[1] feroque E[1]q
659 pendas EBkq: perdas PR *cum dett.*   **661** *om.* PEBKR; *secl. Kohlmann*
662 Ostupuit R[1]: Obstupuit KQR[2]   **663–4** *spurios censuit Garrod*   **663** comminus ipsum] luminis ignem *Koch*   **664** paventis E   **665** suo E parenti *ex*
patenti KQ   **666** acervas PE   **667** Ausurum KR[1]   **669** furto R

altricem sociam, precibus quae victa duorum   **670**
adnuit. illa astu tacito raptumque pudorem
surgentemque uterum atque aegros in pondere menses
occuluit, plenis donec stata tempora metis
attulit et partus index Lucina resolvit.

II, I   Iamque per Aegaeos ibat Laertia flexus   **675**
puppis, et innumerae mutabant Cyclades oras;
iam Paros Olearosque latent; iam raditur alta
Lemnos et a tergo decrescit Bacchica Naxos,

5   ante oculos crescente Samo; iam Delos opacat
aequor: ibi e celsa libant carchesia puppi   **680**
responsique fidem et verum Calchanta precantur.
audiit Arquitenens Zephyrumque e vertice Cynthi
inpulit et dubiis pleno dedit omina velo.

10   it pelago secura ratis: quippe alta Tonantis
iussa Thetin certas fatorum vertere leges   **685**
arcebant aegram lacrimis ac multa gementem,
quod non erueret pontum ventisque fretisque
omnibus invisum iam tunc sequeretur Ulixem.

15   Frangebat radios humili iam pronus Olympo
Phoebus et Oceani penetrabile litus anhelis   **690**
promittebat equis, cum se scopulosa levavit
Scyros; in hanc totos emisit puppe rudentes
dux Laertiades sociisque resumere pontum

670 quae *om.* B que vita E   **671** astuta cito EBKQR pudorem *supra* dolorem K   **672** Surgentem PBKQ: Turgentem ER messes B   **673** plenisque P statuta R   **675** *incipit in plurimis codd. dett. liber secundus* paeregeos P lerthei E¹: lertheia E² fexus E: fluctus BQ²R *cum dett.*   **676** innumerae mutabant Cyclades oras *scripsi*: innumerae mutabant cyclades auras PEBKQ: innumeras mutabat ciclades (-es *ex* -as) auras R: innumerae (-as *Köstlin*) mutabant Cycladas aurae *edd. vett.*: innumerae mutabat Cyclados oras *Garrod*; *v. adn.*   **678** et *om.* K canaxos bacchi P *cum signo transl.* brachia B¹: bachia B²K: bachea R   **680** e celsa PKQ: excelsa EBR puppi P: puppe EBKQR   **682** arquitenens P: arcitenens (archi-) EBQR *et ex* arcu- K e] a B vertere Q¹   **683** plena E **684** it] Et Q¹ pelago PBQ¹R: pelagi EK *et fort. corr.* Q sonantis P   **685** thetim P **686** gementem EBKR: gementem *ex* legentem Q: timentem P: tumentem *Klotz*; *v. adn. ad 232*   **687** exueret R   **688** sequetur (re *sup. lin.*) E **689** Fragebat P   **691** permittebat *D. Heinsius* e scopulusa P   **692** inanc E **693** lertheiades E sociisque PB: sociosque EKQR pontum EBKQR: portum P

20   imperat et remis Zephyros supplere cadentes.

accedunt iuxta, et magis indubitata magisque   **695**
Scyros erat placidique super Tritonia custos
litoris. egressi numen venerantur amicae
Aetolusque Ithacusque deae. tunc providus heros,
25   hospita ne subito terrerent moenia coetu,
puppe iubet remanere suos; ipse ardua fido   **700**
cum Diomede petit. sed iam praevenerat arcis
litoreae servator Abas ignotaque regi
ediderat, sed Graia tamen, succedere terris
30   carbasa. procedunt, gemini ceu foedere iuncto
hiberna sub nocte lupi: licet et sua pulset   **705**
natorumque fames, penitus rabiemque minasque
dissimulant humilesque meant, ne nuntiet hostes
cura canum et trepidos moneat vigilare magistros.
35   Sic segnes heroes eunt campumque patentem,
qui medius portus celsamque interiacet urbem,   **710**
alterno sermone terunt; prior occupat acer
Tydides: 'Qua nunc verum ratione paramus
scrutari? namque ambiguo sub pectore pridem
40   verso, quid inbelles thyrsos mercatus et aera
urbibus in mediis Baccheaque terga mitrasque   **715**
huc tuleris varioque aspersas nebridas auro?
hisne gravem Priamo Phrygibusque armabis Achillem?'
illi subridens Ithacus paulum ore remisso:
45   'Haec tibi, virginea modo si Lycomedis in aula est

---

694 retus E supplere] -re *sup. lin.* P   **695** iuxta PE: iussi Q¹: iussis BKQ²R
et PER: *om.* B: *del.* Q: et iam K   **699** terreret BKQ¹   **700** iuvet P remanere
ex -eret E arduo (o *in ras.*) E: arida R   **701** praeveneret E   **703** se graia Q:
secreta B tectis Q   **704** succedunt B (procedunt *in mg.*) iuncte P
706 rabiemque EBKQR: labemque P   **707** neunt R hostes *ex* hostet E
708 moneant K: maneat Q   **709** erunt E   **710** medius EBKQR: medios P
711 terunt PE: ferunt B: serunt *ex* ferunt KQR   **712** paramus *ex* paramur Q
713 pridem P: quidem Q (? B¹): quiddam *ex* quidem B²K: quid scit (?) R
714 inbello E   **716** Hauc P variosque P   **717** priamo phrigibusque (fr-) ER:
priamo phrigibus (-ri- *huius v. in ras.*) P: phrygibus priamoque BKQ *cum dett.*
armavis P: armamus EBKR *cum dett.*: armatus (? *ex* -mus) Q achillę P
718 Illeque Q² ait paulum R   **719** molo P si *om.* E

fraude latens, ultro confessum in proelia ducent   **720**
Peliden; tu cuncta citus de puppe memento
ferre, ubi tempus erit, clipeumque his iungere donis,
qui pulcher signis auroque asperrimus astat;
50 nec sat erit: tecum lituo bonus adsit Agyrtes
occultamque tubam tacitos adportet in usus.'   **725**
  Dixerat, atque ipso portarum in limine regem
cernit et ostensa pacem praefatus oliva:
'Magna, reor, pridemque tuas pervenit ad aures
55 fama trucis belli, regum placidissime, quod nunc
Europamque Asiamque quatit. si nomina forte   **730**
huc perlata ducum, fidit quibus ultor Atrides:
hic tibi, quem tanta meliorem stirpe creavit
magnanimus Tydeus, Ithaces ego ductor Ulixes.
60 causa viae—metuam quid enim tibi cuncta fateri,
cum Graius notaque fide celeberrimus?—: imus   **735**
explorare aditus invisaque litora Troiae,
quidve parent—' medio sermone intercipit ille:
'Adnuerit Fortuna, precor, dextrique secundent
65 ista dei! nunc hospitio mea tecta piumque
inlustrate larem.' simul intra limina ducit.   **740**
nec mora, iam mensas famularis turba torosque
instruit. interea visu perlustrat Ulixes
scrutaturque domum, si qua vestigia magnae
70 virginis aut dubia facies suspecta figura;
porticibusque vagis errat totosque penates,   **745**

---

721 Pelidem E nunc tacitus P   **722** clipeisque B his *om.* R   **723** *post* auroque *rasura in* Q, *v.* asperrimus *primum male scripto* astat ER: hasta P: ardet BKQ; *v. adn.*   **724** nec *Garrod*: Haec PBKQR: Hoc E erunt tecumque R assit R **727** *om.* R[1] ostensa PER[2]: ostenta BKQ[1]: ostentans Q[2] praefatur E *cum dett.* **728** -que *om.* R tuas] vestras *sup. lin.* Q[2] (pridem vestras *dett.*)   **730** Europam (*om.* -que) E   **731** ultior P   **732** tibi] est ille R   **733** Ithaces *scripsi*: ithacus P *et dett. quidam*: ithacis EBKQR ducor E: ultor R   **734** quid enim metuam R cuncta tibi P   **735** cum] Dum Q[2] graius BKR: gravius P: grais E: gravis Q[1]: (gravis) es Q[2] *sup. lin.* imus] unus B[2] *cum dett.*   **736** littera Q   **738** Annuat ut R dextrisque P   **739** sibi *et in mg.* dei (i *supra* e) Q   **740** Inlustare Q[2] **741** toros *supra* domosque Q   **743** Scrutaturque *ex* Sertaturque K   **744** facies PER: facie BKQ figurae P

ceu miretur, obit: velut ille cubilia praedae
indubitata tenens muto legit arva Molosso
venator, videat donec sub frondibus hostem
75 porrectum somno positosque in caespite dentes.
    Rumor in arcana iamdudum perstrepit aula,   750
virginibus qua fida domus, venisse Pelasgum
ductores Graiamque ratem sociosque receptos.
iure pavent aliae, sed vix nova gaudia celat
80 Pelides avidusque novos heroas et arma
vel talis vidisse cupit. iamque atria fervent   755
regali strepitu et picto discumbitur auro,
cum pater ire iubet natas comitesque pudicas
natarum. subeunt, quales Maeotide ripa,
85 cum Scythicas rapuere domos et capta Getarum
moenia, sepositis epulantur Amazones armis.   760
tum vero intentus vultus ac pectora Ulixes
perlibrat visu, sed nox inlataque fallunt
lumina et extemplo latuit mensura iacentum.
90 at tamen erectumque genas oculisque vagantem
nullaque virginei servantem signa pudoris   765
defigit comitique obliquo lumine monstrat.
quid nisi praecipitem blando complexa moneret
Deidamia sinu nudataque pectora semper
95 exsertasque manus umerosque in veste teneret

746 obit *Heinsius*: adit PEBKQ² *et in ras.* R: alit (? alet) Q¹   747 muto
PER: multo BKQ arma P *rec. man.*   748 videat donec *cum signo transl.* Q
749 summo E in specie E¹   750 dudum (iam *sup. lin.*) P   751 domos Q
pelasgos E   752 graiasque E rates (-es *in ras.*) R   753 *om.* K¹ Iure PBK²R:
I/re (-u-) Q: Lurea *ex* Laurea E: aure *Garrod*: inde *Baehrens* sua gaudia differt K²
754 avidosque P: avidus K¹ novos] suos *Garrod* heroas] o *sup. lin.* P   756 auro
ex aulro P: ostro EBKQR   757 Tum Q²: Tunc R   758 Natorum E¹ qualis
KQ¹, *corr.* Q² mareotide Q²: meotica B: meotida K ripam BK   759 capta
EBKQR: rapta P   760 sepositis (*ut conj.* Schrader) *Ambros. Hex.* 166: suppositis
PBKQR: sub positis E amazonis E   761 Tunc BKR intentus EBKR: intentos
ex -us Q: intentos P   762 Perlibrat P: Perlibat EBKQ: Prelibat R *cum dett.*
763 extimplo ER: exemplo K iacentum P: iacentis EBKQ: iacuiꝉ (?) R
764 erectum (*om.* -que) E   765 pudoreis P: puris E   767 Quid P: Quod
EBKQR *cum dett.* maneret R   768 sinu] virum Q² pectora EBKQR: tempora P

et prodire toris et poscere vina vetaret 770
saepius et fronti crinale reponeret aurum?
[Argolicis ducibus iam tunc patuisset Achilles.]
    Ut placata fames epulis bis terque repostis,
100 rex prior adloquitur paterisque hortatur Achivos:
'Invideo vestris, fateor, decora inclita gentis 775
Argolicae, coeptis; utinam et mihi fortior aetas,
quaeque fuit, Dolopas cum Scyria litora adortos
perdomui, fregique vadis, quae signa triumphi
105 vidistis celsa murorum in fronte, carinas!
saltem si suboles, aptum quam mittere bello— 780
nunc ipsi viresque meas et cara videtis 782
pignora: quando novos dabit haec mihi turba nepotes?'
110 dixerat, et sollers arrepto tempore Ulixes:
'Haut spernenda cupis; quis enim non visere gentes 785
innumeras variosque duces atque agmina regum
ardeat? omne simul roburque decusque potentis
Europae meritos ultro iuravit in enses.
115 rura urbesque vacant, montes spoliavimus altos,
omne fretum longa velorum obtexitur umbra; 790
tradunt arma patres, rapit inrevocata iuventus.
non alias umquam tantae data copia famae
fortibus aut campo maiore exercita virtus.'
120 aspicit intentum vigilique haec aure trahentem,
cum paveant aliae demissaque lumina flectant, 795
atque iterat: 'Quisquis proavis et gente superba,

770 vetaret *ex* iactaret K   772 *om.* PK¹Q¹; *secl. Kohlmann*; *versum* 592 *substituit
Goold*; Pelides ducibus foret hic detectus achivis Vat. 3281: Ductoribus danaum
iam proditus esset achilles *Par.* 8282 tum Q²   773 fames *ex* -as E reportis K
775 incli *sine ras.* E   776 utinam // mihi K: utinam mihi B *cum dett.*
777 adhortos *ex* -as E: adortus B: adortos *ex* -us K   779 celsa PER¹: celsas
BKQR²   780 sobolos Q¹: soboles EBQ²R aptum PEBK¹R: aptam K²Q *cum
dett.*: aptem *Menke*   781 *non exstat in* PEBKQR: Possem plena forent mihi
gaudia namque iuvarem *codd. dett. nonnulli*   782 meos Q   784 arrepto
EBKQR: abrepto P   785 Haut] Aut E   786 *om.* K¹, *add. in mg.* K²
787 potentes P: potentis *ex* pat- Q   788 Europę P: Europe R: Europes EBKQ
790 longe BK (? Q¹)   791 rapit] (vel) ruit Q² (ruit *dett.*)   792 tanta P
794 trahente P¹: bibentem *Gronovius*   796 superba P: superbus EBKQR *cum dett*

quisquis equo iaculoque potens, qui praevalet arcu,
omnis honos illic, illic ingentia certant
125 nomina: vix timidae matres aut agmina cessant
virginea; o multum steriles damnatus in annos   800
invisusque deis, si quem haec nova gloria segnem
praeterit.' exisset stratis, ni provida signo
Deidamia dato cunctas hortata sorores
130 liquisset mensas ipsum complexa. sed haeret
respiciens Ithacum coetuque novissimus exit.   805
ille quoque incepto paulum ex sermone remittit,
pauca tamen iungens: 'At tu tranquillus in alta
pace mane carisque para conubia natis,
135 quas tibi sidereis divarum voltibus aequas
fors dedit. ut me olim tacitum reverentia tangit!   810
is decor et formae species permixta virili.'
occurrit genitor: 'Quid si aut Bacchea ferentes
orgia, Palladias aut circum videris aras?
140 et dabimus, si forte novus cunctabitur auster.'
excipiunt cupidi et tacitis spes addita votis.   815
cetera depositis Lycomedis regia curis
tranquilla sub pace silet, sed longa sagaci
nox Ithaco, lucemque cupit somnumque gravatur.
145 Vixdum exorta dies et iam comitatus Agyrte
Tydides aderat praedictaque dona ferebat.   820
nec minus egressae thalamo Scyreides ibant
ostentare choros promissaque sacra verendis
hospitibus. nitet ante alias regina comesque
150 Pelides: qualis Siculae sub rupibus Aetnae
Naidas Hennaeas inter Diana feroxque   825

---

799 vix *ex* vis E   800 o multum ER: multum PK¹Q: et multum BK² *cum dett.*:
a multum *Baehrens*   803 cuncta P   806 quoque PER: quidem BKQ   incerto P
807 At] et *in ras.* Q   At tu] ait hic K (*ex* ait tu) *et* B² *in ras.*   808 sacrisque ER
811 Is PBKQ¹: His EQ²: Hiis R   virilis *Krohn*   812 aut *om.* BKQ: *del.* R²
814 dabitur R, (-tur *in ras.*) Q   novos (u *supra alt.* o) P   cunctavitur P: cunctatur
E: (vel) cantabitur Q² *in mg.*   815 cupidi PR: cupide EBKQ   816 dispositis
ER   817 agaci P   818 Mox E   ithaco *supra* itaque P   somnoque ER *cum dett.*
820 praedicta] c *sup. lin.* P   824 quales P   825 Naides KQ¹ Ennaeas *Gronovius*: aetneas (ethn-) *codd.* ferosque P: ferosque *ex* feroxque R: feroxve *Damsté*

Pallas et Elysii lucebat sponsa tyranni.
iamque movent gressus thiasisque Ismenia buxus
signa dedit, quater aera Rheae, quater enthea pulsant
155 terga manu variosque quater legere recursus.
tunc thyrsos pariterque levant pariterque reponunt   830
multiplicantque gradum, modo quo Curetes in actu
quoque pii Samothraces eunt, nunc obvia versae
pectine Amazonio, modo quo citat orbe Lacaenas
160 Delia plaudentesque suis intorquet Amyclis.
tunc vero, tunc praecipue manifestus Achilles   835
nec servare vices nec bracchia iungere curat;
tunc molles gressus, tunc aspernatur amictus
plus solito rumpitque choros et plurima turbat.
165 sic indignantem thyrsos acceptaque matris
tympana iam tristes spectabant Penthea Thebae.   840
    Solvuntur laudata cohors repetuntque paterna
limina, ubi in mediae iamdudum sedibus aulae
munera virgineos visus tractura locarat
170 Tydides, signum hospitii pretiumque laboris,
hortaturque legant, nec rex placidissimus arcet.   845
heu simplex nimiumque rudis, qui callida dona
Graiorumque dolos variumque ignoret Ulixem!
hic aliae, qua sexus iners naturaque ducit,
175 aut teretes thyrsos aut respondentia temptant
tympana, gemmatis aut nectunt tempora limbis;   850
arma vident magnoque putant donata parenti.
at ferus Aeacides, radiantem ut comminus orbem

826 lucebant R   827 Namque R Ismenia] in moenia P   828 entea P: euhia
(euchia) EBKQR   829 recursu/ (-s) K   831–3 quo...modo om. B¹, quo...
amazonio suppl. B² in mg.   831 curtes E¹ (en add. sup. lin. E²): curre/tes Q:
curretur K   832 Quoque piideis amothraces P   835 Tum vero P tunc alt.
om. R¹   838 rupitque R   839 matri R   840 Penthea Thebae] penthebae P
841 lauda K¹ vel K²   842 ibi ex ubi BQ media E   843 Numera P usus
tactura R locabat Q²   844 labor sine ras. P   846 quis Q²   847 vafrumque
Heinsius ignoret PBQR¹: ignorat (e supra a) E: ignorat KR² cum dett.
848 Tunc R qua P: qua ex quas B: quas EKQR iners EBKQR: inest P ducit
ex docet Q   849 teres E   850 tempora] timpora ER   851 dona E¹
852 Aut ferus E ut] que R¹: del. R²

caelatum pugnas—saevis et forte rubebat
180 bellorum maculis—adclinem conspicit hastae,
infremuit torsitque genas, et fronte relicta   855
surrexere comae; nusquam mandata parentis,
nusquam occultus amor, totoque in pectore Troia est.
ut leo, materno cum raptus ab ubere mores
185 accepit pectique iubas hominemque vereri
edidicit nullasque rapi nisi iussus in iras,   860
si semel adverso radiavit lumine ferrum,
eiurata fides domitorque inimicus, in illum
prima fames, timidoque pudet servisse magistro.
190 ut vero accessit propius luxque aemula vultum
reddidit et simili talem se vidit in auro,   865
horruit erubuitque simul. tunc acer Ulixes
admotus lateri summissa voce: 'Quid haeres?
scimus' ait, 'tu semiferi Chironis alumnus,
195 tu caeli pelagique nepos, te Dorica classis,
te tua suspensis exspectat Graecia signis,   870
ipsaque iam dubiis nutant tibi Pergama muris.
heia, abrumpe moras! sine perfida palleat Ide,
et iuvet haec audire patrem, pudeatque dolosam
200 sic pro te timuisse Thetin.' iam pectus amictu
laxabat, cum grande tuba sic iussus Agyrtes   875
insonuit; fugiunt disiectis undique donis
inplorantque patrem commotaque proelia credunt.
illius intactae cecidere a pectore vestes,
205 iam clipeus breviorque manu consumitur hasta—
mira fides—Ithacumque umeris excedere visus   880

---

853 /rubebat E: rudebant K   **854** astam ER (acclivem...hastam *dett.*)
855 licta E   **857** troiae K[1] est *om.* EK[1]   **858** cum] qui ER   **859** pecti (*om.*
-que) K iuvas E   **860** rapi nisi] rapini E nisiussus P   **862** Eiurata P: Abiurata
ER: It iurata BK: Et iurata Q in *om.* K[1]   **863** pudet servisse E[2]BKQR[2]: pudet
servesse E[1]: pudet fuisse R[1]: iuvet servire P (servire *dett.*): rubet servire *Krohn*:
iuvat saevire *Baehrens*   **864** accessit *om.* Q[1], add. sup. lin. Q[2] -que *om.* R
867 voco E   **869** dori E[1] (ca *add. sup. lin.* E[2])   **871** Isaque (p *sub lin.*) P
mittant (*primum* t *punctis not.*) E   **872** Eia rumpe ER *cum dett.* ide EBR: idę
KQ: idem P   **873** iuvat KQ   **879** clipeus breviorque] brevior clipeus P
880 mira] Ma/a (?) E[1]: *corr.* E[2]

Aetolumque ducem: tantum subita arma calorque
Martius horrenda confundit luce penates.
inmanisque gradu, ceu protinus Hectora poscens,
210 stat medius trepidante domo, Peleaque virgo
quaeritur.
       Ast alia plangebat parte retectos   885
Deidamia dolos, cuius cum grandia primum
lamenta et notas accepit pectore voces,
haesit et occulto virtus infracta calore est.
215 demittit clipeum regisque ad limina versus
attonitum factis inopinaque monstra paventem,   890
sicut erat, nudis Lycomedem adfatur in armis:
'Me tibi, care pater—dubium dimitte pavorem—,
me dedit alma Thetis: te pridem tanta manebat
220 gloria; quaesitum Danais tu mittis Achillem,
gratior et magno, si fas dixisse, parente   895
et dulci Chirone mihi. sed corda parumper
huc adverte libens atque has bonus accipe voces:
Peleus te nato socerum et Thetis hospita iungunt
225 adlegantque suos utroque a sanguine divos.
unam virgineo natarum ex agmine poscunt: 900
dasne? an gens humilis tibi degeneresque videmur?
non renuis? iunge ergo manus et concipe foedus
atque ignosce tuis. tacito iam cognita furto
230 Deidamia mihi; quid enim his obstare lacertis,
qua potuit nostras possessa repellere vires?   905

881-2 *om.* B¹K¹Q¹, *add. in mg.* B²K²Q²   **882** Martis horrendi B²: Martis et
horrenda R   confudit R: perfudit K²Q²   **883** Inmanesque P: Inmanusque K
gradu *ex* -us Q poscent K   **884** peleaque PE: peleia BQR *cum dett.*: pelegia K:
Peleiaque *Baehrens*   **885** hastalia P   **886** gradia P   **887** Amenta P
888 colore Q¹: dolore R   **889** Dimittit BQ *cum dett.*   **890** factis PER: fatis BKQ
891 nudis P: nudus ER: mediis BKQ inermis R: inertus E¹   **892** Mettibi P
dudum demitte ER pavorem PER: timorem BKQ   **893** primum Q¹ manebit E
894 danais *om.* Q¹   **895** *om.* K¹, *add. in mg.* K² Gratior es et E parentem P
900 virginea E natorum E¹ examine E   **901** Visne R an gens PE²: agens E¹:
age R: age an BKQ *cum dett.* humilis EB¹K: humiles PB²QR *cum dett.*; *cf.* 559
902 remis R¹: remus E   **904** quis R   **905** Qua P: Qui E: Qui *ex* Quid K: Quid
BQ: Que R repellere vir (*sine ras.*) P: evadere flammas EBKQR

me luere ista iube; pono arma et reddo Pelasgis
et maneo. quid triste fremis? quid lumina mutas?
iam socer es'—natum ante pedes prostravit et addit—
235 'iamque avus. inmitis quotiens iterabitur ensis,
turba sumus.' tunc et Danai per sacra fidemque   910
hospitii blandusque precum conpellit Ulixes.
ille, etsi carae conperta iniuria natae
et Thetidis mandata movent prodique videtur
240 depositum tam grande deae, tamen obvius ire
tot metuit fatis Argivaque bella morari;   915
fac velit: ipsam illic matrem sprevisset Achilles.
nec tamen abnuerit genero se iungere tali:
vincitur. arcanis effert pudibunda tenebris
245 Deidamia gradum, veniae nec protinus amens
credit et opposito genitorem placat Achille.   920
     Mittitur Haemoniam, magnis qui Pelea factis
impleat et classem comitesque in proelia poscat.
nec non et geminas regnator Scyrius alnos
250 deducit genero viresque excusat Achivis.
tunc epulis consumpta dies, tandemque retectum   925
foedus et intrepidos nox conscia iungit amantes.
     Illius ante oculos nova bella et Xanthus et Ide
Argolicaeque rates, atque ipsas cogitat undas
255 auroramque timet. cara cervice mariti

---

906 pelascis *ex* pell- P: pelasgus K   907 mutas BKQ: mutus P: volvis ER
908 prostravit ER: prostavit P: proiecit BKQ   909 enses P   911 conpellit
PER: compellat (con-) BKQ   912 nata (e *sup. lin.*) P   913 videtu *sine ras.* P
914 ire *om.* P   916 *versus fortasse spurius; v. adn.* velut P achille P   917 *versum
eicere voluit Barth* Nec PE: Ne/ KR: Ne BQ abnuerit P: abnueret EBKQR
tali] ali P   918 archanas R effer P tenebris *ex* -as P: tenebras R   919 Deidama P
veniam R am P (ament *rec. man.*)   920 achillem P *rec. man.*   921 haemoniam
(emon-) EBKR: haemoniae P: haemonia Q magnis P (? K²): magni EBK¹QR
proelia K factis P *rec. man.*: facti P¹EBK¹QR: facto K²   922 Impleant P pos P
(cā *rec. man.*): posca/t K: poscant Q   923 regnatore P¹: regnatur (?) R¹
924 Deducit *ex* Dedicit P   925 retectum P: receptum EBKQR   926 nox
coniungit P   927 et xanthos Q: exanthus E   928 atque ipsas PER: atque iam
Q¹: atque tam Q²: /////iam K: ast hec iam B   928–9 *lacunam inter hos vv.
ponendam censuit Baehrens*   929 -que *om.* K timet et R

fusa novi lacrimas iam solvit et occupat artus: 930
'Aspiciamne iterum meque hoc in pectore ponam,
Aeacide? rursusque tuos dignabere portus,
an tumidus Teucrosque lares et capta reportans
260 Pergama virgineae noles meminisse latebrae?
quid precer, heu! timeamve prius? quidve anxia mandem, 935
cui vix flere vacat? modo te nox una deditque
inviditque mihi. thalamis haec tempora nostris?
hicne est liber hymen? o dulcia furta dolique,
265 o timor! abripitur miserae permissus Achilles.
i—neque enim tantos ausim revocare paratus—, 940
i cautus, nec vana Thetin timuisse memento,
i felix nosterque redi! nimis improba posco:
iam te sperabunt lacrimis planctuque decorae
270 Troades optabuntque tuis dare colla catenis
et patriam pensare toris, aut ipsa placebit 945
Tyndaris, incesta nimium laudata rapina.
ast egomet primae puerilis fabula culpae
narrabor famulis aut dissimulata latebo.
275 quin age, duc comitem; cur non ego Martia tecum
signa feram? tu thyrsa manu Baccheaque mecum 950
sacra, quod infelix non credet Troia, tulisti.
attamen hunc, quem maesta mihi solacia linquis,
hunc saltem sub corde tene et concede precanti
280 hoc solum, pariat ne quid tibi barbara coniunx,
ne qua det indignos Thetidi captiva nepotes.' 955
talia dicentem non ipse inmotus Achilles
solatur iuratque fidem iurataque fletu

932 rursumque R dignavere PE portus PEBKQR: partus *codd. dett., edd.*
933 tumidos R teucrousque E   **934** noles PE: nolis BKQR   **935** timeamne
R -ve prius…mandem *om.* Q¹: -ve prius quidve inde precabo Q² anxia
mandem *om.* K¹ mandem EBK²R: tandem P   **936** vocat Q¹   **938** est *om.* R
hymen *om.* E   **940** Non etenim tantos ER   **941** Incautus K¹ i *om.* ER ne R
thetim PBKQ: thetidem ER   **942** Infelix K¹   **943** decore Q   **944** ob/ta-
buntque (-s-) Q: obtabuntque B   **945** placebat B   **947** egomet] ego et K¹Q
(aut *add.* K²): ego quae B   **948** narrabor, thalamis aut *Schrader*   **950** Signo E
tu] si B thyrsa P: pensa EBKQR   **952** mihi *om.* R¹

spondet et ingentis famulas captumque reversus
285   Ilion et Phrygiae promittit munera gazae.
inrita ventosae rapiebant verba procellae.   960

958 ingenuas *Damsté* famulos R   959 gazae EBKQ: pugnae ca/e (? -z-) P:
pugnae R   960 *versus in* B *deletus; spurium censuit Damsté*

LIBER SECUNDUS

EXUIT implicitum tenebris umentibus orbem
Oceano prolata dies, genitorque coruscae
lucis adhuc hebetem vicina nocte levabat
290 et nondum excusso rorantem lampada ponto.   5
et iam punicea nudatum pectora palla
insignemque ipsis, quae prima invaserat, armis
Aeaciden—quippe aura vocat cognataque suadent
aequora—prospectant cuncti iuvenemque ducemque
295 nil ausi meminisse pavent; sic omnia visu
mutatus rediit, ceu numquam Scyria passus   10
litora Peliacoque rates escendat ab antro.
tunc ex more deis—ita namque monebat Ulixes—
aequoribusque austrisque litat fluctuque sub ipso
300 caeruleum regem tauro veneratur avumque
Nerea: vittata genetrix placata iuvenca.   15
hic spumante salo iaciens tumida exta profatur:
'Paruimus, genetrix, quamquam haut toleranda iuberes,
paruimus nimium: bella ad Troiana ratesque
305 Argolicas quaesitus eo.' sic orsus et alno
insiluit penitusque Noto stridente propinquis   20
abripitur terris: et iam ardua ducere nubes
incipit et longo Scyros discedere ponto.
Turre procul summa lacrimis comitata sororum

---

3 bebetem P: ebetem E   4 nondum] non B: nunc R   lampata (d *supra* t) P
5 nudatum PKR²: nodatum EBQR¹ *cum dett.*   6 inmiserat Q¹   7 Aeaciden
(Eac-) EBQ: Aeacidem PKR   aurora R   suadent *ex* suadet E: *ex* sudant K   10 abiit
R²   11 -que rates excendat P (*corr. Baehrens*): -que rates descendat E: raptusque
ascendit Q¹: raptus descendit Q²: raptus descendat BK *cum dett.*: raptus discedat R
13 Aequoreis B *cum dett.*: Equoreisque R   lita E   15 iuvenca PE: iuvenca est
BKQR   16 Sic R   17 tolleranda P   iuberes ER²: iube*ris* (*puberis*) (*eraso*
i *priore; v. adn.*) P: iubes R¹: iubebas BQ: iubebar *ex* -as K   19 quaesitus] -ae- *in*
ras. P²: quesit *sine ras.* E   21 Abripitur EBKQR: Arripitur P   ducere PE: cernere
BKQ¹: crescere Q²R *cum dett.*   22 longo scyros (sci-, schi-) PER: scyros longo
BKQ   descendere E: decedere R: decrescere Q² *cum dett.*

69

310 commissumque tenens et habentem nomina Pyrrhum
pendebat coniunx oculisque in carbasa fixis   25
ibat et ipsa freto, et puppem iam sola videbat.
ille quoque obliquos dilecta ad moenia vultus
declinat viduamque domum gemitusque relictae
315 cogitat: occultus sub corde renascitur ardor
datque locum virtus. sentit Laertius heros   30
maerentem et placidis adgressus flectere dictis:
'Tene' inquit, 'magnae vastator debite Troiae,
quem Danaae classes, quem divum oracula poscunt,
320 erectumque manet reserato in limine Bellum,
callida femineo genetrix violavit amictu   35
commisitque illis tam grandia furta latebris
speravitque fidem? nimis o suspensa nimisque
mater! an haec tacita virtus torperet in umbra,
325 quae vix audito litui clangore refugit
et Thetin et comites et quos suppresserat ignes?   40
nec nostrum est, quod in arma venis sequerisque precantis;
venisses—' dixit; quem talibus occupat heros
Aeacius: 'Longum resides exponere causas
330 maternumque nefas; hoc excusabitur ense
Scyros et indecores, fatorum crimina, cultus.   45
tu potius, dum lene fretum Zephyroque fruuntur
carbasa, quae Danais tanti primordia belli,
ede: libet iustas hinc sumere protinus iras.'

24 Commissumque P: Confessumque EBKQR phyrrum P   25 Pendebat P:
Tendebat EBKQR   26 freto PE: fretum BKQR *cum dett.* puppim Q² iam
om. R   27 delecta ER¹   28 relicta P   29 renancitur (s *sup. lin.*) P   ardor]
amor E   30 sentit P, *cod. Helmstad.*: sensit EBKQR   31 Herentem E *cum dett.*
et *om.* K¹Q¹: *add. sup. lin.* K²Q²   32 victor R debita E: dedite B   34 in limine
BKQR: in limite P: limine E   35 violavit PR: violabit E: velavit BKQ
36 -que *om.* K illis P: illis *ex* ullis Q: ullis EBKR furta] membra ER   37 nimis
o Q (*ras. post* o), B: nimis P: nimio K: animo E: statis (?) R suspesa minisque E
38 an] ut B tacita PEBQR: tanta K torpescet ER: torpet K   39 clamorefugit E
42 dixit PER: ultro BKQ; *v. adn.*   43 Aeacius P: Aeacides (Eac-) EBKQR
longum P: longum est EBKQR   44, 45 *transp.* E *et dett. quidam*   44 ense *ex*
entese P   46 zephyroque PR: zephyrisque (-phi-) BKQ: et zephirisque E feruntur
Brux. 5338 cum dett.   48 iustas EBKQR: iussas P hi/c Q protinus sumere R

335　　Hic Ithacus paulum repetito longius orsu:　　　　　　　　
　　　'Fertur in Hectorea, si talia credimus, Ida　　　　　　　50
　　　electus formae certamina solvere pastor
　　　sollicitas tenuisse deas, nec torva Minervae
　　　ora nec aetherii sociam rectoris amico
340　lumine, sed solam nimium vidisse Dionen.
　　　atque adeo lis illa tuis exorta sub antris　　　　　　　55
　　　concilio superum, dum Pelea dulce maritat
　　　Pelion, et nostris iam tunc promitteris armis.
　　　ira quatit victas; petit exitialia iudex
345　praemia; raptori faciles monstrantur Amyclae.
　　　ille Phrygas lucos, matris penetralia caedit　　　　　　60
　　　turrigerae veritasque solo procumbere pinus
　　　praecipitat terrasque freto delatus Achaeas
　　　hospitis Atridae—pudet heu miseretque potentis
350　Europae!—spoliat thalamos, Helenaque superbus
　　　navigat et captos ad Pergama devehit Argos.　　　　　65
　　　inde dato passim varias rumore per urbes,
　　　undique inexciti sibi quisque et sponte coimus
　　　ultores: quis enim inlicitis genialia rumpi
355　pacta dolis facilique trahi conubia raptu
　　　ceu pecus armentumve aut vilis messis acervos　　　70
　　　perferat? haec etiam fortes iactura moveret.
　　　non tulit insidias divum imperiosus Agenor
　　　mugitusque sacros et magno numine vectam
360　quaesiit Europen aspernatusque Tonantem est

---

49 repetito *ex* -os P　orsu EBKQ¹R: orso Q²: ortu P　　50 ida P: ora KQ: hora
EBR　　51 certamine E　　52 minerva E　　53 *om.* EB¹K¹Q: *add.* B²K² *in mg.*
54 Lumina EB¹K¹Q　velisse K　　56 peleum dum R　　57 promitteris *ex*
promisseris P: *ex* promiseris B²　　60 friges R　cedit E　　61 veritasque P: vetitasque
EBKQR; *v. adn.* pinos BKQ²　　63 pudet *add.* E² *in mg.* (*om.* E¹)　misereque E¹
64 spolia E¹　　65 agros E¹R¹　　66 Unde E　sparsim R　rumore *ex* -es E
67 inexenti E　　68 inlicitis genialia (gene- P) rumpi PR: genialia (geni/alia Q)
foedera (foedere K¹) rumpi EBKQ　　69 pacta] Flucti E　-que *om.* R　　70 Geu P
armentumque R　vilis P: viles EBKQR　acervo/ (-s) Q　　71 haec etiam] et non
hec E　movera/ (-t) Q　　73 nomine KQR　　74 aspernatemque (tus *supra* tem) E
tonanteme (st *add.* P²) P

71

ut generum; raptam Scythico de litore prolem   75
non tulit Aeetes ferroque et classe secutus
semideos reges et ituram in sidera puppim:
nos Phryga semivirum portus et litora circum
365 Argolica incesta volitantem puppe feremus?
usque adeo nusquam arma et equi, fretaque invia Grais?   80
quid si nunc aliquis patriis rapturus ab oris
Deidamian eat viduaque e sede revellat
attonitam et magni clamantem nomen Achillis?'
370 illius ad capulum rediit manus ac simul ingens
inpulit ora rubor; tacuit contentus Ulixes.   85
    Excipit Oenides: 'Quin, o dignissima caeli
progenies, ritusque tuos elementaque primae
indolis et, valida mox accedente iuventa,
375 quae solitus laudum tibi semina pandere Chiron
virtutisque aditus, quas membra augere per artes,   90
quas animum, sociis multumque faventibus edis?
sit pretium longas penitus quaesisse per undas
Scyron et his primum me arma ostendisse lacertis.'
380   Quem pigeat sua facta loqui? tamen ille modeste
incohat, ambiguus paulum propiorque coacto: 95
'Dicor et in teneris et adhuc reptantibus annis,
Thessalus ut rigido senior me monte recepit,

75 vi generum *Gronovius* raptam EBKQR: rapta P scytico P: serchio R¹: et scythico (scith-, scit-, schit-) EBKQR²   76 aetes P   77 *om.* E itura P: ituram *ex* iteram Q litore puppem R   78 frigas E   79 Argolicae P volitante E   81 Quodsi E   82 Deidamia E a sede R: essede P¹: sede E¹ revellet Q¹   84 redit Q magnus P¹   85 rubet E contentes (u *supra alt.* e) P achilles B (*corr. in mg.*)   86 Excepit P qui/ B   87 alimentaque R 88 Idolis P accendente P iuven///ca E   90 movere R   91 vultumque E edis P: ede EBKQR   92 penitus pr. longus R   93 *om.* E primum me arma ostendisse lacertis *Schenkl*: primum arma ostendisse lacertis (*ex* -tos) P: primumque arma tendisse lacertis B¹ (Scyron et ista tuis prima arma dedisse lacertis B² *in mg.*): primum armos (arm/ K¹) tendisse lacertis K¹Q: primum graia arma aptasse lacertis K²: primum arma extendisse lacertis R: armis primum tendisse lacertis (-tos *alt. man.*) *Brux. 5338*: primos arma ostendisse lacertis *Wilamowitz*; *v. adn.* 94 factu E   95 propriorque P: propriorque EB: priorque R   96 Ducor R² tene/ris (-b-) KQ reptantibus PE: rectantibus R¹: restantibus BKQR²

non ullos ex more cibos hausisse nec almis
385 uberibus satiasse famem, sed spissa leonum
viscera semianimisque lupae traxisse medullas. 100
haec mihi prima Ceres, haec laeti munera Bacchi,
sic dabat ille pater. mox ire per invia secum
lustra gradu maiore trahens visisque docebat
390 adridere feris nec fracta ruentibus undis
saxa nec ad vastae trepidare silentia silvae. 105
iam tunc arma manu, iam tunc cervice pharetrae,
et ferri properatus amor durataque multo
sole geluque cutis; tenero nec fluxa cubili
395 membra, sed ingenti saxum commune magistro.
vix mihi bissenos annorum torserat orbes 110
vita rudis, volucris cum iam praevertere cervos
et Lapithas cogebat equos praemissaque cursu
tela sequi; saepe ipse gradu me praepete Chiron,
400 dum velox aetas, campis admissus agebat
omnibus, exhaustumque vago per gramina passu 115
laudabat gaudens atque in sua terga levabat.
saepe etiam primo fluvii torpore iubebar
ire supra glaciemque levi non frangere planta.
405 hoc puerile decus. quid nunc tibi proelia dicam
silvarum et saevo vacuos iam murmure saltus? 120
numquam ille inbelles Ossaea per avia dammas
sectari aut timidas passus me cuspide lyncas
sternere, sed tristes turbare cubilibus ursos

98 non ullos] Nullos K hausisse PR: habuisse EBKQ almi/ (-s) Q 99 saciasse E
100 semianimisque (-esque R) lupae PR¹: semianimesque libens EBKQR²
transisse E 102 invia P: avia EBQR: via K 106 arma P: arma erant R: hasta
(h *sup. lin.* E: *ex* haste K) EBKQ 107 preparatus Q multum E 108 -que
om. E cunctis R flexa R 112 equos P (? R¹): equo EBKQR² praemissaque *ex* -seque P 113 pe///ipse (sae *sup. lin.*) P 115 exhaustumque PR *et in*
ras. B: exhaustoque KQ: exaustoque E 116 in *om.* E terga PR: colla EBKQ
117 prono fluvi E iubebar BR: iubebar *ex* -bat PE: iubar K: iubebat Q
118 supra P: super EBKQR -que *om.* E 119 quit B nunc] dn̄s E
120 saltos (u *supra* o) P 121 ossa ea K: cessans Q devia Q dammas (dam-) PR:
linces EBKQ *cum dett.* 122 lincas (-ch-) PR: dammas BKQ *cum dett.*: damnas E
123 tristes turbare *ex* tristesunt bare E ursos P: ursas EBKQR *cum dett.*

410 fulmineosque sues, et sicubi maxima tigris
    aut seducta iugis fetae spelunca leaenae.   125
    ipse sedens vasto facta exspectabat in antro,
    si sparsus nigro remearem sanguine; nec me
    ante nisi inspectis admisit ad oscula telis.
415 iamque et ad ensiferos vicina pube tumultus   ·
    aptabar, nec me ulla feri Mavortis imago   130
    praeteriit. didici, quo Paeones arma rotatu,
    quo Macetae sua gaesa citent, quo turbine contum
    Sauromates falcemque Getes arcumque Gelonus
420 tenderet et flexae Balearicus actor habenae
    quo suspensa trahens libraret vulnera tortu   135
    inclusumque suo distingueret aëra gyro.
    vix memorem cunctos, etsi bene gessimus, actus.
    nunc docet ingentes saltu me iungere fossas,
425 nunc caput aërii scandentem prendere montis,
    quo fugitur per plana gradu, simulacraque pugnae   140
    excipere inmissos curvato umbone molares
    ardentesque intrare casas peditemque volantis
    sistere quadriiugos. memini, rapidissimus ibat
430 imbribus adsiduis pastus nivibusque solutis
    Sperchios vivasque trabes et saxa ferebat,   145
    cum me ille immissum, qua saevior impetus undae,

---

124 Fulmineosque *ex* Flum- P   125 deducta E   126 expectat E   ab R
127 si *om.* K¹: An *add.* K²   nigro P: magno EBKQR necne R   128 ad
oscula telis] bscula tellis E¹: a *ante* bs- E²   129 et ad ensiferos BK: et in
ensiferos R: etensiberos (f *supra* b) P: ad ensiferos Q *cum dett.*: et ad enferos E
131 Praeteriit PER: Praeterit et BKQ   penes EB: meones Q   132 macetes R
gaesa] tela ER   citen' E¹ (*corr.* E²): manu (*sic*) Q   134 baleiaricu̧s P:
balearius (c *sup. lin.*) E   auctor B (au- *in ras.*), KR²: hautor E   135 vultnera P
tractu E *cum dett.*   136 Inclusumque suo P, *Paris. 11324*: Inclusumque ciens
K¹ (quo K²): Inclusum (? Inclusn E) quotiens EBQR distingueret PR:
distingeret E: discingeret BKQ   137 bene PR: modo EBKQ   138 decet
(o *sup. lin.*) P ingentes P: ingenti EBKQR fossos Q   139 praendere P
141 et inmissos R   curvato EBKQR²: curato R¹: scutato P   142 Ardentesque
intrare EBKQR: Ardentesque errare P: ardentes penetrare *Robertson; v. adn.*
145 Sperchiosque K   vivasque P: vulsasque EBKQR   146 me ille] mille K:
ille R   senior E   impetus *om.* K

stare iubet contra tumidosque repellere fluctus,
quos vix ipse gradu totiens obstante tulisset.
435 stabam equidem, sed me referebat concitus amnis
et latae caligo fugae; ferus ille minari   150
desuper incumbens verbisque urgere pudorem.
nec nisi iussus abi: sic me sublimis agebat
gloria, nec duri tanto sub teste labores.
440 nam procul Oebalios in nubila condere discos
et liquidam nodare palen et spargere caestus,   155
ludus erat requiesque mihi; nec maior in istis
sudor, Apollineo quam fila sonantia plectro
cum quaterem priscosque virum mirarer honores.
445 quin etiam sucos atque auxiliantia morbis
gramina, quo nimius staret medicamine sanguis,   160
quid faciat somnos, quid hiantia vulnera claudat,
quae ferro cohibenda lues, quae cederet herbis,
edocuit monitusque sacrae sub pectore fixit
450 iustitiae, qua Peliacis dare iura verenda
gentibus atque suos solitus pacare biformes.   165
hactenus annorum, comites, elementa meorum
et memini et meminisse iuvat: scit cetera mater.'

147 ibuet (*sic*) *ex* iuvet P   tumidusque P[1]: midosque E   **149** sed P: set R: ne B[1]: nec EB[2]KQ   refebat (*corr. sup. lin.*) P: ferebat E   annis K   **150–167** *suppl.* q, Q *nihil habente nisi v.* 150, *qui deletus est*   **150** fugae P: viae (vie) EBKR: me q **152** sibi iusus K   abii PR   **153** tantos P   **154** lam Bq   abalios E: cubalios q **155** E   liquidam P   nodare P: nudare EBKqR *cum dett.*   palem q   cestos (u *supra* o) P   **156** istis *ex* illis P   **157** plectro *ex* plector P   **158** mirare E **160** quo] quo et E   medicamina E   **161** somnus q   **162** cederet inerbis E: deficit herbis R   **164** paeliagis (c *supra* g) P   iure E[1]   **165** solitos P: solet hic R pacare EBKQ: pacare (l *sup. lin.*) P (placare *codd. dett.*): arcere R   bimembres q **166** alimenta R   **167**a Aura silet puppis currens ad litora venit EB *rec. man.*, R[2] *et dett. quidam*

NOTES

BOOK I

1-13 INTRODUCTION

1f. Magnanimum Aeaciden formidatamque.... This type of opening for an epic owes its origin to Virgil's *arma virumque*; similarly in *Th.* I, 1 *fraternas acies alternaque regna....*

Magnanimum. Used by Virgil as an epithet of Aeneas, *Aen.* I, 260; V, 17, 407; IX, 204; by Ovid of Achilles, *Met.* XIII, 298; by St. of various heroes.

Aeaciden. A frequent Homeric patronymic for Achilles, derived, like *Alcides*, from a grandfather.

formidatamque Tonanti progeniem. The earliest literary reference to this story available to St. would have been the *Cypria* (see *RE* s.v. 'Thetis', sect. H). A mythological summary is given by ps.-Apollod. III, 13, 5. There are three forms of the legend: (*a*) in Pind. *Isthm.* VIII (VII), 27 ff. and others, Zeus and Poseidon, rival suitors of Thetis, are warned by Themis (or, as Ov. *Met.* XI, 221 ff., Proteus) that any son born to Thetis will be mightier than his father, and therefore neither of the two will marry her; (*b*) according to Aesch. *P.V.* 908 ff. and others, only Zeus is involved, and Prometheus knows the secret; in the Πρ. Λυόμενος he may have divulged it as the price of his freedom; (*c*) the alternative story in ps.-Apollodorus, that Thetis was given in marriage to a mortal because she refused to consort with Zeus, had its origin, according to a fragment from Herculaneum, in the *Cypria* and in Hesiod (O.C.T. Homer, vol. V, *Cypria* II, discussed by R. Reitzenstein, *Hermes*, 1900, 73). St. is evidently thinking of (*b*), not of (*a*), as there is no mention of Neptune (Poseidon) as a suitor.

patrio...caelo. 'Id est Iovis, qui Achillis pater fuisset ni a Thetide abstinuisset' (Delph.).

succedere. Here the sense is 'succeed to', as in *regno succedere*; cf. *Th.* II, 398. Thus *patrio caelo* implies overlordship of the gods, not (as *accedere caelo* Ov. *Met.* XV, 818, 870; Virg. *Georg.* IV, 227 *alto succedere caelo*, of individual spirits joining the divine whole) a mere place among them.

3 refer. Cf. *Th.* I, 33 f. *nunc tendo chelyn satis arma referre Aonia.* Brinkgreve incredibly says: '*referre* cum obj. directo insolite dictum est.' For its use with a personal obj. cf. *Silv.* II, 1, 96 ff.; V, 3, 126 f.

multum. Although *multa* would give a stronger contrast with *plura vacant*, there seems no need to change. St. is fond of the adverbial *multum*, as in l. 800 *multum steriles*.

4f. ire per omnem...heroa. 'To recount the whole life of...'; cf. Ov. *Fast.* I, 15 *adnue conanti per laudes ire tuorum*.

Scyro. For the sources available to St. for Achilles' connection with Scyros see introd. pp. 10–12.

6f. Dulichia...tuba. 'With Ulysses' trumpet'; cf. l. 725. In the Homeric catalogue, Dulichium is an island near Ithaca with its own king Meges (*Il.* II, 625 ff.);

but in Latin poets it is merged into Ulysses' kingdom or confused with Ithaca. The adj. *Dulichius* as applied to Ulysses is first used by Virg. *Ecl.* VI, 76 (= *Ciris* 60).

proferre. The writer is said to do the actions which he describes, as in Virg. *Ecl.* VI, 46 *Pasiphaen...solatur*, 62–3; Hor. *Sat.* I, 10, 36 *turgidus Alpinus iugulat dum Memnona*; Juv. I, 163 f. *securus licet Aenean Rutulumque ferocem committas*; *Silv.* II, 7, 77 *qui per freta duxit Argonautas.*

nec in Hectore tracto sistere. This outlines the intended scope of the *Achilleid*, and makes it clear that it was planned on a scale comparable with that of the *Thebaid*, ending with Achilles' death.

tota Troia. Not, as Nisard (following Lemaire), 'c'est loin de Troie que je veux montrer le jeune héros', since this is an introduction to the complete epic planned by St., not to the extant portion alone. The phrase means 'throughout Troy', an abl. of place often found with *totus* (Kühner, *Lat. Gr.*², II, i, 351), and thus by metonymy 'throughout the Trojan war'; the transference from place to time is helped by the fact that the abl. can be used of 'time throughout which', as Cat. CIX, 5f. *tota perducere vita...foedus amicitiae.*

iuvenem. The whole active life of a warrior can be described by the term *iuvenis*. Clearly St. does not follow the account (ps.-Apollod. III, 13, 8) whereby Achilles was only nine years old when he went to Scyros. In the Pompeii frescoes (see Introd. p. 11, n. 6) he looks distinctly mature. St. gives us the best idea of the intended age at l. 163 below, *necdum prima nova lanugine vertitur aetas.*

iuvenem deducere. The phrase is parallel to *ire per...heroa* above, the person being substituted for his deeds; cf. Philostr. *Hero.* XIX, 1 (vol. II, p. 196, 22 in Kayser's 1870–1 ed.), of Achilles, διεξελθὼν αὐτὸν ἐκ νηπίου. *Deducere* is probably in origin a metaphor from weaving, as remarked by Duff on Juv. VII, 54, who compares Hor. *Epist.* II, 1, 225 *tenui deducta poemata filo.* Cf. also Manil. I, 1 ff. *carmine divinas artes...deducere.*

8 veterem. For the dates of completion of the *Thebaid* and beginning of the *Achilleid* see Introd. pp. 4, 6f.

deplevimus. *Depleo* is used, literally, of draining anything dry; so of draining blood from animals, Pliny, *N.H.* XVIII, 148. Its metaphorical use is found only here and in Scaliger's emendation to Manil. IV, 13 (MSS. *deflere*), where the abl. is one of separation.

haustu. For *haustus* of poetic inspiration cf. Lucr. I, 412; Hor. *Epist.* I, 3, 10.

9f. da fontes. Cf. Prop. IV, 9, 58 *di tibi dent alios fontes.*

fronde secunda necte comas. So in *Th.* VII, 170 *nectere fronde comas*; Virg. *Aen.* VIII, 274 *cingite fronde comas*; ll. 288f. below. *Fronde secunda* either 'a second crown', the *Thebaid* being the first, or perhaps 'a propitious crown'.

Aonium nemus. Cat. LXI, 28 *Aonios specus* is the first extant use in Latin of the adj. *Aonius* as applied to Mt Helicon. In St. it is found frequently both in the sense 'Boeotian' and as applied to Helicon or the Muses. For *Aonium nemus* cf. Prop. III, 3, 42.

advena pulso. Here, as in *Silv.* V, 2, 20 *advena pulsasti* (of seeking admission to the senate), I, 5, 1 *Helicona...pulsat chelys*, and V, 3, 209f. *me quoque vocales lucos*

Boeotaque (see app. cr.) *tempe pulsantem*, the metaphor is from knocking on a door; though in connection with a grove there is a mixing of metaphors. *Pulsare* in the sense of seeking admission is also found in *Silv.* I, 2, 48; IV, 8, 62; *Th.* V, 97.

11 augescunt. Similarly in *Th.* VI, 71 *parvique augescunt funere manes.* The old reading *albescunt* is equally suitable but has poor MS. support.

12f. For Statius' bold claim to be regarded as equal to the bards of old cf. the epilogue to the *Thebaid* (XII, 810–19); there is a marked contrast to the diffidence expressed in *Silv.* I, pref.

Dircaeus. 'Theban', from the fountain and stream Dirce (cf. *Th.* VI, 907f. *Dircaeus...campus*), which according to ps.-Apollod. III, 5, 5 derives its name from Dirce wife of Lycus; for her death at the hands of Amphion and Zethus see *Oxf. Class. Dict.* s.v. 'Amphion'. Amphion is very literally the founder of Thebes, as having, according to the legend, caused the stones of the city walls to pile up of their own accord by playing his lyre (Ap. Rh. I, 740f.; *Th.* I, 9f.; II, 454f.).

meque. This may be an example of *-que* in the sense of *quoque*, found regularly with *hodie* and rarely, in poetry, with monosyllabic pronouns: Prop. III, 1, 35 *meque inter seros laudabit Roma nepotes* (corresponding to Ov. *Pont.* III, 2, 35 *vos etiam seri laudabunt saepe nepotes*); Cat. XXXI, 13 *vosque* (*vos quoque* MSS.); CII, 3 *meque*; Prop. III, 21, 16 *tuque*.

14–19 DEDICATION TO DOMITIAN

14ff. The address to the emperor, with its mixture of flattery and apology, is very similar to *Th.* I, 17f. At least in the earlier part of his principate Domitian interested himself in poetic composition: see Quint. X, 1, 91; Tac. *Hist.* IV, 86; Suet. *Dom.* 2; Sil. III, 619ff. In Val. Fl. I, 12ff. it is implied that Domitian contemplated writing a poem on the siege of Jerusalem. The *Capitolini caelestia carmina belli* mentioned in Mart. V, 5, 7 may have been written by Domitian or (less probably) by his librarian Sextus, to whom the epigram is addressed. Clearly he cannot have abandoned all interest in poetry later, as stated by Suet. *Dom.* 20, but he probably contented himself with being a patron of poets. Domitian's military achievements were not so slender as his poetic efforts; for an appreciation of them see B. W. Henderson, *Five Roman Emperors*, p. 98. A. W. Verrall, *Collected Literary Essays*, pp. 161 ff., makes rather sweeping conclusions from the omission of any mention of the emperor's godhead in this address, together with other evidence, to try to show why Dante thought St. a convert to Christianity.

stupet, with direct obj., 'is astonished at', is a poetic constr.: cf. Virg. *Aen.* II, 31; *Th.* II, 564; IV, 282, 448, etc.

virtus. 'The prowess of', an almost personified usage. Cf. Virg. *Aen.* XII, 827 *Itala virtute*, though the sense is different. St. scans *Ītalus* normally, but *Ĭtalus* at *Th.* VIII, 411; *Silv.* V, 1, 223.

16 olim has its Silver Latin meaning of 'long since', equivalent to *iamdudum* (see Mayor on Juv. IV, 96, Langen on Val. Fl. I, 35), as in *Th.* I, 312 *olim vagus exul*; VI, 387; VII, 304 (?), 779; X, 362, 781; *Ach.* I, 810; *Silv.* II, 1, 76. St. is representing

Domitian as possessing a real genius for poetry, which (personified) has long been sorry that his military genius has overshadowed it: *altera* means 'the former', not 'each in turn' as Jannaccone interprets.

dolet...vinci. Perhaps a reminiscence of Hor. *Od.* IV, 4, 62 *vinci dolentem*; *doleo* with inf. is a rare poetic constr. (Ov. *Trist.* III, 12, 49; *Pont.* I, 3, 67), used also by Suetonius, commoner being acc. and inf., e.g. *Silv.* IV, 3, 102 *Appia se dolet relinqui.*

17f. Both **sudare** and **pulvere** are metaphors from the arena, and are so used by Cicero: e.g. Cic. *Sest.* 139 *sudandum est iis pro communibus commodis.* Similarly in *Silv.* IV, 7, 24f. *primis meus ecce metis haeret Achilles* we have a metaphor from the stadium. St. was not only disturbed at having neglected his proposed epic on the emperor's achievements (see next note); he was also, as shown by the last quotation, anxious about the magnitude of his present theme: cf. *temptatur* in *Silv.* IV, 4, 94.

18f. In *Th.* I, 17ff. St. promises to write an epic on Domitian, and gives a brief summary of some of the events it will touch upon. In *Silv.* IV, 4, 94ff. he says he is working on the *Achilleid*, but feels he must also attempt the *arma...Ausonii maiora ducis.* Four lines from Statius' poem *de bello Germanico quod Domitianus egit*, quoted by a scholiast on Juv. IV, 94, are reproduced at the end of the O.C.T.; but evidently St. contemplated an epic on a far larger scale than anything he actually completed.

praeludit. *Praeludere* can mean not only to act a prelude but, as in *Silv.* I, pref. (l. 10 O.C.T.), to write a preface, or as here to form a preface to.

20–29 THETIS' CONCERN AT THE CONSEQUENCES OF THE RAPE OF HELEN

20 Oebalio. Oebalus, variously called the son of Cynortas, Perieres or Argalus, was a member of the Spartan royal family, according to most accounts king of Sparta; Tyndareus is said to be either his eldest son or the son of Perieres: see *RE* s.v. Oibalos. As an adj. meaning Spartan in general, *Oebalius* is found in Virg. *Georg.* IV, 125, of Tarentum, and in other poets; cf. *Th.* II, 164; VIII, 429; IX, 690; X, 503; in *Silv.* I, 2, 151 *Oebalis* (fem.). It is also used frequently to denote particular Spartans; e.g. *Silv.* II, 6, 27f. *nec Paris Oebalios talis visurus amores rusticus invitas deiecit in aequora pinus*; see also *Ach.* II, 154.

pastor. Paris is also called *pastor* in *Ach.* II, 51, where the story is given in more detail; cf. Virg. *Aen.* VII, 363; Hor. *Od.* I, 15, 1; *Silv.* I, 2, 213f., etc.

21 blande populatus. 'After suavely plundering', a pretty oxymoron.

Amyclas. Amyclae, situated south of Sparta in the Eurotas valley, is often a synonym for Sparta in Latin poetry; similarly *Amyclaeus* = Spartan.

22 plena...referens. 'Reproducing in their fullness' (*referre* is frequently used of reproducing something old); but there is also an idea of Paris bringing Helen back to Troy.

praesagia somni. Cf. *Th.* V, 620 *o dura* (*vera* Müller) *mei praesagia somni.* Hecuba had dreamt, before the birth of Paris, that she had given birth to a torch which had set fire to the whole city. The interpretation of this dream (variously ascribed to Cassandra, Apollo and others) led to the exposure of the infant. Cf. ps.-Apollod. III, 12, 5; Ennius (?) in Cic. *Div.* I, 42; Virg. *Aen.* VII, 319 f.

23 f. culpatum. Perhaps a reminiscence of Virg. *Aen.* II, 602 *culpatus...Paris*; cf. *Th.* III, 702.

relegebat iter. 'Retracing his journey', as in Val. Fl. IV, 54 *relegit...vias*.

qua...Helle. Phrixus and Helle were son and daughter of Athamas and Nephele. To save them from being sacrificed, Nephele gave them the ram with the golden fleece, given her by Hermes. According to several writers, they rode on it through the air until they reached the Hellespont, where Helle fell into the sea and was drowned (ps.-Apollod. I, 9, 1; Tzetzes, schol. Lycophr. 22, etc.). But others, e.g. Diod. Sic. IV, 47, make no mention of flying, and Lactantius on this passage says: *Cum Phrixus et Helle per mare Hellespontum transirent, Phrixus ascendit in arietem pellem auream habentem. Helle natans ad caudam ipsius arietis se tenebat. fessa tandem ponto submersit.* The double tradition of swimming and flying is exhaustively covered by D. S. Robertson in *CR*, 1940, 1–8, who quotes *Th.* V, 475 as proving that St. adhered to the former.

condita ponto. Probably not, as Brinkgreve, 'buried', for Helle is here said to have been changed into a Nereid rather than to have died from drowning: 'deep sunk below the sea' (Mozley).

Nereis. For the short second syllable see Housman in *CQ*, 1933, 72.

26 vitreo sub gurgite. J. Henry, *Aeneidea* I, 368 ff. argues that *gurges* means simply a body of water; and certainly in Sil. IV, 87 we have *lucenti gurgite*, and in *Silv.* IV, 3, 94 (cf. *Th.* IV, 818; Lucan IV, 380) *puro gurgite*, of rivers; so that if the original meaning did contain an idea of turbulence it is often forgotten. For *vitreo* cf. *Silv.* I, 3, 73 f. *vitreas...aquas*; II, 2, 49 *vitreo...ponto*; II, 3, 5.

27 nec mora et. St. has a variety of constructions after *nec mora*. Commonest are inverted *cum* (*Th.* I, 533; VI, 887; IX, 834; *Silv.* III, 1, 117; III, 4, 47) or asyndeton (*Th.* I, 310; VI, 813; *Ach.* I, 558, 741). In *Th.* II, 513 it is followed by *quin*, here by *et*: cf. *Th.* XII, 414 f. *vix ille sepulcro conditus, et...*; similarly *Silv.* III, 1, 135 f.

28 f. fervent. 'Seethe' (with activity): cf. Virg. *Aen.* IV, 409 f. *litora fervere late prospiceres* (but IV, 567 *fervere litora flammis* is in the literal sense); Lucan VI, 67; *Silv.* IV, 3, 61. The use in ll. 443, 755 below is very similar.

coeuntia. 'Narrowing': whereas Pliny, *N.H.* IV, 92 says that the Symplegades appeared to come together, *coeuntium speciem praebebant*, Statius' use of the verb is metaphorical; cf. Prop. II, 1, 22, of Xerxes' bridge, *bina coisse vada*.

Phrixi litora. Cf. l. 409 *Phrixi...semita*; for *litus* see n. to ll. 75 f.

non explicat. Gives them no room to move; cf. *Th.* I, 146 *atria, congestos non explicitura clientes*; and for the sense, ll. 445 f. below, *ipsum iam puppibus aequor deficit.*

30–51 THETIS' MONOLOGUE

30 discusso...ponto. Not, as Mozley, 'as soon as she had shaken the brine from off her', but 'having parted the waters'; cf. Pliny, *N.H.* X, 9, of the osprey swooping upon a fish, *discussis pectore aquis.*

32 Cf. *Th.* I, 491 f. *divina oracula Phoebi agnoscens monitusque datos.* O. Müller, *Quaestiones Statianae,* p. 9, pointed out that Statius' regular habit is to scan final *-o* of the 1st sing. pres. ind. short in the middle of a sentence but long at the end. To the first part of the rule this line and ll. 34, 530, 775 are exceptions; but *agnosco* differs from the other examples in the *Achilleid* in being a molossus (*-ŏ Silv.* v, 1, 239); for in verbs such as *video* the long *-o* is necessary for the metre. The incidence of the word-accent seems not to affect the quantity of the final syllable.

33 f. facibus...levatis. This refers to the wedding torches for Paris and Helen (not, as the Dresden scholiast and the Delphin ed. would explain, signals from the ship); but there may be a double significance, i.e. *faces* = Bellona's instrument of war. Contrast *Th.* IV, 5 ff.

34 mille carinis. Virg. *Aen.* II, 198; Ov. *Met.* XII, 37; XIII, 182.

35 f. nec...Atridis. 'And it is not enough that the whole land of the Greeks is swearing allegiance to the angry sons of Atreus.' Cf. *Silv.* III, 2, 98, of Phoenix, *imbellis tumidoque nihil iuratus Atridae*; Ov. *A.A.* I, 687. *Coniurat* is used in the technical sense of military allegiance, as in Hor. *Od.* I, 15, 6 f. *Graecia...coniurata tuas rumpere nuptias.*

38 f. quid...magistri? Thetis regrets having sent Achilles to Chiron's cave in Mt Pelion. If *committere* here meant 'entrust', as editors give, we should have to accept an extraordinary inversion of the trust and the trustee, since the constr. is invariably as in II, 36 *commisit...illis tam grandia furta latebris.* Perhaps therefore the sense is, rather, local, 'connect', where the acc. and dat. are more easily interchangeable.

40 ni fallor. The reading of P, *nil fallor*, is not paralleled in classical writers (though Ter. *Andr.* 204 has *nil me fallis*), while *ni fallor* is common; cf. *Th.* II, 656. For the story of the battle between the Centaurs and Lapiths see Ov. *Met.* XII, 210 ff.

41 inprobus. A favourite adj. of Statius'. J. Henry, *Aeneidea* II, 175 is right in saying that it is never a mere synonym for *magnus, ingens,* etc., but is over-simplifying when he says it always means simply 'wicked'. The basic idea is usually indifference to the rights or feelings of others. In St. we may roughly classify the usages as follows: (1) 'naughty', of children: here and *Th.* IV, 796; (2) 'naughty', of love: *Th.* I, 253; II, 292; VII, 300; IX, 423; *Ach.* I, 569; *Silv.* I, 2, 75; II, 3, 11; V, 1, 233; (3) 'shameless', of intervention: *Th.* IX, 836; XI, 485; XII, 300, 766; (4) 'shameless', of anything unnatural: *Th.* VIII, 442; IX, 126, 754; *Ach.* I, 535; *Silv.* I, 6, 54; II, 1, 2; (5) 'cunning': *Th.* VI, 644, 804, 892; (6) 'headstrong': *Th.* VI, 839 (almost 'monstrous'); VIII, 582; IX, 744; (7) various meanings applied to abstract nouns: *Th.* IV, 319; XI, 505 (cf. *Ach.* I, 942); XII, 260, 441; *Silv.* II, 3, 67; (8) of the sun and of cold, *Silv.* I, 5, 46; I, 3, 7; of a torrent, *Th.* III, 675; of a wolf, VIII, 693; of a flower lifting its head though doomed to perish, *Silv.* II, 1, 107; of Jocasta's eyes, wretched in comparison with Oedipus' blindness, *Th.* XI, 334; of Phorbas delaying his death for the sake of Antigone, VII, 364.

patria...se metitur in hasta. 'Measures his strength with his father's spear': he is already strong enough to wield a full-sized weapon. The same idea in Val. Fl. I, 266 f. (Peleus speaking to Chiron) *sub te...magistro...nostram festinet* *ad hastam.* The use of *in* is akin to that in *Th.* I, 712; IV, 221; VII, 669; but in these passages the emphasis is more on the carrying of the weapons.

43 non potui infelix. A reminiscence of Dido's speech in Virg. *Aen.* IV, 600 ff. (*infelix* IV, 596). Lactantius' note on l. 39, COMMISIMUS *re properantis est* (read *reprobantis est,* as suggested by R. D. Williams), really belongs here, as shown by his quotation of *non potui* from *Aen.* IV, 600.

gurgite nostro. *Th.* IX, 377 *sic nostro in gurgite regnas?* Note the abl. in spite of motion being implied: cf. II, 16; *Th.* V, 388; IX, 536; *Silv.* I, 2, 109; V, 5, 69. St. is very free with his use of the abl.: examples are given by L. Lehanneur, *De P.P.S. Vita et Operibus,* p. 67; R. D. Williams, *CQ*, 1951, 143.

44 f. Rhoeteae. 'Trojan', from the city and promontory of Rhoeteum in the Troad.

cecidere trabes. Although ships were built on land, poetry could speak of the timber itself falling into the sea (*cadere* as applied to *trabs* normally, however, refers to felling, as in Varro, *Sat.* 391; Ov. *Met.* X, 373 f.; Quint. V, 10, 84, on Enn. *Medea*). Thus in *Silv.* II, 6, 28 St. writes (*Paris) invitas deiecit in aequora pinus.*

attollere magnum aequor. Cf. l. 445 below.

45 f. incesti praedonis. Both *incestus* and the metaphorically applied *praedo* are used elsewhere of abductors, e.g. Hor. *Od.* III, 3, 19 *fatalis incestusque iudex;* Virg. *Aen.* VII, 362 *perfidus...praedo;* Ov. *Fast.* IV, 591 *praedone marito;* and in *Ach.* II, 79 *incestus* is applied to Paris's ship; cf. also l. 946.

profunda tempestate. Here *profundus* is 'deep-penetrating', as in Hom. *Il.* XI, 306 βαθείη λαίλαπι: see also *Th.* X, 837 f., where *profundae caedis* is 'thick slaughter' with the idea of heaped up bodies.

cunctas...sorores. The Nereids are usually said to be fifty in number, though a few authors mention a hundred; but the lists given in Hom. *Il.* XVIII, 39 ff., Hes. *Theog.* 243 ff., ps.-Apollod. I, 2, 7 and Virg. *Georg.* IV, 336 ff. do not correspond, and altogether between seventy and eighty names are preserved. Thetis's name appears only in the lists of Hesiod and ps.-Apollodorus. See *RE* s.v. Nereiden.

47 nunc quoque—sed. A favourite aposiopesis, with *nunc* or a personal pronoun, as in *Th.* VII, 210; VIII, 60; *Ach.* I, 502.

iniuria raptae. Lit. 'the wrong done in carrying off the woman'; for the gen. defining *iniuria* cf. Virg. *Aen.* I, 27 *spretae...iniuria formae; Th.* I, 247. The past participle is used as in l. 6 above.

48 f. secundi...Iovis. Just as Pluto is Ζεὺς καταχθόνιος (Hom. *Il.* IX, 457), so Neptune is *Iuppiter secundus;* but in Cat. IV, 20 f. the same phrase denotes a favourable wind.

49 quod superest. Used by Virgil (*Aen.* V, 796; IX, 157; cf. J. Henry, *Aeneidea,* III, 196) in the same parenthetical constr. at the beginning of the line; St. has it thus in *Th.* IX, 215; X, 47; and in the second foot XII, 161.

Tethyos annos. Tethys, wife of Oceanus, is said to have been the mother of Nereus, and thus the grandmother of Thetis.

50 grandaevum...patrem. Not 'his aged sire' (Mozley), since Kronos (Saturn) had long been overthrown by his children, but Oceanus, i.e. her ancestor.

51–60 ARRIVAL OF NEPTUNE

51 in tempore. Equivalent to ἐν καιρῷ: see Lewis & Short s.v. tempus II, F; Kühner, *Lat. Gr.*², II, i, 357.

52 Oceano veniebat ab hospite. A very similar passage is *Silv.* IV, 2, 53 ff.; and cf. Hom. *Il.* XIII, 23–31; Virg. *Aen.* V, 816 ff.

53 aequoreo diffusus nectare vultus. Cf. *Silv.* IV, 2, 54 *sacro diffusus nectare vultus* (this parallel argues against Koch's conjecture *aequoreos*, and *aequoreo nectare* is also found in Paul. Nol. *Od.* II, 9); Ov. *Met.* III, 318 *Iovem...diffusum nectare.* St. is fond of the 'acc. of the part affected': see Introd. p. 17.

54 unde. Has a causal rather than local force, and refers perhaps more to *veniebat* than to l. 53; the winds are hushed because Neptune is coming.

quieto. E's *soluto* is perhaps due to a desire for euphony, but for examples in St. of *-que qu-* see G. B. A. Fletcher in *CR*, 1938, 165.

55 armigeri. Has almost the medieval sense of 'squire', as in Virg. *Aen.* IX, 564 *(aquila) Iovis armiger*; Ov. *Met.* XV, 386. Mozley translates 'who bear his armour', and others explain 'quia ferunt tridentem Neptuni'; but (*a*) he had no known armour, although it is true that in l. 58 the trident is spoken of as *telum*; (*b*) a number of Tritons could not carry one trident; (*c*) the Tritons are normally represented (e.g. Virg. *Aen.* X, 209) as carrying *conchae*, trumpets in the form of a shell, while Neptune, as in l. 58 below, carried the trident himself.

Tritones. Originally (Hes. *Theog.* 930 ff.), as elsewhere in St., only one Triton, a son of Poseidon, is mentioned; but Virg. *Aen.* V, 824 speaks of Tritons, and in later writers and in art we find Tritons, Centauro-Tritons and even Tritonesses: see Daremberg-Saglio, s.v. Triton.

scopulosa...cete. So in Hom. *Il.* XIII, 27f. ἄταλλε δὲ κήτε' ὑπ' αὐτοῦ πάντοθεν ἐκ κευθμῶν, οὐδ' ἠγνοίησεν ἄνακτα, and Virg. *Aen.* V, 822. *Cete* is the only form of the nom. and acc. pl. in classical Latin. *Scopulosa* is translated by Forcellini and Lewis & Short (cf. Garrod on Manil. II, 224) as 'projecting like a rock', by Mozley as 'rock-like', by Brinkgreve as 'in scopulis habitantia'. But H. L. Wilson, *The Metaphor in the Epic Poems of St.* (Baltimore, 1898), following Forcellini's second alternative, may be right in suggesting that the reference is rather to roughness of surface, comparing Val. Fl. II, 518 *scopulosa...terga* (referring to the sea-monster of Sigeum). See also K. Prinz, *Philol.* LXXIX, 189, who compares Enn. scenica *(Andromeda)* 115 Vahlen³; Langen on Val. Fl. *loc. cit.* For adjectives in *-osus*, of which St. is very fond, see Heuvel on *Th.* I, 217.

56f. Note the number of r's in *Tyrrheni—rege*, which portray rolling, as in Virg. *Aen.* XI, 627 they portray ebbing waves on the shore. *Tyrrheni greges* is a periphrasis for dolphins, from the story of Dionysus and the Tyrrhenian pirates, as told in *Hymn. Hom.* 7; Ov. *Met.* III, 582 ff., etc. For *greges* of aquatic animals cf. *Silv.* V, 3, 280 *Hydrae...greges.*

57 arduus. Cf. *Th.* IX, 418 f., of Ismenos, *stetit arduus alto amne.*

58 Imitated by Claud. *Rapt. Pros.* III, 138 *tardos queritur non ire iugales.* In l. 78 and *Th.* II, 46 they are called *equi.* For *triplici telo* see n. to l. 55.

59 f. spumiferos glomerant a pectore cursus. 'In front they prance, raising foam as they go': *a pectore* refers to the front part of Neptune's horses, as opposed to *pone*, which denotes their fish-like rear part; cf. *Th.* II, 46 f. *prior haurit harenas ungula, postremi solvuntur in aequora pisces.* *Glomero* is used almost as a technical term for movements of horses' legs, first in Virg. *Georg.* III, 117 (see Lewis & Short), where Macr. *Sat.* VI, 9, 8 explains that the phrase refers to the horse, not to the rider; cf. *glomeratio*, Pliny, *N.H.* VIII, 166; Sil. III, 336; X, 461 *rapidum glomerans cursum*; Val. Fl. II, 499, of the Sigean sea-monster, *adglomerare fretum.* The word is carefully analysed by W. H. Semple in *CR*, 1946, 62, who argues that it denotes repetitive rather than circular motion. The reading of EBKQR, *fluctus*, looks like the interpolation of a scribe who did not understand *cursus.* *Spumifer* is used by Ovid as an epithet of waters; elsewhere in St. applied only to the Aegean, *Th.* v, 56, and to the Hebrus, IX, 438.

pone. Although Quint. VIII, 3, 25 calls this word archaic, it is frequently used in post-Aug. poetry; by St. six times as adv. and once as prep., always at the beginning of the line.

delent...cauda. Borrowed from Virg. *Georg.* III, 59 *gradiens ima verrit vestigia cauda.*

61–76 THETIS' APPEAL TO NEPTUNE

62 ff. The customary wish that ships had never been invented; for passages illustrating this see H. Frère (Budé ed.) on *Silv.* III, 2, 61. A. Ker, *CQ*, 1953, 10 suggests the punctuation *in qualis (miserum!)*....

63 crimina. Applied to the person or thing bringing discredit on something; cf. Manil. IV, 665 *crimina terrae*, referring to snakes; Prop. I, 11, 30 *a pereant Baiae, crimen amoris, aquae!*; Ov. *Trist.* IV, 9, 26; Sen. *Oed.* 875.

terrarum. Objective gen.

64 iura freti. Each element has its own natural laws, as *Th.* I, 297 f. *profundi lege Erebi.*

repostam. Not 'hallowed' (Mozley), but 'distant' (cf. Virg. *Aen.* III, 364; VI, 59), referring to the remoteness of the Euxine. For the syncope, common in past participles of compounds of *pono*, cf. *Th.* I, 227; IV, 478, 832; V, 551; VII, 197; *Ach.* I, 773; *Silv.* IV, 4, 36.

65 The Argo, according to the usual account, was built by Argus at Iolcus on the gulf of Pagasae. For *puppis Pagasaea* cf. Ov. *Met.* VII, 1; XIII, 24; in Val. Fl. I, 422 the form is *Pagaseia.*

66 It is easiest to take *scelus* as joint obj., with *spolia hospita*, of *portans, furto* (quasi-adverbial, as in *Th.* I, 313; III, 164; VIII, 61; IX, 133; XI, 758) being loosely attached to the phrase, which is a poetic equivalent of 'spolia ex scelere furtim commisso portans' (cf. l. 22 *referens praesagia*).

67 Cf. *Silv.* I, 2, 43 f. *nec si Dardania pastor temerarius Ida sedisses.*

68 quos gemitus...daturus. Here the meaning is of causing sighs among gods and men, a different sense from Virg. *Aen.* IV, 409 (of Dido) *quosve dabas gemitus*; cf. *Th.* VI, 107, 527 *dat gemitum tellus.* Examples of *dare* with a noun (*vulnera*, etc.), as a circumlocution for a verb, a constr. which St. frequently has, are given by Lewis & Short s.v. do II, E, Langen on Val. Fl. IV, 49.

69 The reading of EBKQR, *praemia*, has perhaps crept in from Virg. *Aen.* V, 70 *cuncti adsint meritaeque exspectent praemia palmae.* For confusion of dactylic words see Markland, pref. to *Silvae*, pp. ix–xi; Housman on Manil. I, 416; II, 780. Thetis is complaining that she and others are having to pay dearly for Venus' victory on Mt Ida.

70 gratae munus alumnae. Mozley renders 'her gift to her dear ward', i.e. Helen, but the phrase is best interpreted with subjective gen., 'the gift of our grateful nursling' (*gratae* ironical), i.e. Venus, this being a reference to her birth from the sea.

71 semideos. So *Th.* III, 518 *semideos...reges,* also of the Argonauts. Theseus was often regarded as a son of Poseidon (Plut. *Thes.* 6, etc.). No other writers speak of him as having accompanied the Argonauts; but it is clear from ll. 156f. below that St. thought he did.

72 undis honor, sc. *est. Honor,* in the sense of 'esteem', is regularly applied to inanimate things: cf. Ov. *Met.* X, 170 *nec citharae nec sunt in honore sagittae.* The sense of *adhuc* (=*etiam nunc*) is one not used by Cicero, and the form of the sentence may have been suggested by Virg. *Aen.* IV, 318f. *istam, oro, si quis adhuc precibus locus, exue mentem.*

73f. aut permitte fretum. 'Or entrust the command of the sea to me'; the omission of *mihi* is perhaps compensated by its emphatic position (after *fas sit*) at the end of the sentence. The reading of P, *haut permitte,* which E. Baehrens, *Bursians Jahresber.* X, 53 supports, and which Kohlmann and Brinkgreve adopt, has no parallel and is, as pointed out by Housman, introd. to Manil. I, p. xxxviii, n. 1, and Garrod, *CR,* 1914, 67, quite untenable; cf. also P's readings at ll. 194, 198, 885.

nulla inclementia, sc. *me movet.* Thetis can achieve her purpose by a slight storm causing no undue hardship or suffering. Cf. Virg. *Aen.* II, 602 *divom inclementia*; *Th.* XI, 684 *timida inclementia regum.*

timuisse. After *fas est* St. uses either the pres. or perf. inf., the latter in l. 895 below; *Silv.* II, 1, 82; V, 3, 265 (never in the *Thebaid*); in *Silv.* V, 3, 275f. he has both pres. and perf., *fas mihi sic patrios contingere vultus, fas iunxisse manus.* This last example shows that J. Ae. Nauke, *Observationes criticae,* etc., p. 32, was wrong in distinguishing between the use of pres. and perf. inf. after *fas.*

74 da. St. often has *da* with inf.: *Th.* VII, 93; IX, 624f.; XI, 96; similarly *des, Th.* VIII, 332; *dabo,* l. 92 below, etc. Cf. Val. Fl. I, 604f. *da mergere Graios insanamque ratem.*

da pellere luctus. This is the reading of P, while BKQR have *da tollere fluctus* and E¹ *adtolle fructus.* After ll. 71–3 *da tollere fluctus* would be repetitive; it is more reasonable to suppose that the reading of BKQR has crept in from l. 92 than that the reading of P is due to a conjecture intended to avoid the repetition *fluctibus* in l. 75.

75f. Line 75 has been variously emended, as (*a*) the sense of *de tantis...fluctus* has been held not to be clear; (*b*) those who consider *tollere fluctus* the correct reading in l. 74 suspect *fluctibus* here; (*c*) P has *unam*, EBKQR *unum*. In support of the latter, *litus* badly needs an epithet, as admitted by A. Klotz, *Philol.* LXI, 294, who nevertheless prefers *unam*. Arguments in favour of *unum* are given by R. Helm, *Berl. Phil. Woch.* 1902, 973; cf. Housman, introd. to Manil. I, p. xxxviii, n. 1. St. is evidently following the account (Strabo XIII, 1, 32, etc.) by which Achilles' tomb was said to be on Cape Sigeum; and reading *unum*, we may construe: 'And do not destine me to live on one shore, the rocks of a Trojan tomb, out of such great waters you possess.' *Tantis* cannot equal *tot* (thus Baehrens' conjecture must be wrong), in spite of Lewis & Short s.v. tantus I, B and Mozley on *Silv.* V, 3, 119; this seems to be a post-classical usage: see references in Krebs-Schmalz, *Antibarbarus*, s.v. tantus. The apparent contradiction between *fluctibus* and *litus* is removed by assuming that Thetis foresees herself confined to the waters immediately below Achilles' tomb (Sen. *Tro.* 1121f. *tumulumque Achillis, cuius extremum latus Rhoetea leni verberant fluctu vada*). Moreover *litus* can mean the waters near the shore, as in ll. 29, 226f. *pleno litore*, 690 (cf. E. Wistrand, *Nach innen oder nach aussen?* appendix I, reviewed in *CR*, 1948, 91; M. P. Cunningham in *Class. Philol.* 1949, 5ff.). For the topography of Cape Sigeum see W. Leaf, *Strabo on the Troad*, p. 165. There is a curious parallel to these two lines in *Silv.* II, 2, 15f. *dat natura locum montique intervenit unum litus et in terras scopulis pendentibus exit*; where *unum*, although suspected, is probably correct.

77–94 NEPTUNE'S REPLY

77 laniata genas. Virg. *Aen.* XII, 606.

pectore nudo. *Th.* XI, 418.

79 invitat curru. The abl. with *invitare* is an instrumental rather than a local abl.; for alongside *invitare tecto ac domo* (Cic. *Verr.* II, 4, 11) we have also *invitare hospitio*. In Plautus and other early writers the normal meaning is 'entertain' rather than 'invite'; e.g. Plaut. *Rud.* 362 *Neptunus magnis poculis hac nocte eum invitavit*; and H. Nettleship, *Contributions to Lat. Lexicography*, p. 495, is perhaps correct in deriving *invito* from *vita* (but see A. Walde, *Lat. Etym. Wörterbuch*). Cf. *Silv.* II, 3, 61 (where *gurgite* goes more naturally with *invitat* than, as Slater, with *exclusos*); III, 1, 138; V, 3, 282.

dictis...ita mulcet amicis. *Dictis...amicis* is a Virgilian phrase, e.g. *Aen.* II, 147; V, 770; VIII, 126; X, 466; St. uses the whole of this phrase in *Th.* III, 294, and has the verb with *dictis* also in *Th.* I, 478; III, 178; *Silv.* I, 2, 194.

81 fata vetant. Lucan X, 485; *Th.* III, 316 (Mars' speech); V, 179; IX, 254.

ratus ordo deis. 'It is a decree of fate fixed for the gods that...'; cf. *Th.* II, 169 *longo...ordine fati*.

82f. consulta and **edixit** are terms applicable respectively to the senate and to magistrates; *edicere* as applied to a god can be paralleled only in Christian writers.

84f. quem...natum. 'What a son...!' Cf. Virg. *Aen.* IV, 47.

Sigeo in pulvere. There is no need to alter the MS. reading, as Lachmann; see my note in *CR*, 1949, 50. Ll. 84–7 clearly derive their inspiration from Cat.

LXIV, 343 ff., esp. 344 *cum Phrygii Teucro manabunt sanguine campi*, and 349; cf. *Il. Lat.* 384 *sanguine Dardanii manabant undique campi*; *Culex*, 322 f.

quanta...funera. This phrase occurs also in *Th.* II, 460 f. and Hor. *Od.* I, 15, 10, where Wickham remarks: 'This use..., where we should expect *quot*,... is poetical, and seems to include the notion of magnitude as well as of number.'

funera. See n. to l. 88.

87 undabit. There appears to be no parallel for the transitive use of *undare*, for in Claud. *Ruf.* II, 67, quoted in dictionaries as a parallel, it is clearly intransitive. But *undabit* for *inundabit* seems possible; e.g. in *Th.* III, 719 St. has *cunctor* transitive, which is found elsewhere only in Claudian. For Statius' verbal innovations see M. Schamberger, *De P. P. Statio verborum novatore*, diss. Halle, 1907, and the reviews by Klotz in *Berl. Phil. Woch.* 1909, 137, and T. Stangl, *Woch. f. Klass. Phil.* 1908, 707. The contrast with *modo crassa exire vetabit flumina* is made far stronger if, while the rivers are made solid, the plains are said to run with rivers of blood: thus *turpabit* (suggested by Garrod) is weaker. St. confines *undare* to the pres. part. except here and *Silv.* IV, 3, 138.

crassa. *Crassus* as applied to waters means 'thick', often with mud; but it is commonly used of blood, and in *Th.* IX, 257 f. *crasso vada mutat uterque sanguine* there is the same notion of a stream being made thicker.

exire. 'Flow out into the sea', not, as the Thesaurus interprets, 'overflow', which is contrary to the sense.

88 funere. 'Corpse': so used by St. over twenty times. The variant *pondere* given by Lactantius is, however, possible, and *funere* may have been supplied from l. 85.

89 inpellet. 'Will overthrow.'

nostros. Apollo and Poseidon were said to have been commissioned by Laomedon to build the walls of Troy (Hom. *Il.* VII, 452 f.). Apollo's share in the work is mentioned in *Th.* I, 699 f.

opera inrita. Cf. Ov. *Met.* XII, 587 *irrita qui mecum posuisti moenia Troiae*. The god is not, as Lactantius suggests, complaining of the fact that Laomedon refused to pay for the walls when built, but is calling them useless because they are soon to be overthrown.

90 ff. Thetis is comforted by being told that, in spite of her marriage to a mortal, Achilles will be thought to be the son of Jupiter; and that although she will mourn for him, she will be able to wreak her vengeance in her 'kindred waters' when the Greek fleet sails back: see n. on l. 93.

nec...-que. 'Not...but' (*nec* with *inulta*): see Kühner, *Lat. Gr.*², II, ii, 48, 3; Owen on Ov. *Trist.* II, 347.

92 dabo. See n. on l. 74.

tollere fluctus. Virg. *Aen.* I, 66, 103; cf. J. Henry, *Aeneidea* I, 294.

93 f. reduces Danai. Note the ellipse of *erunt* in this subordinate clause.

nocturna...exseret. Nauplius, an Argonaut (said by ps.-Apollod. II, 1, 5 to be a son of Poseidon, but by Ap. Rh. I, 133 ff. to be a descendant of the Nauplius who was a son of Poseidon), to avenge the death of his son Palamedes, condemned by the Greeks as a traitor, lit beacons on Cape Caphereus in the south of Euboea, which caused the Greek ships to be wrecked: cf. Eur. *Hel.* 1129 ff.; Virg. *Aen.* XI, 260; Prop. IV, 1, 115; Ov. *Met.* XIV, 472 ff.; Q. Smyrn. XIV, 614 ff.

exseret. A favourite verb of Statius', used twenty-one times including the part. *exsertus*; here 'reveals'.

dirum...Ulixem. Virg. *Aen.* II, 261, 762.

quaeremus. 'Seek out', for punishment, as *Th.* I, 648, Neptune being hostile to Ulysses because of the blinding of Polyphemus, Thetis because Ulysses had taken Achilles to Troy.

95–125 THETIS VISITS CHIRON

95 vultum demissa. Virg. *Aen.* I, 561; similarly *demisso...vultu*, *Th.* IV, 769.

96 bellare with dat. is confined to post-Aug. poetry and later Latin: *Th.* VII, 320f.; VIII, 505; IX, 15, 791; Sil. IX, 503; XVI, 564.

97 animo. *Iterum* (EBQR; K seems originally to have read *iterum animo*) is most likely a makeshift, as in *Th.* XI, 21, where Q reads it for *campo*; see also Garrod's app. cr. to *Th.* III, 710.

paratus. For the pl. in the sense of 'preparations' cf. Ov. *Pont.* III, 4, 5 *opus exiguum vastisque paratibus impar*; *Th.* II, 104; *Ach.* I, 940.

98 Haemonias. 'Thessalian', from the Thessalian tribe Haemones: so *Haemonia*, 'Thessaly'.

detorquet. 'Turns aside'; so *Th.* IV, 487; VII, 737.

99 f. Thetis is swimming towards Thessaly, as shown by l. 98 *detorquet bracchia* (later, l. 383, *abnatat*). St. makes no mention of Thetis flying, as in Hom. *Il.* I, 496 f.; nor does *gressus*, as thought by Jannaccone, here refer to a walking motion. Three arm strokes and three leg strokes bring the goddess to the shore of Thessaly.

ter...ter. Hom. *Il.* XIII, 20 says of Poseidon τρὶς μὲν ὀρέξατ' ἰών, τὸ δὲ τέτρατον ἵκετο τέκμωρ. Claud. *Nupt. Hon.* 147 f. *ter pectora movit; iam quarto Paphias tractu sulcabat arenas.* For the ritual significance of such phrases see Slater in *CR*, 1909, 252 f.

conata. Used absolutely in the sense of *nixa*.

reppulit. *Repello* can be used of soaring upwards from land or sea, as in Virg. *Georg.* IV, 233; Ov. *Met.* IV, 710; but it is not here so used, and we should translate *reppulit* 'thrust back' rather than 'spurned' (Mozley).

niveas...plantas. Barth and others recall the Homeric ἀργυρόπεζα Θέτις.

feriunt vada. The shoals hit the soles of her feet (note the change of subject), i.e. she feels the bottom (Lewis & Short, s.v. vadum I, B, 2) under her feet. For *ferio* thus applied to a motionless object cf. Lucan VIII, 698; IX, 336; *Silv.* II, 2, 80.

101 ff. conubialia...antra. *Conubialis* is first found in verse, with consonantal *i* as always, in Ov. *Her.* VI, 41; then in St., here and *Th.* V, 112. *Conubium*, except in nom. and acc. pl., is scanned similarly (not with *-ŭ-*, as implied by Jannaccone on *Ach.* II, 69). The description of the cave on Pelion, where the marriage of Peleus and Thetis was celebrated, is inspired mostly by Ov. *Met.* XI, 229 ff.; see n. to l. 108.

We should observe that (l. 109 below) St. equates this cave with that of Chiron. The cave itself is said to open wide its recesses in joy at the approach of Thetis.

102 f. Sperchios. This, not *Spercheos*, is the form found in the MSS. here. At l. 239 P has *Spercheos*; at l. 628 the MSS. except q have *Sperchie*; at 11, 145 the MSS. have *Sperchios*; at *Silv.* III, 4, 85 M has *Sperchio*; at *Th.* IV, 839 (O.C.T. numbering) P has *Spercheus*. Although St. always uses *Alpheos*, not *Alphios*, P has *Lyrcius, Lyrcie* at *Th.* IV, 117, 711; Priscian, however, notes *Lyrceus* as a variant. In general *Sperchius* is the commoner form in Latin, and St. may have adhered to it.

dulci. 'Fresh'; cf. *Th.* VIII, 362, where the sea water is said to be 'fresh', from the flooded Nile pouring into it; *Silv.* II, 2, 18 f.

circuit. Cf. l. 408 *undisonae quos circuit umbo Maleae.*

104 fatigat. Whereas in l. 217 the object is Thetis herself and the subject her anxiety, here the constr. is virtually reversed. Cf. Virg. *Aen.* VIII, 94 *olli remigio noctemque diemque fatigant,* 'give no respite to'.

105 sollers pietate magistra. 'Scheming under the guidance of her devotion (to Achilles).'

106 domus ardua. *Silv.* I, 1, 7 *attoniti...domus ardua Daci.*

107 longo suspendit Pelion arcu. Cf. *Th.* X, 83 *longo suspenditur arcu*; Claud. praef. *Nupt. Hon.* I *ducto...Pelion arcu. Suspendo* is commonly used of arching or vaulting; cf. also *suspensio, suspensura.*

108 This description is similar to that of Ov. *Met.* XI, 235 f. *est specus in medio, natura factus an arte ambiguum, magis arte tamen*: see note to l. 101.

exhausta. 'Excavated'; cf. Hor. *Epod.* V, 30 f. *ligonibus duris humum exhauriebat*; Colum. I, 6, 15; similarly *terrae...immurmurat haustae* Ov. *Met.* XI, 187. Sen. *Tro.* 831 speaks of Chiron's cave as *montis exesi...antro.*

109 f. signa. Tokens (rather than arms and insignia, as the Dresden schol. implies) of the gods and goddesses present at the marriage of Peleus and Thetis, consisting of the *tori* on which they reclined.

sacrarit. P has *sacravit*, the other MSS. *sacrarat*. Menke's *sacrarit* (indirect question) would account for both readings, and is likely also because (*a*) Priscian has *sacrasset*, evidently quoting from memory, (*b*) the parallel in *Th.* IV, 162 ff. *parvo...ostenditur arvo, robur ubi et laxos qua reclinaverit artus ilice, qua cubiti sedeant vestigia terra* has the same constr.

accubitu. Perhaps first used by St., here and *Th.* I, 714 (the ref. in Isid. *Orig.* XX, 11, 19 does not prove that he found the noun in Varro).

genio has not its normal meaning of tutelary deity (as *genium...loci,* Virg. *Aen.* VII, 136, and *genio loci* in inscriptions), but almost equals *numine.*

111 Centauri stabula. Virg. *Aen.* VI, 286 *centauri in foribus stabulant.*

non aequa. 'Very different from those of': *comparatio compendiaria.* Chiron is dissociated from the battles with the Lapiths.

112 ff. nullos...nec...aut. Similarly *neque...aut,* *Silv.* I, 4, 66, a constr. found mostly in poetry.

cruores. This poetic pl., as Virg. *Aen.* IV, 687, occurs in St. also at *Th.* VI, 102; VIII, 405; XII, 595, 719.

genialibus, of things connected with a marriage, as *Silv.* I, 2, 224; II, 7, 82 (*genitalibus* LM); here the marriage of Pirithous.

orni…crateres. Some of the traditional weapons of the Lapiths and Centaurs; for *orni* cf. Juv. I, 11; for *crateres Th.* II, 564; VI, 537, etc.

115 inania terga. St. uses *inanis* of skins of dead animals: *Th.* I, 483 *inanem…leonem*; VI, 722 *tigrin inanem*; also *vacua ora leonum*, VII, 276; *vacuorum terga leonum*, IX, 589. Mozley incredibly translates 'mighty hides' (is he thinking of *immania*?). For *terga ferarum* cf. l. 415, and Virg. *Aen.* VII, 20.

117 Hyg. 274, 9 says that Chiron *artem medicinam chirurgicam ex herbis primus instituit*; the therapeutic herb *centaureum* was named from him, and another called Χιρώνειον is mentioned by Theophr. *Hist. Plant.* IX, 11, 1 (Sir A. Hort in Loeb ed. wrongly translates 'that of Chaeronea': cf. Pliny, *N.H.* xxv, 66). His medicinal lore is mentioned also in *Silv.* I, 4, 98 f., and more fully in *Ach.* II, 159 ff.

dubiis. 'In danger' (of dying), as Ov. *Her.* xx, 199.

animantibus. A Lucretian word (e.g. Lucr. III, 96), also in *Silv.* III, 2, 61; *Th.* I, 501; III, 552; XI, 465; XII, 503 *animantibus aegris*.

118 Cf. I, 186 ff.; II, 157 f.; Sil. XI, 449 ff. *quae Peliaca formabat rupe canendo heroum mentes et magni pectora Achillis, Centauro dilecta chelys.* Other allusions to Chiron's musical skill are quoted by Langen on Val. Fl. I, 138.

120 serenat. A poetic verb (once in Cic.) mostly describing weather: 'brightens up'.

123 The origin of the dactylic lines representing galloping, made famous by Virg. *Aen.* VIII, 596 *quadrupedante putrem sonitu quatit ungula campum*, is Enn. *Ann.* 224, 277 (Vahlen³) *quatit ungula terram*, 439 *cava concutit ungula terram*; but in Ennius, as here, only the ending is dactylic. Other examples in St. are: *Th.* VI, 401, 459; XII, 656; *Silv.* V, 3, 55.

desueto. Here in the passive sense, as Virg. *Aen.* II, 509 *arma…desueta*, not as *Th.* V, 231. Note the juxtaposition of the two contrasting adjectives *nota* and *desueto*.

124 f. imos demissus in armos. EBQ have *summissus*, which is paralleled by Sil. x, 464, of a horse, *inclinatus colla et submissus in armos*; but *demissus*, as in *Silv.* V, 5, 83, is probably correct. It signifies stooping to the level of Thetis (*ungula* and *armos* are reminders of Chiron's equine nature) rather than, as Brinkgreve, because the entrance to the cave was low; nor does *admonet antri* imply this. K. Prinz, *Philol.* LXXIX, 189 f. suggests that the latter refers to the darkness of the cave, and the line is quoted by Heuvel, on *Th.* I, 518, as an example of *hysteron proteron*. But Thetis had been to the cave before, and Chiron is perhaps simply reminding her that it is only a cave. *Admoneo* with gen. also in *Th.* VIII, 35 f.

inducit. *Induco* in its literal sense with dat. is mostly poetic: Virg. *Georg.* I, 316; *Th.* II, 200; XII, 326, 464 f.; *Ach.* I, 548.

126-158 THETIS' REQUEST TO CHIRON AND HIS ANSWER

127 pignora. Pl. for sing., as in l. 384. 'Pledge' in the sense of a child is found in English from Spenser to Dickens and his contemporaries.

129 te sine. For the anastrophe (Virg. *Aen.* XII, 883, etc.) cf. ll. 269, 654, *te propter.*

129 ff. See following note for translation.

130 et magnos utinam mentita timores? To place *utinam mentita* in brackets, as Brinkgreve does and as Mozley's translation implies, involves the ellipse of two verbs, *atra...signa* being nom. and *magnos...timores* acc. *Mentita* must govern *timores*, with sense rather as Prop. II, 17, 1 *mentiri noctem* ('to promise falsely'); and *utinam mentita* is a compressed equivalent of *minantia* (*utinam falso*). We may thus translate ll. 129 ff.: 'Is there not just cause for my sleep being disturbed, and for signs from the gods coming upon his mother, signs black and portending (I hope falsely) great fears?' K. Prinz, *Philol.* LXXIX, 190 ff. comments soundly on this passage; but there is no need to adopt his emendation *iam merito* (omitting question-mark).

131 namque. Garrod reads *iamque*, and his app. cr. implies that this is the reading of PEKQ; but actually PEBKQR all read *namque*, only Brux. 5338 (first hand) *iamque.*

utero mihi. There is a slight awkwardness of constr. in the two datives, *utero* being governed by *infensos* and *mihi* dat. of disadvantage, as (dat. of advantage) Plaut. *Cas.* 337 *quis mihi subveniet tergo aut capiti aut cruribus?* Klotz would have *utero* abl. ('in utero contuor') and *mihi* dependent on *infensos*, but the order of the words is against this.

contuor. This is the conjugation used by Plautus; Lucretius has both 2nd and 3rd conj., while Cicero and later writers almost always have *contueor.* St. also has *tuor*, *Th.* III, 152, and *intuor*, III, 533.

133 f. Thetis is pretending that in her dreams she seems to re-enact the dipping of Achilles into the waters of Styx (*ipsa* agrees with *Tartara*). Homer does not mention the legend by which Thetis made her son invulnerable except for his heel; in later writers it appears variously as dipping him into the Styx or treating him with fire or with boiling water in an attempt to make him immortal (Ap. Rh. IV, 867 ff.; ps.-Apollod. III, 13, 6). The version in which he is dipped into the Styx does not occur in any extant poet earlier than St.: see Kürschner, *op. cit.* pp. 16–22; Legras, *REA* X, 41 n. 4. Nevertheless, as Legras *ibid.* 39 points out, the legend of partial invulnerability must have been known early, as a lost Chalcidian amphora from Vulci (600–550 B.C.; E. Pfuhl, *Malerei und Zeichnung*, Abb. 163; id., *Masterpieces of Greek Drawing and Painting*, p. 19, fig. 13) shows Achilles dead pierced by an arrow in the heel. For immersion in the Styx see also O. Weser in Roscher, *Lex. Mythol.* IV, 1576; Waszink on Tert. *de Anima* L, 3. For *inania Tartara* cf. Ov. *Met.* XI, 670; XII, 523 f., 619; *Th.* IX, 654 f.

Stygios...fontes. Val. Fl. VII, 364.

fero mergere. The poetical use of the inf. in a final sense is perhaps not paralleled with *fero* meaning 'carry'. Examples of it in the *Achilleid* with other verbs of motion are ll. 210, 288 f., 735 f., 821 f.

135 ff. St. seems clearly to have in mind the scene in Virg. *Aen.* IV, 480 ff. where Dido, who is deceiving Anna about her real intentions, tells her that she has found an Ethiopian sorceress who will cure her of her love, and asks her to put relics of Aeneas on a funeral pyre. The language is in many points similar. *Hos abolere metus...iubet...Carpathius vates* is inspired by *Aen.* IV, 497 f. *abolere nefandi cuncta viri monimenta iubet*, where the reading *iubet* should be accepted rather than *iuvat*, as St. has clearly copied the former. *Magici* is perhaps borrowed from *Aen.* IV, 493, *sacri* from *ibid.* 500; while *litora summa Oceani* corresponds to *Oceani finem* and *ultimus...locus, ibid.* 480 f.

Carpathius vates. Proteus, one of whose abodes was the island of Carpathos: Ov. *Met.* XI, 249. St. is the first to attribute this particular prophecy to him (see Legras, *REA* X, 41 n. 5).

sub axe peracto, the reading of P, is a curious phrase, but may represent a conscious variation of Virgil's *Oceani finem iuxta solemque cadentem* (*axem, ibid.* 482, is in a slightly different sense, of the whole heavens). Garrod notes that at ll. 199 f. below Thetis is undecided where to hide Achilles; but this is of no consequence, since she is now only inventing a false story. In *Silv.* IV, 3, 107 *sub axe primo* indicates the East, and just as this refers to the beginning of the sun's course, so *sub axe peracto* can refer to its end (cf. *Th.* V, 180 *perfecto sole*); other examples of *primus* in the sense of 'east' are given by Vollmer *ad loc.* and Heuvel on *Th.* I, 200 (*primaeque occiduaeque domus*).

138 inlabentibus astris. Avien. *Arat.* 1057 *omnibus iste* (*sol*) *noctibus inlabens pelago sex inserit astra, sex reparat* (an expansion of Aratus, 554 ff.). The stars are picturesquely said to warm the Ocean as they fall in (*Pontus*=Oceanus, not the Euxine).

140 longum (sc. *est*). Cf. II, 43; *Th.* II, 163 *longum enumerare.*

141 magis. In the sense of *potius*, as Cat. LXVIII, 30; Virg. *Ecl.* I, 11; *Th.* IV, 543; also *sed magis*, Lucr. II, 428, 869.

neque enim ille dedisset. *Th.* I, 578 f.

142 tegmina foeda. Cf. ll. 652 f., where the words again refer to Achilles' feminine attire.

143 ausa, sc. *esset.* St. quite often omits the subjunctive of *sum*, as in ll. 477, 776, 780; II, 89.

144 infringe. 'Break down (their opposition).'

145 nam (not *non* as Garrod) is the reading of PEBKQR. Chiron is warning Thetis that her desires are such as may kindle the envy or enmity of other gods. Barth, giving *iam* as an alternative reading, says that *tua vota* means 'filius tuus'; but this is unwarrantable.

147 patria omina. This is usually taken to mean 'the prophecies of a father'— either because Chiron was the foster-father of Achilles, or simply as denoting prophecies by which fathers were often deceived. But a comparison with *Th.* IX,

662 *nec te de dubiis fraterna oracula fallunt* suggests that this applies to the gift of prophecy, perhaps bestowed on Chiron by his father Saturn (Kronos) even if taught him by Apollo.

148 vis festina. Cf. *Th.* IX, 716 *festina...virtus*.

> **tenues.** Similarly *Th.* IV, 512; and in *Silv.* V, 2, 13 *angustis...annis*.

> **supervenit.** 'Surpasses', i.e. 'goes beyond', not, as Lewis & Short, 'attacks'.

150 procul haut. For *haud* after the adv. it modifies, cf. Lucan VI, 286.

151 non capit. 'Cannot contain.' Barth and others compare Apollo's words to Iulus in Virg. *Aen.* IX, 644, *nec te Troia capit*.

152 Pharsaliae. This is the reading of P, and should be retained, -*iae* being scanned with consonantal *i*: see my note in *CR*, 1949, 50. Klotz in *Philol.* LXI, 295 remarks: 'Similiter variant libri Anth. 110. 2 Baehr., ubi haud scio an *Pharsaliam*, quod Probi codex Parisinus exhibet, genuinum sit.'

156f. Cf. *Th.* III, 517ff. *prima cum pube virentem semideos inter pinus me Thessala reges duceret.* *Argoos* is adj. from *Argo*; it cannot mean 'Greek', as Brinkgreve would have it.

157 The original omission of this line by P was due to the similarity between *Thessala* and *Thesea*, which led the scribe by haplography to telescope 156–7 into ...*pinus cum Thesea vidi*; there is thus no MS. support for Garrod's suspicion of l. 157 as spurious. For Theseus and the Argonauts see n. on l. 71.

158 sed taceo. Cf. the aposiopesis in *Th.* IV, 517, *illum—sed taceo.*

158–177 ARRIVAL OF ACHILLES

158 gelidus...pallor. Ov. *Trist.* I, 4, 11; *gelidus* is quite commonly used in poetry with abstract nouns, e.g. *horror*, Sil. V, 390f.; IX, 122; *tremor*, Virg. *Aen.* II, 120f.; VI, 54f.; XII, 447f. Cf. Val. Fl. IV, 226 *pavor et gelidus defixit Castora sanguis.*

159 sudore et pulvere. *Th.* IX, 710.

> **maior.** Mozley translates 'made larger'; but the implication is rather 'more impressive', as Sil. XII, 280, and *magnus*, Sen. *H.F.* 418.

160 festinatos. In much the same sense as *festinos*.

161f. natat ignis in ore. *Silv.* II, 1, 17f. *lacrimis en et mea carmina in ipso ore natant* (so M: *carmine in ipso ora* Friedrich); for parallels see Vollmer *ad loc.* The meaning is roughly 'suffuses the surface of', and is different from the common use, of streaming eyes, as in *Th.* II, 337. For *ignis in ore* cf. *Silv.* I, 2, 61f. *puer...cui plurimus ignis ore.*

> **purpureus.** A reddish colour, as commonly: cf. Hor. *Od.* III, 3, 12 *purpureo...ore.*

162 gratior. Sen. *Phaedr.* 769. Kürschner, *op. cit.* p. 39 n. 5 observes the extraordinary similarity of language in Philostr. *Hero.* XIX, 5 (vol. II, p. 200, 10 in Kayser's 1870–1 ed.) τὴν μὲν δὴ κόμην ἀμφιλαφῆ αὐτῷ φησιν εἶναι καὶ χρυσοῦ ἡδίω.

163 Not so strictly confined as Isid. *Orig.* XI, 2, 2 *prima aetas infantia est...*, *quae porrigitur in septem annos.* See n. to *iuvenem*, ll. 6f.

164f. faces. Similarly of a snake *Th.* v, 508 *livida fax oculis*; of horses and riders *Th.* VI, 396 *face lumina surgunt*; and in apposition Prop. II, 3, 14 *oculi, geminae... faces.* The use of *fax* with an adj. meaning 'gentle' is unusual.

plurima vultu mater inest. An attractive phrase, cf. Claud. *Rapt. Pros.* II, 27f. *multus in ore frater erat.*

165f. The simile is inspired by Virg. *Aen.* IV, 143 ff. *qualis ubi hibernam Lyciam... deserit ac Delum maternam invisit Apollo instauratque choros,* etc.; cf. Hor. *Od.* II, 10, 18 ff. The chief town in Lycia associated with Apollo was Patara.

saevis permutat plectra pharetris. 'Exchanges his fierce quiver for the quill' (Mozley): 'quits' would render even more of the alliteration. *Pharetris* abl. of price (or instrumental; see Roby, §§ 1197 n. 2, 1198).

167 gaudia subject, **formae** dat. For the parenthesis cf. l. 122 *dant gaudia vires.*

168 Cat. LXIV, 154 *sola sub rupe leaena*; Virg. *Aen.* VIII, 295 *vastum Nemeae sub rupe leonem.* There are two mountains called Pholoe, one (*Th.* x, 228, etc.) in Arcadia, this one in Thessaly, *populum...mentita biformem* according to Lucan III, 198.

170 incitat ungues. Achilles, carrying the lion cubs, teases them so that they use their claws: cf. Cat. II, 4 *acres solet incitare morsus.*

171 fido...in limine. The epithet can be paralleled by Prop. IV, 4, 8 *fida...castra,* Sil. IV, 24 *fidos...obices,* and by l. 751 below *virginibus qua fida domus.* Similarly *Th.* IX, 321 *in gurgite fido*; x, 318 *subter iuga fida.*

173 gravis amplexu. Lit. 'heavy in his embrace', *amplexu* being either abl. of respect or supine.

174ff. St. follows the account whereby Patroclus was already Achilles' companion in Chiron's cave; so also does Val. Fl. I, 407ff. In *Silv.* II, 6, 54 St. calls Patroclus *Haemonium Pyladen* (if we retain the reading of M). H. Kürschner, *P.P.S. quibus...fontibus,* pp. 28ff., discusses the mythology and its bearing upon Statius' sources.

175 extenditur. *Se extendit* in prose (Caes. *B.C.* III, 77, 3, etc.).

176 aevi...modis. *Th.* VII, 296f. *aevi confudere modos* has a slightly different meaning.

sed robore longe. Lewis & Short (cf. F. Hand, *Tursellinus* III, 548f.) compare *Th.* x, 140, saying that in both places *longe=valde,* and would have *impar* understood here. But this is clearly unsound: one cannot supply the opposite epithet to the one used. In *Th.* x, 140 *longe* must mean 'from afar'; for the use as *valde,* as opposed to that as *multo,* is post-class. and rare. *Longe esse* can be used for *abesse, distare,* and *longe* here has an 'adjectival' force, being equivalent to *distans*; cf. Quint. VIII, praef. 3 *ut...ab eloquentia longissime fuerint,* i.e. 'far removed' (see R. G. Austin on Quint. XII, 9, 8). *Th.* XI, 432 *nec tu mihi sanguine longe* is perhaps the nearest parallel in St., but cf. also *Th.* v, 25; *Silv.* III, 3, 121.

178–197 ACTIONS OF ACHILLES THE SAME DAY

179 fumantis. A favourite epithet of Virgil's (participle occurs ten times) and Statius' (twelve times), denoting steam rising from sweat.

novatur. 'Is refreshed': *genas crinemque* may be acc. of the part affected (see Kühner, *Lat. Gr.*², II, i, 288 ff.), or could, if the verb is used as a middle, be considered direct obj.

180 f. anhelo...equo. Virg. *Georg.* I, 250; *Aen.* v, 739, etc.; cf. l. 690 below.

fessumque sui iubar excitat astri. St. conceives Castor as still being a horseman after his deification, and pictures him refreshing the beam of his constellation in the Eurotas. The expression is very similar to *Th.* x, 136, where Iris *obtusum multo iubar excitat imbri*. *Fessus* as applied to stars is found in *Th.* II, 36; Manil. II, 249; III, 60.

182 pectora mulcens. Elsewhere the phrase is not used literally as here; see note on l. 275 below.

184 libare dapes. Virg. *Aen.* v, 92; Hor. *Sat.* II, 6, 67; *Silv.* III, 3, 199.

185 *Silv.* III, 5, 95 *nec desunt variae circa oblectamina vitae.*

186 elicit. An extension of the use of *elicio* with *vocem*, etc.; cf. Cic. *N.D.* II, 150 *ad nervorum eliciendos sonos ac tibiarum.*

extremo. A very rare adverbial form on the analogy of *postremo*, found in Corn. Nep. *Ham.* (*Vir. Illus.*) II, 3.

chelyn. *Chelys*, a lyre (lit. tortoise, from which it was originally made), occurs no fewer than twenty-seven times in St. Cf. Val. Fl. I, 139 *pulsatque chelyn post pocula Chiron*; Sil. XI, 451 *Centauro dilecta chelys.*

187 f. expertas pollice chordas. Jannaccone gives parallels, to which may be added Tib. II, 5, 3; Ov. *Am.* II, 4, 27; *Fast.* II, 108; by *chordas* St. means the whole instrument as obj. of *dat*, but the strings in connection with *expertas*, 'tested' to tune them.

188 f. immania. The force of this adj. is often weakened in St. by employment in such phrases as *telum immane*, *Th.* IX, 547, 802; *certamen immane* XII, 662.

laudum semina. 'Origins of glorious deeds.' Cf. II, 89; *Th.* XII, 546 f. Ov. *Her.* IX, 83 is perhaps a scribe's insertion borrowed from this passage (see Palmer's ed.; Planudes translates a different line).

189 novercae. The labours imposed on Heracles by Eurystheus were really due to the jealousy of Hera, who had caused Eurystheus to be born a day earlier than Heracles, in order that he and not Heracles should have the supremacy which Zeus had promised to a descendant of Perseus born that day (Hom. *Il.* XIX, 95 ff.).

190 f. Amycus, king of the Bebryces, a Bithynian tribe, is frequently called Bebryx as their eponymous founder. He was said to have killed (sacrificed, according to most authors) foreigners whom he had defeated in boxing, but was himself defeated and killed by Pollux (Ap. Rh. II, 1 ff.; Val. Fl. IV, 99 ff., which St. probably knew). Other references to this story in St. are *Silv.* IV, 5, 27 f.; *Th.* III, 352 f. For the form of the indirect questions (*quo caestu obruerit* for the ordinary *quomodo obruerit caestu*) cf. II, 131–5.

crudum. This is the reading of all except E, which has *crudo*, perhaps inspired by Virg. *Aen.* v, 69. It may have not only the meaning of 'savage', 'cruel', but also a reference to its original etymology (cognate with *cruor*), as with *vulnus*, etc.; cf. Mart. iv, 49, 4 *cenam, crude Thyeste, tuam* (for *Thyeste* see Housman in *Journ. Philol.* xxxi, 252); *Th.* iii, 352 f.

192 St. refers to the struggle of Theseus with the Minotaur in *Th.* xii, 668 ff.

193 gravatum. Mozley translates 'trodden by the gods'; certainly the reference is still to the marriage of Thetis, but *gravo* implies 'weighing down'. Just as the gods were often spoken of as of superhuman size, so also as regards weight: Barth aptly quotes Juv. xiii, 48 f.

194 'Then Thetis, though worried, mastered her face and smiled.'

195 collabitur. The compound perhaps denotes putting his arms round the rock; cf. Val. Fl. i, 348 f. *ille suo conlapsam pectore matrem sustinuit.*

197 adsuetaque pectora mavult. Ov. *Met.* iv, 596 *assuetaque colla petebat.*

198–216 THETIS DECIDES TO HIDE ACHILLES IN SCYROS

198 undisonis. Val. Fl. iv, 44 *ab undisoni...crepidine saxi.*

199 quibus abdere terris. So also ll. 505 *quibus abditus oris*, 529 *latebris quibus abdere*; the case is probably abl., as in *Th.* xii, 228 f., rather than dat., though in Sil. xiii, 406 we have *reclusae...abdere terrae.*

200 destinet. *Destino* with inf. even in Caes. *B.C.* i, 33, 4; in St. *Th.* vi, 933; x, 80.

huc illuc divisa mente. Virg. *Aen.* viii, 20 (=iv, 285, which is perhaps spurious) *atque animum nunc huc celerem, nunc dividit illuc.*

201 proxima seems curious as applied to Thrace, which is further from Pelion than either Macedonia or Scyros. But the poet's knowledge of Greek topography is undoubtedly second-hand: see n. to ll. 677 ff.

202 f. Macetum. *Macetae* or *Macedae* is used *metri gratia* in dactylic poetry for *Macedones*: see P. Kohlmann in *Philol.* xxxiv, 570 f.

laudumque daturi Cecropidae stimulos. 'Nor the Athenians, likely to incite to renown', a slight anachronism. Baehrens's *laudumve* is not necessary, as -*que* is often used where we should render 'or', 'nor': cf. l. 225 below, and see Housman on Manil. i, 475.

opportuna. The literal sense (derivation *ob-portus*) is noteworthy.

204 ire per. Not literally but mentally.

artas. P's reading is usually discarded because of *Cycladas altas* in l. 530; but *altas* is perhaps less suitable here, where Seriphos is called *humilis*: for the opposite error see *Th.* iv, 805 app. cr. The epithets *crebrae* (*Th.* v, 182), *innumerae* (*Ach.* i, 676) and *vadosae* (i, 389) likewise suggest a crowded archipelago.

205 Myconosque humilisque Seriphos. In Ov. *Met.* vii, 463 it is Myconos which is called *humilis*; though not very appropriately, as it rises to over 1000 ft.

206 Lemnos non aequa viris. Refers to the story told by Hypsipyle in *Th.* v, 49 ff.

hospita. With dat. here and *Th.* xii, 618; with gen. *Th.* v, 336; ix, 228; *Silv.* iii, 5, 75f.; v, 3, 168.

207 ff. For the origins of the legend concerning Lycomedes, king of Scyros, and Achilles see Introd. pp. 11–12. The only other connection in which he is mentioned is that he killed Theseus by throwing him down from a rock (Plut. *Cim.* viii, 5; id. *Thes.* xxxv, 4; Paus. i, 17, 6). We learn from Thuc. i, 98, 2 that at the time of Cimon the inhabitants of Scyros were Dolopes, a Thessalian tribe; but evidently St. does not consider Lycomedes and his people as Dolopes, as in ll. 777ff. the king says he fought against the Dolopes when they attacked the island.

inbelli. There is a sharp contrast with *Mavortia Thrace*, l. 201; similarly in l. 625 Achilles complains of *imbelli carcere*.

208 persona. A rare adj.: the only other examples seem to be Val. Fl. iv, 418; Petron. 120 (*Bell. Civ.* 72); Mamert. *Grat. Act.* 10. In all four passages the form *persona*, either fem. sing. or neut. pl., and no other is found.

209 f. Aegaeon or Briareus, son of Uranus, was with his brothers imprisoned in the earth by Uranus till Zeus released them, according to Hesiod to fight the Titans. In Hom. *Il.* i, 396ff., however, Achilles reminds Thetis that she saved Zeus, when the other Olympians wanted to put him in bonds, by releasing 'the hundred-handed one, whom the gods call Briareus, but all men Aegaeon'. St. evidently envisages Aegaeon as still in bonds shortly before the events described here. It would seem that he connects Aegaeon etymologically with the Aegean Sea (as Eustathius on Dionys. Per. 132; others give various other connections); cf. *Th.* v, 288f., where the dat. is *Aegaeōni*.

laxantem. 'Trying to undo.'

numerare catenas. A typically exaggerated attention to detail, which in this case sounds somewhat ludicrous. For the infinitives see n. to ll. 133f.

211 Perhaps borrowed from Virg. *Aen.* iii, 78f. *huc feror; haec fessos tuto placidissima portu accipit.* Note the alliteration.

212f. This simile is imitated by Claud. *Rapt. Pros.* iii, 141ff.

vicino seems to mean 'approaching', a sense paralleled by *Th.* xi, 149 *fati monitus vicinaque funera sentit*; Lucan vii, 50 *mortis vicinae properantis admovet horas*; cf. *vicinia mortis* (Lucan viii, 569; Petron. 93). If *vicino* has this meaning, *inanem* is 'empty', i.e. without fledglings; if not, *inanem* has to be 'insubstantial'. For *domus* of birds' nests cf. Lucr. i, 18. Another simile about the anxious mother and her fledglings is in *Th.* x, 458ff.

216 vix...et. A poetic constr., as in *Th.* v, 263f.

217–241 THE DEPARTURE

217f. consilio. 'Deliberation.'

fatigat cura. Sil. vii, 302; xiii, 467f.

sinu conplexa. Cf. ll. 767f.

219 magno Tritone. Instrumental (on the instr. abl. applied to persons see T. Maguire, *Journ. Philol.* iii, 232ff.); for Triton see n. on l. 55.

220 Iris, personifying the rainbow, is said to drink up the sea water and replenish the clouds, as in Ov. *Met.* I, 270 f.; cf. *Th.* IX, 404 ff. *arcano...in antro, unde aurae nubesque bibunt atque imbrifer arcus pascitur.*

221 f. murice...acuto. Virg. *Aen.* V, 205 and Sil. XVII, 276 use *acuto murice* as meaning a sharp edge of rock. Here the meaning is more literal, the shell of the murex serving as a bit for the dolphins.

frenat...delphinas. Tib. I, 5, 46 *vecta est frenato caerula pisce Thetis*; Ov. *Met.* XI, 237 *frenato delphine sedens, Theti nuda.*

biiugos. See app. cr.; Virgil uses *biiugus* seven times, *biiugis* twice (not counting the *Culex*); St. only *biiugus*, here and in *Th.* II, 723.

222 maxima Tethys. *Th.* III, 34; Val. Fl. II, 317.

224 f. glaucae...formae. *Glaucus* is used once by Lucretius (I, 720) of the sea, then by Virgil and others, especially of sea gods, etc.

226 pectoris humani. Manil. I, 28, 717.

iubet hos subsistere. Military phraseology.

226 f. pleno litore. See n. on ll. 75 ff. Pliny, *N.H.* IX, 22 says: *solent (delphini) in terram erumpere incerta de causa, nec statim tellure tacta moriuntur.* Note the alliteration.

contagia terrae. Ov. *Met.* XV, 195.

228 f. toto resolutum pectore. There is no need to emend to *corpore*; for *toto pectore* had become a stock phrase for the whole of one's conscious being; a parallel, though with a more suitable verb, is *Th.* VII, 88 f., where after the simile of an abating storm St. adds *nondum...toto respirant pectore nautae*—they are still dazed. There is also perhaps an imitation of Virg. *Aen.* IX, 326 *toto proflabat pectore somnum*, which Servius calls a euphemism for snoring! Here the phrase merely means a deep sleep, and St. amplifies it by the clause *qui pueris sopor* (see n. to l. 287). Note the unusual metrical break in l. 229.

231 effulgurat. Otherwise found only in late Christian writers. *Cynthia = luna* is post-Aug. (in Ov. *Her.* XVIII, 74 we should perhaps emend with Palmer to *numen*).

232 f. In l. 233 P has *rotat*, the other MSS. *rogat*. If we read *rotat*, the phrase must mean that Chiron, after entering the sea, swiftly leaves it again. As Mozley remarks, this has no point. Furthermore *celeres recursus* is used elsewhere with the meaning of 'a speedy return', so that here it can appropriately refer to the return of Thetis and Achilles if we read *rogat*; e.g. Ov. *Met.* VI, 450 *celeres missae spondere recursus*; Pliny, *Paneg.* LXXXVI, 4 *precatus...celerem...recursum.* In *Th.* IX, 678 P has *natant* or *notant* for *negant*, a similar corruption, while in l. 686 below P has *timentem*, EBKR *gementem*, which is probably correct. Schenkl's *notat* has the objection that *noto* 'to hint at' is used with acc. of person only.

securus pelagi. Virg. *Aen.* VII, 304.

235 erecto prospectat equo. The same phrase in *Silv.* I, 2, 217 *erecto prospexit equo*, but of Chiron watching Thetis' approach before her marriage. *Equo* means the equine part of Chiron, just as *viro* in Claud. *Gigant.* 89 refers to the human portion of Mimas. St. is fond of emphasising the double nature of Chiron and other centaurs, e.g. *Th.* VII, 638f.; *Silv.* I, 4, 98 (cf. Ov. *Met.* VI, 126); *Th.* I, 457; *Ach.* II, 165.

236 orbita is properly speaking the track left in the earth by a chariot wheel, as in *Th.* VI, 415f., etc.

237 Thessala Tempe. Ov. *Met.* VII, 222; Hor. *Od.* I, 7, 4; Sen. *Med.* 457; *Silv.* I, 2, 215. Elsewhere in St. *tempe=valles.*

238 Pholoe. See n. on l. 168. Note the 'pathetic fallacy' in ll. 237–41.

Othrys. In addition to the Thessalian mountain mentioned here and at l. 426, also *Th.* III, 319, St. mentions a Mt Othrys in Thrace, *Th.* IV, 655.

239 tenuior. Postgate's emendation should be accepted; the corruptions are perhaps due to scribes thinking it unmetrical. For examples of *tenuis, tenuior* and other words involving irregular scansion of *-ui-*, see my note in *CR*, 1949, 50. The Spercheus is said to overflow (l. 102) with joy at the coming of Thetis, and now to contract at the departure of her and Achilles. For the frigidity of sentiment see J. Wight Duff, *Literary History of Rome in the Silver Age*, p. 483.

Sperchios. See n. on l. 102.

242–282 ARRIVAL AT SCYROS; THETIS ATTEMPTS TO PERSUADE ACHILLES

242f. Cf. *Silv.* II, 6, 79f. *quinta vix Phosphorus hora* (so M, perhaps rightly) *rorantem sternebat equum.*

premit. Has the double sense of 'chases' and 'presses down upon' (cf. W. H. Semple in *CQ*, 1937, 16). The sun-god is called *Titan* as being considered son of the Titan Hyperion.

243f. The sun's horses are still dripping (*rorantes*) from their immersion in the ocean, and *pelagus* refers to the salt water, still clinging to the chariot on its upward journey through the heavens.

magno. Brinkgreve connects this with *curru*, but from its position it belongs more naturally to *aethere*: cf. *Th.* X, 456; XII, 4.

248 aëre primo. 'At his first glimpse of the air': the air and climate are very different from his normal surroundings, where he would have woken up in Chiron's cave.

251 occupat. Ov. *Fast.* III, 509 *occupat amplexu.*

252 Barth recalls the imitation in Claud. IV *Cons. Hon.* 214f. *si tibi Parthorum solium fortuna dedisset, care puer....*

sors aequa. *Th.* I, 661.

253f. dabat. 'Offered.'

aetheriis...plagis. Virg. *Aen.* I, 394; IX, 638 (sing.).

255 humiles. Having power over the earth, *humilis* being applied by gods to earthly matters (*Th.* X, 664; *Ach.* I, 268).

256f. inpar...genus. This phrase is used, for example in Sall. *Jug.* XI, 3, of illegitimate sons or the like; in Tac. *Hist.* II, 50 *maternum genus impar* means 'his mother's family was of less distinction'.

praeclusaque leti…via est. Ov. *Met.* I, 662 *praeclusaque ianua leti.*

a matre. 'On your mother's side': cf. *utroque a sanguine,* l. 899.

258 extremis…metis. Here the metaphor is from the turning-point in a stadium; the crisis has reached its turning-point. Contrast *plenis…metis,* l. 673, where the metaphor is from the winning-post.

260 dignare. St. often has *dignor* with acc., 'to deem a thing worthy': *Th.* VII, 505; IX, 783; XII, 579, 737, 785; *Ach.* I, 932; *Silv.* I, 4, 46; III, 2, 115; V, 3, 156 (in *Silv.* III, 1, 155 *invicta…manu* is perhaps constructed with *dignare* rather than instrumental as Mozley).

260f. Hercules served Omphale, queen of Lydia, for three years as a recompense for the murder of Iphitus. The language is extremely similar to that of Prop. III, 11, 19f. *ut…tam dura traheret mollia pensa manu.* Cf. also *Th.* x, 646ff.; *Ach.* I, 582, 654 (of Deidamia and Achilles). *Lydia* agrees with *pensa, dura* with *manu.*

hastas. This does not mean loom shuttles ('radii', Brinkgreve), for which there is no parallel, but thyrsi; for in *Th.* x, 649, after describing Hercules' efforts with the distaff, St. adds *et tympana rumpere dextra,* a similar reference to Bacchic revels, and in ll. 654f. below Achilles says *tibi pensa manu, tibi mollia gesto tympana.* For *hasta = thyrsus* cf. Virg. *Ecl.* v, 31; *Th.* IX, 796.

262 The **palla** is properly speaking a woman's garment, but the term was applied also to actors' and singers' robes (e.g. that of Apollo), etc. A very similar passage is Sen. *H.F.* 472–5.

263 Jupiter disguised himself as Diana (*a*) when in love with Callisto, daughter of the Arcadian king Lycaon (Ov. *Met.* II, 425); (*b*) according to Lactantius on this passage (but perhaps wrongly), when in love with Antiope daughter of Nycteus.

264 ambigui…sexus. In l. 337 *ambiguus…sexus* is said of Achilles; here the pl. is more appropriate owing to Caeneus' change of sex. The story of Caeneus is given in Ov. *Met.* XII, 171ff., and is apt here owing to the connection with Peleus (*Met.* XII, 193). *Magnum* perhaps refers to the fact that Caeneus, like Achilles apart from his heel, was invulnerable (*Met.* XII, 171). See J. T. Kakridis, 'Caeneus', in *CR*, 1947, 77ff.

265 hac. Postgate's emendation, *hac* going closely with *exire,* improves the sense and accounts for P's reading. It appears to be the corrected reading in B.

nubem…malignam. *Nubes* in the metaphorical sense also *Th.* I, 124; II, 321; IV, 512; *Silv.* I, 3, 109; III, 3, 147; V, 3, 13 (*nubila*). *Malignus* is also a favourite word of Statius' (twelve occurrences, often of natural phenomena).

exire. Probably transitive, governing *minas nubemque,* 'evade' (cf. *Th.* XI, 138f. *incertum leto tot iniqua fugane exeat*), rather than, as the Thesaurus gives, intransitive, *sine* governing *minas nubemque.*

266f. mox. See n. on II, 88.

lustra. 'Wild tracts', as *lustra ferarum,* Virg. *Georg.* II, 471; *horrentia lustra, Aen.* XI, 570; *lustra habitata feris, Silv.* III, 1, 169; *invia…lustra, Ach.* II, 102f.; and elsewhere in St.

267ff. per ego…. The same formula in Virg. *Aen.* IV, 314ff. With *ego* we should understand *te oro;* with *experta, sum;* with *utinam, armavissem.*

iuventae gaudia. Val. Fl. vii, 3391. *nec videris ulla iuventae gaudia?*
humilem...maritum. Cf. l. 255 *humiles Parcas.*

severo. 'More poetarum de omnibus rebus quae ad inferos pertinent'
(Heuvel on *Th.* i, 88); cf. Virg. *Georg.* iii, 37f., of Cocytus; *Aen.* vi, 374f.; *Th.* iv,
53f. For the immersion of Achilles in the Styx see n. to ll. 133f.

271 ora reducis. *Th.* xi, 494. Similar questions in l. 907 *quid triste fremis?*
quid lumina mutas? and *Th.* vii, 508 *quid aufers lumina?*

273 cognata...aequora. Cf. ii, 7, and i, 92 *cognatis...fretis.*

274 horrida pectora tractat. 'Handles his uncouth heart.'

275 mulcens. Virg. *Aen.* i, 153, 197, etc.; *Silv.* ii, 1, 56f., 230.

275f. genitorque...nutritorque. Concrete for abstract, *genitor* standing
idiomatically for the thought of his father; cf. *Th.* i, 591f. *pulsi ex animo genitorque*
pudorque et metus; v, 658ff. *faxo omnis fabula Lemni et pater et tumidae* (dat., sc. *Hypsi-*
pylae) *generis mendacia sacri exciderint.* In these two parallels the concrete noun is
coupled with abstract nouns. Among other examples are Ov. *Met.* viii, 463
pugnant materque sororque; xiii, 187.

279 campis fluviisque. Cf. l. 154; the *et* couples concrete and abstract nouns
in zeugma.

honore. 'Grace', a poetic meaning; cf. Hor. *Epod.* xvii, 17f. *tunc mens et*
sonus relapsus atque notus in voltus honor; Th. ii, 160 (of Adrastus' daughters);
vii, 225 (of rose-gardens).

280 colla. St. has the pl. form always in nom. and acc. (forty-six times), the
sing. only in dat. and abl.

281 lupis. Bits with sharp teeth are called (*a*) *freni lupati* (Hor. *Od.* i, 8, 6);
(*b*) *lupati* or *lupata* (n. pl.) (Virg. *Georg.* iii, 208; *Th.* iv, 731; vi, 303); (*c*) *lupi*
(Ov. *Trist.* iv, 6, 3).

fremit. Used with inf. also in *Th.* v, 696, but in the sense 'clamour to'.
But the lack of parallel for the meaning here, 'loudly protests at having to', does
not argue in favour of *gemit*, the reading of EBKQR; for *fremo* is found both literally
of horses neighing (e.g. Virg. *Aen.* xi, 496, 599) and metaphorically of grumbling,
with acc. or acc. and inf.

282 miratur discere. *Miror* with prolate inf. *Th.* ii, 14. There seems to be no
mention in grammars or dictionaries of this constr. parallel to *gaudeo, indignor,* etc.

283–317 ACHILLES WATCHES THE MAIDENS OF SCYROS AT THE FESTIVAL OF PALLAS

283f. attonitae...parenti contulit. 'Bestowed upon the bewildered mother.'

quae mens. Emendations have been proposed, but are unnecessary. *Mens*
simply 'plan', 'design', as often.

detraxit. *Distraxit* might rather have been expected; but St. evidently
means 'pulled down' from the high pedestal of his stubborn refusal and inde-
pendence.

285 f. The passage is reminiscent of Ov. *Met.* II, 711 ff. *illa forte die castae de more puellae vertice supposito festas in Pallados arces pura coronatis portabant sacra canistris*; and Virg. *Aen.* VIII, 102 ff. *forte die sollennem illo rex Arcas honorem Amphitryoniadae magno divisque ferebat ante urbem in luco.*

Palladi. St. uses the gen. *Pallados*, not *Palladis*; hence dat. *-ĭ*, as *Doridi*, *Silv.* IV, 2, 28 (Politian's correction of *Doride*); *Iasoni*, *Th.* III, 521 (Barth's correction of *Iasone*); but *Thetidis*, *Thetidī* (l. 955).

litoreae. Cf. ll. 696 ff. below.

honorum. Probably from *honor* rather than, as Brinkgreve, from *honorus*; some parallels are given by the Thesaurus s.v. *dies* IV, B.

287 quae rara licentia. For other examples in St. of short parenthetical relative clauses without verbs see Heuvel on *Th.* I, 169 f., Vollmer on *Silv.* I, 4, 90 f., and cf. *qui pueris sopor*, l. 229 above.

288 f. dare veris opes. 'To offer the riches of the spring'—not merely flowers, as H. L. Wilson, *The Metaphor in the Epic Poems of St.* For the inf. see n. to ll. 133 f.

divaeque severas...comas. Not, as Mozley, 'bind their grave tresses with the leaf of the goddess', but 'bind the austere locks of the goddess (i.e. of her statue) with foliage'. See n. to l. 9 (*fronde*).

spargere floribus. *Th.* V, 580.

hastam. The spear of Pallas, not, as Bernartius interpreted, thyrsi.

290 eximium formae decus. *Silv.* III, 3, 113.

292 virginitas...annique. Cf. *Th.* V, 82; but there *anni* implies that Hypsipyle is younger than her companions. Claud. *Epithal.* 125 f. has *matura tumescit virginitas*.

293 ff. The same simile in *Silv.* I, 2, 115 f. *quantum Latonia nymphas virgo premit quantumque egomet Nereidas exsto.* These are inspired by Hom. *Od.* VI, 102 ff., the only simile of any length in the *Odyssey* introducing gods (about forty brief similes such as 'like a god', 'like Aphrodite'), and Virg. *Aen.* I, 498 ff., which almost translates the Homeric passage; cf. Ov. *Met.* III, 181 f. Just as in Egyptian art kings are portrayed of superhuman size, so are gods often so depicted in Greek art and poetry (e.g. Demeter and Persephone as opposed to Triptolemus in the Eleusinian relief, Athens, Nat. Mus. no. 126; Demeter in *Hymn. Hom.* II, 188 f.).

294 obruit. 'Eclipses': used in prose also, *M. Brutus Vatinium dignitate obruerat*, Vell. II, 69. The formula *tantum...obstat, obruit...quantum* occurs in Val. Fl. I, 318 f., quoted below.

umeris. See n. to l. 880 (*umeris excedere*).

295 f. regina...chori. *Th.* IV, 379. The leader in boys' games was called *rex*; there is no reference to princely birth.

obstat. *Obstare* here means 'eclipse' or 'outshine', as in Val. Fl. I, 318 f. *femineis tantum illa furens ululatibus obstat, obruit* (Baehrens: *obruat* S) *Idaeam quantum tuba Martia buxum*, and somewhat as in Livy II, 33, 9 *sua laude obstitit famae consulis Marcius.* The original meaning of *obstare* is 'to stand in the way of', and in Enn. *Ann.* 163 (Vahlen³) *soli luna obstitit* it is applied to a literal eclipse.

297 'The bright colour flames upon her rosy countenance' (Mozley); cf. *ignis...purpureus* in ll. 161 f. Editors explain *purpura* as a purple or purple-edged garment,

Barth comparing Juv. XI, 154f., an allusion to the *toga praetexta*. But that meaning is not easily understandable from the context, and the normal effect of a rosy face would be to make a red or purple dress seem less bright. Cf. Claud. *Rapt. Pros.* I, 270 *niveos infecit purpura vultus*, borrowed from this passage and ll. 161f.

298 'And her jewels have more radiance and more fetching gold.' *Aurum* probably refers to the gold attachments of Deidamia's jewels; and the comparatives evidently contrast her with her sisters. The explanation given by H. L. Wilson, *op. cit.*, that *aurum* refers to the colour in her face, is hardly possible.

299 forma. Deidamia's beauty (not Minerva's, as Mozley), which St. compares here with that which the goddess would have if depicted in a less warlike manner. For the type of conditional sentence cf. *Th.* IV, 550, and for the sense *Th.* I, 535f.

pectoris angues. The same phrase in *Th.* VIII, 518; it refers to the Gorgon's head, bristling with snakes, on Minerva's shield; cf. l. 486.

300 vultus. Acc. of the part affected, here with a finite pass. verb; see Introd. p. 17.

301 agmina. See n. to l. 900. There is a reminiscence of Virg. *Aen.* X, 721 *hunc ubi miscentem longe media agmina vidit*, applied to a different context.

302 trux puer. Sen. *Tro.* 832 *trucis Chiron pueri magister*; *Th.* VII, 342.

nullo temeratus pectora motu. Cf. *Silv.* II, 1, 156 *et nullo temeratus corpora damno*. Festus says: *Temerare: violare sacra et contaminare, dictum videlicet a temeritate*; and there is an etymological connection, *temere* being loc. of **temus*, 'darkness', and *temerare* the verb formed from it. *Motu* = 'emotion'.

303 deriguit. Although the MSS. mostly have *diriguit*, the better form is *derigesco*: there is no separative force to justify *di-*. In the three other occurrences in St., *de-* is preferred (but *di-* P *Th.* IX, 36).

totisque...ignem. The metaphor is from drinking a fiery poison which permeates the body, and is similar to several Virgilian passages: *Aen.* V, 172 *tum vero exarsit iuveni dolor ossibus ingens*; VII, 354ff. (cf. I, 660); I, 749 *longumque bibebat amorem*; also Ov. *Met.* II, 410 *accepti caluere sub ossibus ignes*.

304f. Virg. *Aen.* VIII, 389f. *Vibrare* is used, in the literal sense, of torches in Claud. *Epithal.* 97.

redit. 'Duly appears'; i.e. becomes visible on the cheeks, as opposed to *latet*.

306 inpulsam. Agreeing with *lucem genarum*, which stands for *genas*. This use of *impello* to signify a flush of blood beating upon the cheeks is one apparently peculiar to St., being found also in *Th.* IV, 581 *tenues...impelli sanguine vultus*; *Ach.* II, 84f. *ingens inpulit ora rubor*. Garrod with early editors has *impulsum* (sc. Achillem), which would read equally well but has poor MS. support.

307f. The Massagetae were a Scythian tribe living to the east of the Caspian. The custom of mixing milk with blood is mentioned by Sen. *Oed.* 470 *lactea Massagetes qui pocula sanguine miscet*, and Virg. *Georg.* III, 463, where other Scythian tribes are said to drink the mixture. The simile of staining ivory comes from Hom. *Il.* IV, 141f. (whence Ov. *Am.* II, 5, 40) via Virg. *Aen.* XII, 67f., being ascribed by Homer to Caria or Maeonia, by Virgil to India. Ennius, *Ann.* 352 (Vahlen[3]) has the simile *et simul erubuit ceu lacte et purpura mixta* (*lacte* nom.).

corrumpitur. Perhaps an intentional variation on Virg. *Aen.* xii, 67f. *Indum sanguineo veluti violaverit ostro si quis ebur,* to render Hom. *Il.* iv, 141 ὡς δ' ὅτε τίς τ' ἐλέφαντα γυνὴ φοίνικι μιήνῃ. The impairing force of the verb is not stressed; similarly Virg. *Georg.* ii, 466, Prop. ii, 33, 29 and other passages, where, however, it is used not, as here, of staining, but of mixing, melting or cooking.

309 notis. *Th.* iv, 744; vi, 293; *Silv.* i, i, 15f.

palletque rubetque. Cf. *Th.* i, 537f. There seems no need, with Schenkl, to put these words in brackets, so as to make Achilles subject, as shown by K. Prinz, *Philol.* lxxix, 198, who compares Claud. *Rapt. Pros.* iii, 88.

310ff. The pres. subjunctives give a more vivid picture, as in Virg. *Aen.* vi, 292ff. For *eat atque* cf. ii, 82.

pudor. Brinkgreve understands *pudor matris,* but this is unnecessary.

313ff. Other similes of a bull occur in *Th.* ii, 323ff.; iii, 330ff.; xii, 601ff. When a bull's horns were fully grown they were said to be *lunata; Th.* vi, 267; Pliny, *N.H.* vi, 38.

quondam. Referring to the fut., a poetic usage, as Virg. *Aen.* vi, 876; not elsewhere in St.

toto...gyro. *Th.* xi, 311; ix, 117 *ancipiti circumfert cornua gyro. Gyrus* is used twenty-one times by St.

316f. Note the alliteration.

318–337 THETIS TRANSFORMS AND BEAUTIFIES ACHILLES

320 gelida...Ossa. *Th.* v, 261.

321f. iungere curas. Not 'idem curare quod tu' (Brinkgreve), but 'to match two loving hearts' (Mozley). *Cura* is frequently used in poetry for both love and the loved one. Barth and others compare with these two lines Virg. *Aen.* iv, 328f.

323f. visus...obliquat. Similarly ii, 27 *obliquos...vultus; Silv.* ii, 6, 102 *obliquo...vultu.* Achilles begins to cast sly side-glances, throwing off his hitherto stiff *visus* (cf. *colla rigentia,* l. 326).

325 cogique volentem. The MS. reading *cogitque volentem* can be defended (cf. l. 553 *stimulatque Agamemno volentes*), and K. Prinz in *Philol.* lxxix, 198 gives parallels for both this and *cogique;* but *cogitque volentem* implies rather too much force on Thetis' part, and perhaps more eagerness on Achilles' part than *cogique volentem;* and the latter may have been inspired by Ov. *A.A.* i, 666, 700, a passage dealing with Achilles and Deidamia. For similar MS. corruptions see *Th.* ii, 593 *involvi(t);* iv, 781 *poni(t);* v, 140 *agi(t).*

326 iniecitque sinus. 'And put the (women's) garments upon him': *sinus* of a garment, as *Silv.* ii, 1, 133. The mixing of pres. and past tenses is not uncommon in St.; e.g. *Th.* x, 118ff., 137ff., 140–5, 153ff., 170–5, all within a short space. See also Introd. p. 16.

colla rigentia. *Th.* vi, 482.

329 dilecta cervice. Thetis is putting her own necklace round Achilles' neck. J. Ae. Nauke, *Observationes criticae,* etc., pp. 24f., argued that such a use of the abl. is impossible; and Damsté would read *dilecta sua*. But St. uses the local abl. (see R. D. Williams, *CQ*, 1951, 145; Heuvel on *Th.* I, 532) even where motion is implied, as in ll. 929f.; cf. Juv. II, 85 *toto posuere monilia collo*. In *Silv.* III, 5, 81f. *has ego te sedes...transferre laboro* an acc. of motion is used; elsewhere in St. the normal prose constructions.

330 Cf. Virg. *Aen.* IV, 137 *Sidoniam picto chlamydem circumdata limbo* (and J. Henry, *Aeneidea* II, 292ff.); *Th.* VI, 367 *picto discingit pectora limbo* refers to a belt, not, as here, to the fringe of the dress. See also n. to ll. 849f.

331 incessum. 'Gait', as Virg. *Aen.* I, 405 *vera incessu patuit dea*.

332f. victurae. St. is fond of expressions denoting the appearance of statues as literally living; e.g. *Silv.* I, 3, 47f.; II, 2, 66f.; III, 1, 95f.; IV, 6, 26ff.

cerae. Vollmer implies that these are the same as the *Apelleae cerae* of *Silv.* I, 1, 100; II, 2, 63ff. But the latter are probably encaustic paintings made with wax (see M. H. Swindler, *Ancient Painting*, pp. 425f.), whereas these are clearly waxen images, perhaps of ancestors, as Juv. VIII, 19. Wax melted by a charcoal fire was also used, according to Vitruv. VII, 9, 3, for preserving mural frescoes: see Swindler, *op. cit.* p. 142. Barth compares Juv. VII, 237f. *exigite ut mores teneros ceu pollice ducat, ut si quis cera vultum facit*; Pers. V, 40 *artificemque tuo ducit sub pollice vultum*.

ignemque. The wax is moulded by fire, but to say that the waxen images 'follow the fire' is strange, and emendations have been suggested. Possibly the 'fire' is just a candle, which would be brought up to the instrument held in the other hand.

334 talis erat...imago. *Th.* VII, 808.

336f. invita virtute. Abl. abs. with concessive sense, *virtus* having its original meaning of 'manhood'.

fallitque...sexus. Cf. Hor. *Od.* II, 5, 21ff. *quem si puellarum insereres choro, mire sagaces falleret hospites discrimen obscurum solutis crinibus ambiguoque vultu*: St. must have had this passage in mind, for three important words are reproduced.

tenui...discrimine. 'By only a slight distinction.'

338–348 THETIS' FINAL ADVICE TO ACHILLES

338 fatigans. 'Pressing him', as often in connection with prayers to the gods, e.g. *Th.* II, 244; IV, 633.

340 feres. Fut. with imperative force.

341 misceat. 'Let you join.'

342 'And the deceit of my attempted trick be wasted.'

343 admoto...tactu. *Silv.* II, 1, 13.

non cessat. There is no parallel for P's reading *non distat* (perhaps the scribe's eye wandered back to *dicit*); while *non cessat* is supported by *Silv.* I, 2, 110ff. *nec colla genasque comere...cessavit mea, nate, manus. Distare* is found neither with the inf. nor in any sense suitable here; and the suggestion of Legras (*REA* x, 66, n. 5) to attach *comere* to *admoto* is contrary to the word order. Moreover Klotz's app. cr.

is erroneous: E reads *dixit* for *dicit*, not for P's *distat*, for which it and all the other MSS. have *cessat*.

344 ff. Hecate is here identified with the Arcadian and Spartan Artemis, so that the relations mentioned are Jupiter, Latona and Apollo. See T. S. Duncan, *The Influence of Art on Description*, etc., pp. 95 f. Therapnae in Laconia is associated with Apollo in *Th.* III, 422. The Greek word θεράπνη means either a maidservant or some kind of dwelling; and Strabo IX, 2, 24 mentions a Therapnae near Thebes.

   comes haeret eunti. Val. Fl. VIII, 55; *Th.* V, 98 f.; XI, 357.

   exserta. 'Bare', lit. 'protruding': *Th.* II, 513; IV, 235.

348 tumet. The reading *studet* is clearly a makeshift, being metrically objectionable, and *timet* (PEB) would denote too much hesitation to suit the context. *Tumet* (Gronovius), meaning 'is proud to', could easily account for the two MS. readings.

   conponere crines. Virg. *Georg.* IV, 417.

349–362 THETIS' REQUEST TO LYCOMEDES

350 germanam. According to Hom. *Il.* XVI, 175, Achilles actually had a sister Polydora, betrothed to the river Spercheus.

351 torva genas. Acc. of respect, whereas in *Th.* II, 238, 716 we have *torva genis*; 'eyes' rather than 'face' (see n. to l. 516).

352 animosa. Cf. Ov. *Her.* XIII, 91 *ne sis animosus in armis*. Note the alliteration.

355 frange. So *frangebat*, *Silv.* V, 3, 194 of Chiron disciplining Achilles.

356 f. indocilem. Cf. l. 284.

   sexu...tene. *Tene* = *contine*, the opposite idea being *sexu...relicto*, *Th.* XII, 178.

   dum...pudor. 'Until she is of age to marry and can put off her maidenly modesty': the gerundive has rather a potential force.

357 f. exercere protervas gymnadas. St. is clearly thinking of the training of Spartan girls; for an approval of their stripping for exercise see Prop. III, 14 *passim*, and cf. Plut. *Lycurg.* 14. Naturally Thetis' only worry is that Achilles' sex may be discovered. *Gymnas* in Lat. appears first in St., who uses it five times, elsewhere in the sing.; otherwise only in post-class. writers. It does not, as Lewis & Short and the Thesaurus render, mean simply 'wrestling', but any games or athletics (e.g. boxing in *Silv.* IV, 2, 48), or the contestants collectively in *Silv.* II, 2, 8.

360 A close parallel is Livy XXVII, 30, 7 *ut Attalum...portibus et litorum appulsu arceret.*

361 f. vela Phrygum. It is assumed that Paris' ships called in at Scyros, or at least passed nearby, on their way back to Troy.

   didicere carinae. The ships are said to be responsible for their owners' sins.

363–378 LYCOMEDES RECEIVES ACHILLES

365 supplice dextra. *Th.* XI, 688; *Silv.* I, 2, 67; V, 1, 258.

367 defigere. 'Stare at.' In this sense the normal usage is *oculos defigere*, while *defigere* with acc. of person has a stronger meaning, 'stupefy', 'astound'; the only exact parallel in the sense 'stare at' (with acc. of person) is l. 766 below, while in ll. 584 ff. St. uses *figere*. The indirect question depends on the idea of curiosity implied in *defigere ora*.

369 fundat. 'Extends': Jannaccone compares Livy XXXVIII, 21, 9 *Gallorum fusa et candida corpora*.

370 dehinc. EBKQ have *dein*, which O. Müller, *Quaestiones Statianae*, supports on the ground that *dehinc* is always disyllabic in St.; but Klotz in *Philol.* LXI, 298 points out that P also has *dehinc* in *Th.* II, 100.

sociare choros. 'Join her (i.e. his) dancing to theirs.'

371 ceduntque loco. Garrod says one would expect the girls to advance rather than withdraw, as the simile seems more suited to the former, and proposes *clauduntque locum*, an unlikely corruption; Damsté *ceduntque locum*, but *loco* is equally apt. One must, with the MS. reading, imagine several of them stepping aside to induce Achilles to come forward.

contingere gaudent. Virg. *Aen.* II, 239 *funemque manu contingere gaudent*.

372 f. Idaliae volucres. Doves were sacred to Venus, one of whose chief places of worship was Idalium in Cyprus; the same phrase is used in *Th.* V, 63; XII, 16 (a simile of doves seeing a snake approach).

iam longum caeloque domoque gregatae. The sense is perhaps 'after having long teamed together in their dovecots on high', *caeloque domoque* being a hendiadys. The uncompounded verb *grego* occurs only here and in very late writers; in *Th.* VIII, 667 P's *gregatim* is preferable to the *gregati* of the other MSS. Lucr. VI, 456 has the tmesis *conque gregantur*.

377 plausu. 'Beating of wings'; so also in the simile of a frightened dove in Virg. *Aen.* V, 215.

379–396 THETIS' DEPARTURE

381 tacito...vultu. Either (*a*) 'by facial expression without speech', as Lucan III, 739 *tacito tantum petit oscula vultu*, in which case *verba* is not literal and refers to signs given after the *murmura* of l. 380, or (*b*) Thetis' countenance is so composed that she hardly seems to be speaking.

383 abnatat. This compound is found only here and in the Greek glossary.

384 pignora. See n. on l. 127.

385 depositum...commisimus. A metaphor from entrusting a loan to a friend; cf. Sen. *Benef.* IV, 26, 3 *pecuniam credet aut depositum committet. Depositum* of persons also *Silv.* III, 2, 6; *Ach.* I, 914.

386 f. Another simile from the early years of Jupiter ll. 588 ff. The silence was necessary in order to deceive Saturn (Kronos).

387 honos. See n. on l. 798.

388 instabili...Delo. For descriptions of Delos as a supposedly floating island in primeval times see Call. *Hymn. in Del.* 191 ff.; Ov. *Met.* VI, 191.

389 vadosas. 'Shallow': more appropriately used in *Silv.* IV, 5, 38 of Africa, i.e. of the Syrtes, for the Cyclades do not lie in shallow waters.

390 frangunt. Cf. II, 104 f. *fracta ruentibus undis saxa.*

391 iurandaque nautis. So *dis iuranda palus,* Ov. *Met.* II, 46.

393 "Hic...bellis." These are the words which Thetis asks Scyros to teach Rumour to repeat; Klotz compares *Th.* II, 346.

395 alternum...orbem. Europe (i.e. Greece, as in l. 397) and Asia in turn; so *Th.* II, 183 *alterno...margine,* of the isthmus of Corinth, and elsewhere.

interfurit. A new compound, as *intermicat ignis,* found in *Th.* XII, 252 and Val. Fl. IV, 662.

396 cedo equidem. Virg. *Aen.* II, 704; XII, 818; *Th.* VII, 178; VIII, 516; and conjectured by Menke in *Th.* XII, 77.

397–440 GREEK PREPARATIONS FOR THE TROJAN WAR

398 f. dulcibus...furiis. Oxymoron, cf. *Th.* I, 68.

conquestu. A rare word, only in Livy VIII, 7, 21 before post-Aug. poetry; *conquestio* is commoner in prose.

flammata. Of anger, as *Th.* I, 249; *Silv.* IV, 4, 37.

ambit. 'Solicits aid.'

401 asperat. A favourite verb of Statius'; here 'aggravates': cf. *Th.* I, 642; VII, 496; IX, 705; Tac. *Ann.* II, 29 *ne lenire neve asperare crimina videretur.*

403 calcata. 'Trampled down': the metaphorical sense also in *Th.* III, 208; XI, 679.

404 foedus. Cf. Virg. *Aen.* X, 91.

geminae. Both in sing. and pl. *geminus* is used in poetry for *duo,* but in the sing. usually of abstract nouns, as *Th.* IV, 643; V, 337.

commercia. 'Intercourse' between nations, but with the underlying idea of the obligations of hospitality, as in *Th.* VII, 544.

406 degrassata. 'Has violently attacked', a verb found only here and in post-class. writers. The direct obj. is also unexpected, but can perhaps be paralleled in *grassatus, Th.* VIII, 570, if we read *primum faciles* (but see Housman in *CQ,* 1933, 66).

407 f. bimari. Ov. *Met.* VI, 419 f.; VII, 405.

claustra. In military language *claustra* denotes a key-point of defence, and Cic. *Agr.* II, 87 says: *erat enim posita (Corinthus) in faucibus Graeciae, sic ut terra claustra locorum teneret.*

circuit. To be understood also as the verb of *claustra,* so as to cover all the inhabitants of the Peloponnese: these are designated by the extreme north and south of the peninsula; but even so one would expect *et* joining two places.

umbo. A metaphor from the boss of a shield, more suitably used of a promontory, as here, than of the isthmus of Corinth (*Th.* VII, 15).

Maleae. Second syllable long here and in *Th.* VII, 16, but short *Th.* I, 100; II, 33; IV, 224; X, 537; *Silv.* I, 3, 97.

409 f. The reading *admotas* has been mistrusted because *procul* has been wrongly joined to it: the Thesaurus couples the two. Translate: 'But where, far off, the strait of Phrixus prevents neighbouring Europe and Asia from joining.' *Procul* then means that not only the Peloponnesians but also distant peoples sided with Agamemnon. The constr. changes in this phrase from inhabitants to regions by a rather abrupt ellipse.

admotas. Lucan II, 674 says of Xerxes bridging the Hellespont: *Europamque Asiae Sestonque admovit Abydo.* Cf. also ll. 28 f. above.

Phrixi...semita. A poetic description, lit. 'the pathway of Phrixus'. For Phrixus see n. to ll. 23 ff.

410 f. 'And those peoples in succession whom the waves of the upper sea confine with the shores of Abydos.' We need a reference to European tribes, so cannot translate 'on the shores of Abydos', which would be in Asia. *Silv.* v, 3, 187 *alter Achaemenium secludit Zeumate Persen* may be a similar instrumental abl. Again, however, the geography is vague, for strictly speaking the whole Abydos district has its shores on the Hellespont, which has already been mentioned; while *maris superni* must refer either to the Propontis or the Euxine, or possibly to the Thracian Sea, as the Thesaurus gives. Normally *mare superum* means the Adriatic and Ionian Sea (cf. Virg. *Aen.* VIII, 149 *mare quod supra...quodque adluit infra*), but its use here is logical enough. *Alligat* is perhaps a borrowing from Virg. *Georg.* IV, 480, referring to the Styx: St. has it also at *Th.* II, 182.

412 erigit. Cic. *P. Sest.* 87 *erecta Italia*; *Ach.* II, 34: 'arouses.'

413 f. Temese. In Hom. *Od.* I, 184 Athena, disguised as the king of the Taphians (Ionian islanders), pretends to be on her way to Temese for copper, trading iron for it. Even in ancient times it was disputed whether this referred to Tamassus in Cyprus or to Temesa (Tempsa) in Bruttium. Strabo VI, pp. 255 f. mentions both views, and says there were mines, disused by his time, at the Italian Temesa. But there is more evidence in favour of Tamassus, which Strabo XIV, p. 684 says produced even in his time a plentiful supply of copper; and the whole of Cyprus was renowned for copper, *aes Cyprium* (Pliny, *N.H.* XXXIV, 94, etc.). Moreover the Italian town was not a Greek colony, and all those in Statius' list are Greek towns. On the other hand in *Silv.* I, 1, 42; I, 5, 47 the reference may be to Temesa in Bruttium. See *RE* s.vv. Tamassos, Temesa.

quatitur navalibus. 'Shakes with (the sound of) its dockyards.' Euboea was not well known for dockyards, and had poor harbours, that of Chalcis being treacherous (Livy XXVIII, 6, 8); but possibly Aulis is meant. The form *Eubois* is found also in *Silv.* I, 2, 263; while in *Silv.* V, 3, 137 *Eubois* may perhaps be conjectured (Phillimore suggested *Euboica*) instead of *Euboea* as adj.

415 Nemee. Statius' usage with regard to Greek names is by no means uniform; see notes on ll. 102 f., 422. In the case of Nemea he has, if we may follow the best MSS., the form *Nemeā* as nom. *Th.* I, 355 (but *Nemeae* P); IV, 159, 826 (832); V, 44, 749; VI, 516; but *Nemee* here and *Silv.* III, 1, 143, 182; the acc. *Nemeen* always, but the gen. *Nemees* or *Nemeae*. Similarly both *Tegees* and *Tegeae* occur. The ending *-eā* (nom.) St. has also in *Leucothea*, *Th.* VI, 12; *Malea*, IV, 226; *Midea*, IV, 45; VII, 331; *Pasithea*, II, 286; *Thyrea*, IV, 48. *Argia*, nom. and voc., has six times a short and five times a long final syllable. Prisc. *Gramm. Lat.* II, 287, 12, commenting on *Th.* V, 44, says: *Apud Statium vero Nemea, quia servavit a productam, accentum quoque Graecum servavit, i.e. paenultimam acutam.* Hence Kohlmann and Klotz always write *Nemea* for the nom.

terga ferarum. See n. on l. 115 above.

416 Cirrha. Associated with bows presumably through its connection with Apollo.

sagittiferas...pharetras. Ov. *Met.* I, 468.

417 Cf. *Th.* III, 591 *nec pudor emerito clipeum vestisse iuvenco.* It is difficult to see what connection Lerna has with either shields or cattle; Jannaccone refers it (as in *Th.* III, 348; VIII, 562 and elsewhere) to the whole Argolid, rich in herds, but the separate mention of *Argos* in l. 419 makes this unlikely.

418f. Note the alliteration.

420 Epirus rivalled Thessaly and Argos in rearing horses; cf. Virg. *Georg.* I, 57. Arcadia is mentioned not in connection with horses, as Brinkgreve takes it, but with flocks, to provide food for the army.

421 The sense is that the trees of Phocis (*Phocis = Phoceae umbrae*) and Boeotia lose their branches to make shafts for javelins (*iaculis* dat. of purpose, as *classi*, *remis* ll. 428f.). In *Th.* I, 343 *rarescentibus umbris*, 'as the shadows grow thinner' (contrasting less with the light), is used of the gradual approach of dusk. For the arbitrary apostrophe *metri gratia* cf. Lucan III, 161, 281; *Silv.* I, 3, 131; III, 5, 68; *Th.* I, 398f. and elsewhere.

422 Messena. In *Th.* IV, 179 *Messene.* There probably existed in earlier times a town near Mt Ithome which gave its name to Messenia; the later town was founded only in 370–69 B.C. Possibly St., in connecting it with siege-engines, is thinking of the siege of Ithome by the Spartans in 464–59 B.C., when the Athenians under Cimon, who were experienced in siege warfare, helped the Spartans (Thuc. I, 102).

tendunt. 'Stretch': used in a sense similar to *tendere arcum*.

423ff. This is virtually a condensation of the long passage *Th.* III, 575–91. Cf. especially III, 580ff. *arma paternis postibus...vellere amor*; and XII, 699f. *patriis modo fixa revellunt arma deis*; also Virg. *Aen.* VII, 626–40 (636 *recoquunt patrios fornacibus enses*).

inmunis. Almost in the technical sense of 'free from contributions' towards a war, 'exempt from service'; cf. Virg. *Aen.* XII, 558f. *urbem immunem tanti belli*; *Th.* V, 643 *hic sese Argolicis immunem servat ab armis*.

425 efferat. 'Turns to savage use.' A striking metaphor, in contrast to *superis*; Apul. *Met.* V, 1 (*homo*) *tantum efferavit argentum* uses the verb differently, of fashioning in the shape of animals.

426 sidunt. 'Subsides', i.e. becomes lower through the felling of trees.

427 Taygeta. St. always has the n. pl. form for nom., but *Taygeti* for gen.

exuti...montes. *Silv.* IV, 3, 50 *hi caedunt nemus exuuntque montes.*

428 iam natat omne nemus. Cf. Lucan I, 306 *in classem cadit omne nemus*; and for *natat*, *Th.* VII, 142 f. *iamque natant remi, natat omnis in aequore summo ancora.*

429 silva minor. 'Smaller trees' as opposed to *robora*: not, as Mozley, 'the woods are diminished'.

lassatur. The MS. evidence is in favour of *lassatur* rather than *laxatur*; and the latter is used in *Silv.* V, I, 199, *nunc ferrum laxare cupit*, in the sense of unsheathing a sword. We may compare *aera domat Temese*, l. 413 above.

430 muniat. To strengthen the weapons, e.g. with tips for the javelins mentioned in l. 421.

431f. quod...tunicas. 'For knitting rough coats of mail by a thousand links' (Mozley). There is no need, with Menke, to emend *squalentis* (in any case *squamans* is a non-existent form and *squamatus* post-class.); for *squalens* means 'rough' in Virg. *Aen.* X, 314 *per tunicam squalentem auro* and other places; though St. does not have it elsewhere of garments. The ancients, with Gell. II, 6, 19 ff., probably thought that *squaleo* and *squama* were etymologically connected.

sanguine fumet. *Th.* X, 743; XI, 81.

433 vulneraque alta bibat. Virg. *Aen.* XI, 804, of a spear, *virgineum...alte bibit acta cruorem.*

434f. tenuant. 'They wear away' the whetstones.

attritu. Apul. *Met.* VII, 22 *gladium...cotis attritu parabat. Attritus* is almost always found in the abl.; so *Th.* VI, 271.

addunt mucronibus iras. This striking metaphor, 'impassion listless swords', comes also in Sil. VII, 344 *dant mucronibus iras.* Silius' work and the *Achilleid* were both being written about the same time; for the chronology see F. Buchwald, *Quaestiones Silianae* (Görlitz, 1886), pp. 3 ff.; R. Helm, *De P. P. Statii Thebaide* (Berlin, 1892), pp. 156 ff.; E. Bickel, *Rhein. Mus.* LXVI (1911), 500, who holds that Silius wrote Books VII and following after the death of Domitian; A. Klotz in *RE* s.v. Silius. Claud. *Idyl.* V, 46 has *strictis mucronibus asperat iras* (cf. *Th.* I, 642).

436 nec modus (*est*) with inf.: cf. *Th.* XII, 573 *quis erit saevire modus?*

lentare. 'To make pliant.' In *Th.* I, 703 the meaning is 'to draw a bow', and Lewis & Short wrongly give it this meaning here also. The processes described in this sentence are the manufacture, not the use, of arms.

fundere glandes. *Fundo* is a technical term for melting or casting metals: *Bell. Afr.* XX, 3 *glandes fundere, sudes comparare.* Sil. I, 314 has the same phrase with the meaning 'slinging': *hic crebram fundit Baleari verbere glandem*; and seems wrongly to be thinking of *fundo* and *funda* as etymologically connected. For *glans* as an egg-shaped missile see Daremberg-Saglio and *RE* s.v. glans. St. has the word in this sense in *Th.* VII, 338; VIII, 417; X, 553; never in the sense 'acorn'.

437 torrere sudes. Cf. *Th.* X, 532 *nigras...sudes.*

attollere conis. To raise the height of helmets by adding crests to them:

the opposite in *Th.* xii, 701 *galeas humiles*, of helmets whose plumes have been chopped off.

438 pigram...quietem. *Silv.* i, 6, 91; ii, 2, 7; ii, 3, 66.

439 'Brings a twofold complaint against the Fates' (Mozley).

440 senior Peleus. *Silv.* ii, 1, 90.

441–446 FEVERISH PREPARATIONS IN GREECE

441 exhauserat orbem. *Th.* vii, 25.

442 praecipitans in transtra viros. A colourful phrase, 'hurrying men on to the oar-benches'.

443 fervent. See n. on l. 28.

operta. More emphatic than *plena*, etc.: 'completely covered with.'

444 suas...hiemes. The same phrase in the sing. in Val. Fl. ii, 505, of the Sigean sea-monster.

445 attollit. Cf. l. 44.

446 consumunt. 'Use up'; cf. *Th.* xi, 575 *cunctas Erebi consumite poenas*; Ov. *Her.* vi, 161 *cum mare, cum terras consumpserit, aëra temptet*. See n. to l. 879.

447–466 THE GATHERING AT AULIS

447 ratis...congregat Aulis. Stands by a poetic idiom for *rates congregantur ad Aulidem*; cf. Lucan i, 97 *exiguum dominos commisit asylum*. Hecate = Artemis, as in l. 344; amplified by ll. 449 f.

448 expositis. See W. B. Anderson in *CQ*, 1924, 204.

crepidine. A high projection or bank, as *Th.* ix, 492. W. C. Summers on Sen. *Ep.* lvii, 4 notes: 'Lewis & Short treat this word very inadequately. Its original force is that of the Greek κρηπίς, "a base, foundation, pedestal". Thence it passes to the meanings "ledge" and "edge", and denotes (*a*) a quay or river-bank (Cic. *Verr.* ii, 5, 97, Virg. *Aen.* x, 653, etc.); (*b*) the edge of a causeway, curbstone, gutter (Sen. *Contr.* i, 1, 3, Petr. 9); (*c*) a slope between two terraces (Livy xxvii, 18, 6); (*d*) a ledge, edge of precipice, as Sen. *Ep.* lvii, 4, Val. Fl. iv, 44 and Stat. *Th.* ii, 504 (the Sphinx's).'

dorsi. 'Chine': cf. Val. Fl. ii, 632 f. *longoque sub aequora dorso litus agit*; *Silv.* ii, 2, 31 *longoque domat saxa aspera dorso*.

449 scandens. 'Towering above.' Cf. *Th.* ii, 44 *Taenaros, expositus* (so Baehrens, supported by W. B. Anderson in *CQ*, 1924, 203 f.: MSS. *expositos*) *non audax scandere fluctus*. The geographical use of *scando* can be paralleled by Prop. iv, 1, 125, where, however, the verb is intransitive; similarly Sil. viii, 396 f. *monte nivoso descendens Atina*. St. is wrongly imagining Aulis as being situated on a rock high above the Euripus, perhaps even as being an island, as do Manilius and Servius, also Lactantius on this line (see Housman on Manil. iv, 638).

450 montivagae. A Lucretian epithet, used by St. also in *Th.* i, 581.

451 latratum pelago. 'Barked at by the sea'; cf. Virg. *Aen.* VII, 588 *latrantibus undis*; so Sil. III, 471; V, 397.

453 saevae...praesagia noctis. Refers to the homecoming of the Greeks: see n. on ll. 93 f.

454f. Troiae fatalis. *Fatalis* with dat. is used in prose (e.g. Cic. *Phil.* II, 5, 11 *quod fuit illorum utrique fatale*) as well as in poetry: *Th.* V, 53; XI, 654; *Ach.* I, 475f.

ingens iuratur bellum. Not 'the vast array is sworn' (Mozley), but 'the mighty war is entered on by oaths'.

455f. donec...metas. Cf. Cic. *N.D.* I, 87 *sol...cursus annuos conficit.*

conficeret. The subjunctive is not quite logical; St. simply means that the gathering at Aulis took a year, so that no idea other than of time is involved: but Tacitus has a number of similar examples (see Frost on Tac. *Ann.* I, 13 *oraret* and S. A. Handford, *The Latin Subjunctive*, p. 165). The delay of a whole year seems to be Statius' own invention.

457 dissona. Because of the different Greek races and dialects; cf. Livy I, 18, 3 *per tot gentes dissonas sermone moribusque*; a slightly different use in *Th.* IV. 299.

458 coit. Jannaccone says that St. commonly lengthens final -*at*, -*et*, -*it*, only at the caesura, in accordance with similar lengthenings in Ennius and Plautus. This is misleading, as (*a*) St. treats compounds of *eo* differently from other verbs: in the former, -*it* is commonly scanned long before vowel or *h*, whether present or past (either is possible here) and whether at the caesura or not; (*b*) the long final syllable should be considered as the normal original quantity rather than a lengthening (cf. Kühner, *Lat. Gr.²* I, 113 ff.); (*c*) in verbs other than compounds of *eo*, a 3rd sing. long syllable before vowel or *h* is extremely rare in St.; cf. *Th.* I, 403 *agit* (pause at caesura); VI, 351 *erat* (*erant* Slater).

459 curva...indago. *Silv.* II, 5, 8.

460 artat. Used only here of hunting with nets.

461f. ignem sonitumque. *Ignis* refers to the burning of forests, mentioned by Lucr. V, 1249 as one of the most primitive methods of hunting, but employed also in classical times for hunting lions and elephants. *Sonitus* is probably not the crackling of the fire, but the hunters' shouts (cf. Virg. *Georg.* III, 413; *Aen.* X, 713).

decrescere. This seems to mean that the animals notice an apparent shrinkage in their mountain area, not, as in *Silv.* I, 1, 10 (*decrevit* wrongly indexed under *decerno* by Deferrari and Eagan), that the fire, destroying the trees, makes the mountain seem lower.

464 inque vicem stupuere. 'Are amazed one after another', rather than 'startle each other' (Mozley); similarly *socio...timore* does not mean 'mutual fear' but 'common fear'.

466 cogitur. The sing. verb is due to singular animals representing their species, but is unexpected after -*que*; see, however, n. on l. 469 *premant*. The alliteration is striking.

contempsit. There is poor MS. support for *contemnit*, and as has been seen (Introd. p. 16) St. is fond of varying his tenses.

467-490 THE ARMY CLAMOURS FOR ACHILLES

467 capessant. The subjunctive is rarer than the ind. after *quamquam* in St., but cf. *Th.* XI, 383; *Silv.* V, 1, 53; V, 2, 48; and see n. on *Ach.* II, 17.

469 Sthenelus. Diomede's charioteer.

premant. 'Eclipse', as *Silv.* I, 2, 116. P's *premat* can be justified by *Silv.* III, 1, 131, but there the sing. helps the metre.

annos. 'Youth'; cf. *Th.* V, 82. Antilochus, a son of Nestor, was killed by Memnon at Troy. For his youthfulness see Hom. *Il.* XXIII, 587 ff.

470 f. septem...armenti reges. By a typical exaggeration the seven layers of ox-hide forming Ajax's shield (ἑπταβόειον, Hom. *Il.* VII, 220 ff.) are called the 'seven kings of the herd' (*armenti reges, Th.* XI, 28). Cf. *Th.* IV, 222 *clipeo victum Pythona coruscat*, where the subject of the emblem on the shield is said to be brandished.

aequum moenibus orbem. A rendering of Hom. *Il.* VII, 219 Αἴας... φέρων σάκος ἠΰτε πύργον.

473 f. Achillem. The name is given three times, as *Arcada, Th.* XII, 805 ff.; *Asteris* four times in *Silv.* I, 2, 197 f.; an Ovidian trick.

475 loquuntur. Note the unusual constr. with predicate.

476 fatalem. See n. on ll. 454 f.

477 effossa reptans nive. The snow had to be dug away, either by the infant Achilles or others, before he could crawl.

adortus, i.e. *adortus sit*, 'undertook'. Brinkgreve seems to take this as gen. of the non-existent noun *adortus*. For the omission of the subjunctive see n. on l. 143. Ll. 476-81 form an *or. obl.* explained by l. 482.

478 cruda rudimenta. Virg. *Aen.* XI, 156 f. *belli...dura rudimenta*; *Ciris* 44 f. *aevi prima rudimenta et primos...annos*; *Silv.* V, 2, 8 f. *militiae...primae clara rudimenta* (so M and edd.; but perhaps we may conjecture *dura rudimenta*, which is palaeographically very similar, comparing the passage from the *Aeneid* quoted above; for the confusion see l. 564 below, where k and other MSS. have *clarus* for *durus*).

479 linea. First used by St., here and in *Silv.* III, 3, 44, of genealogical descent.

481 praestruxerit. 'Made impenetrable to' (*ferro* dat.).

483 vinci...fatetur. The simple inf. is not uncommon in poetry.

484 ff. Other similes from the battle with the Giants in *Th.* II, 595 ff.; XI, 7 f.; cf. Sil. IV, 275 f.; *Aetna* 42 has *Phlegraeis...castris*.

pallentes. There is no need to emend: *pallentes* refers to the gods' fear at the battle with the Giants; cf. *Aetna* 54 *Iuppiter e caelo metuit* (*et caelo* Bormans); Claud. *Gigant.* 9 f. *pallescunt subito stellae flectitque rubentes Phoebus equos docuitque timor revocare meatus*. R. Bitschofsky, *De C. Sollii Apoll. Sidonii studiis Statianis* (Vienna, 1881), compared Sid. *Carm.* VI, 15; VII, 133 f. *illic iterum timuit Natura paventem post Phlegram pugnare Iovem*.

Odrysiam. 'Thracian.'

in hastam surgeret. Evidently a borrowing from Virg. *Aen.* IX, 749, XII, 729 *consurgit in ensem*; XI, 283 f. *quantus in clipeum assurgat*. Commentators either render 'rise to the height of his spear' or explain *hasta* as standing for *certamen*. The phrase may, however, be parallel to Virg. *Georg.* III, 232, *Aen.* XII, 104 *irasci in cornua*, where Conington notes: '*In cornua* may be framed on the analogy of *in speciem*, etc., as a sort of modal acc., so that *irasci in cornua* would virtually = *irasci cornibus.*' Cf. *Th.* I, 414 *celsior ille gradu procera in membra*.

486 Libycos...angues, i.e. Pallas' aegis (cf. l. 299): post-Homeric tradition often places the Gorgons in Libya. The epithet *Tritonia* is a reference to the legends which gave as her birthplace Lake Tritonis in Africa: see Smith's *Dict. of Gk. and Rom. Biog. and Mythology* s.v. Athena.

487 Ov. *Am.* III, 3, 29 *flexibiles curvantur Apollinis arcus*.

488 metu. It is possible to defend *metus*, as gen. after *anhela*, from Sil. XV, 718 (see Roby § 1318; Brinkgreve's explanation is weak), but it may well have arisen from the following *s* (cf. l. 499 *cunctis stupeant* PQ: *cuncti stupeant*, better, EBR), and *metu* is far more natural, as in Val. Fl. IV, 514 *letique metu propioris anhelae*; Sil. VI, 188. At *Th.* IX, 699f. P has *pugnae...anhela*, all other MSS. *pugna*.

490 igniferam...Aetnen. *Th.* V, 50. The Cyclopes, as assistants of Vulcan, were often regarded in post-Homeric tradition as living beneath Etna.

491–513 PROTESILAUS' SPEECH TO CALCHAS

492 maris...tempora. 'Tempora navigationis' (Delph.).

493 St. is imitating Virg. *Aen.* II, 122f. *hic Ithacus vatem magno Calchanta tumultu protrahit in medios.* Similarly the hesitation of Calchas in ll. 514–25 is somewhat parallel to *Aen.* II, 127ff.

494 ait. P's reading *agit* would give the sense 'pleads' (sc. *causam, rem*); but although this is the correct reading in *Th.* X, 700, St. does not use it to introduce *oratio recta*. For Protesilaus see n. on l. 502.

496 tripodumque oblite tuorum. *Th.* VIII, 117 *tripodum iam non meminisse meorum*; cf. Ov. *Her.* I, 41; *Th.* VII, 547.

497 deo possessa. Either dat. of agent or instrumental rather than abl. of agent as Brinkgreve; and the examples he gives of abl. of agent without *a* in St. are doubtful, unless we count *Tyrio grege*, *Th.* VI, 145, as personal: see n. to l. 608.

498 quaenam...recludes? To read *quianam...recludes*, with P, and explain *recludes* as 'aperies' with Brinkgreve makes nonsense; for his explanation of *quianam iustius* as 'quam ob causam iustiorem' is not Latin: cf. Garrod in *CR*, 1914, 67. On the other hand Garrod, who reads *quianam...recludis*, is wrong in thinking that St. always uses *recludo* in the sense of 'conceal'; the only certain example is *Silv.* III, 4, 98, unless *reclusit* there is corrupt (*seclusit* Gronovius). Elsewhere it has the opposite meaning, and here, with *quaenam*, will mean 'reveal'. *Quianam* was even in Virgil's time an archaism: Festus says '*quianam*' pro '*quare*' et '*cur*' positum apud antiquos, and Quint. VIII, 3, 25 praises it and other words in Virgil as giving an 'inimitable air of antiquity'; but it is not found elsewhere in St.

499 fremantque. The alternative *premantque* seems unsuitable in Achilles' absence; *fremant*='clamour for', as *Th.* III, 593 *bella animis, bella ore fremunt*; VI, 618 *Arcades arma fremunt*.

500 sordet volgo. 'Is as nothing in the eyes of the crowd' (*volgo* dat., cf. Virg. *Ecl.* II, 44 *sordent tibi munera nostra*). The sing. verb is perhaps to be preferred, as commonly in St., e.g. *Th.* IV, 102 ff. *sensit* followed by a string of place-names.

Calydonius heros. Here and l. 538 of Diomede, but in *Th.* II, 476 of his father Tydeus, who after fleeing from Aetolia to Argos married Deipyle daughter of Adrastus; and Diomede succeeded Adrastus as king of Argos.

502 Garrod's punctuation with aposiopesis (see n. on l. 47) increases the dramatic irony of Protesilaus' hopes for himself at Troy. We are told by Hom. *Il.* II, 701 f. that Protesilaus was first of the Greeks to land and was killed by a Trojan as he jumped from his ship; see *Oxf. Class. Dict.*

Troia arrepta. Garrod explains 'our setting foot on the Troad' (cf. Virg. *Aen.* III, 477; X, 298), while Klotz, reading *abrepta*, interprets 'Troiam vi cito captam'; in the latter sense also, however, *arrepta* would be more suitable (cf. Virg. *Aen.* IX, 13; XI, 531). The Thesaurus perversely comments: '*abrepta* neut. pl., i.e. Graecorum numero sublata.' See also n. on l. 784.

probabunt. Protesilaus means that the war will show whether the Greeks will rely more on Achilles or on himself and the other Greek leaders.

503 pudet heu. A favourite phrase of Statius': *Th.* II, 443; VIII, 57, 626; IX, 389; *Ach.* I, 639; *Silv.* IV, 7, 35.

505 honos. See n. on l. 798.

quibus abditus oris. See n. on l. 199.

507 degere. 'Live': used absolutely also in *Th.* I, 63.

508 inrumpe deos. The suggestion is that the gods, especially Apollo, must be disturbed even if unwilling to prophesy. Cf. *Th.* III, 634 *superum...inrumpere coetus*.

509 laurigerosque ignes...hauri. *Ignes* is not literal, i.e. does not refer to l. 521, but denotes prophetic frenzy, as Ov. *Fast.* I, 473 f. *quae simul aetherios animo conceperat ignes, ore dabat pleno carmina vera dei*; similarly Lucan V, 173 f. *magno... exaestuat igne, iratum te, Phoebe, ferens*.

510 remisimus. 'Excused you': Calchas is never mentioned as fighting, but as it was not unknown for seers to fight, the exemption is represented as having been granted individually.

512 felix, sc. *eris*.

513 The reading and interpretation of this line have been much disputed. Older editors mostly read *pro te portendis* with KQ, but this looks like a scribe's correction. Wilamowitz, *De tribus carminibus Latinis*, p. 9, supported by Vollmer, *Rhein. Mus.* II, 33 and Klotz, was perhaps right in defending P's reading *pro te dependis*, and interpreting this as promising Calchas renown if he exchanges Achilles' service for his own, or 'pays' Achilles to the Greeks in return for his exemption. *Deprendis*, which is virtually E's reading, would also make good sense but is rather commonplace for the context.

514–535 CALCHAS REVEALS ACHILLES' HIDING-PLACE

515 intrantem...deum. For this use of *deus*, the god being supposed to enter into a seer, cf. *Th.* IV, 489f. *illi formidine nulla, quippe in corde deus*; X, 220f.; and for *pallor* of a seer Val. Fl. I, 229.

fatetur. 'Declares' by his facial expression, as Ov. *Trist.* II, 525 *vultu fassus Telamonius iram*.

516 igne genas et sanguine torquens. *Genas*='eyes', as shown by the following line; cf. Virg. *Aen.* II, 210 (of the serpents) *ardentes...oculos suffecti sanguine et igni*; *Ach.* I, 351 *torva genas*, 855 *infremuit torsitque genas*. Mozley renders: 'Rolls fiery, bloodshot eyes.'

517 absens. 'Absent' in the sense of mental wandering; cf. *Th.* XI, 63.

518 superum...coetus. *Th.* III, 634.

deprendit. The seer perhaps visualises himself grasping hold of the gods as they deliberate; cf. *Th.* I, 510 *deprendi, Fortuna, deos!* and such phrases as *Th.* X, 207f. *meos...redde deos*.

519f. sagas. 'Prophetic.'

dura sororum licia. Likewise of the Fates *Silv.* V, 1, 156f.; *Th.* III, 205f. *dura sororum pensa*.

521f. flammarumque apicem rapit. Servius on *Aen.* III, 359 says: *Varro autem quattuor genera divinationum dicit: terram, aërem, aquam, ignem: geomantis, aëromantis, pyromantis, hydromantis*; and Lact. on *Th.* IV, 411 speaks of καπνομάντεις, on X, 599 (perhaps less correctly, since there the poet mentions only fire and 'prophetic vapours', not smoke) of καπνομαντεία. St. gives a fuller description of divination by fire in *Th.* X, 598ff., from which it is clear that normally the seer observed the points of flame (*apex*; cf. Ov. *Met.* X, 279; *Th.* X, 599; XII, 432) and interpreted their shape and movement. See W. Warde Fowler, *The Religious Experience of the Roman People*, pp. 292ff.; W. R. Halliday, *Greek Divination*, pp. 184ff.; Kürschner, *op. cit.* p. 59.

rapit. Mozley translates 'quickly scans', and others interpret similarly: cf. *acie...sagaci, Th.* X, 598. Alternatively St. may be referring only to a mental process.

caligine sacra pascitur. See n. to II, 149f.; here *caligo* refers to the 'prophetic vapours' of *Th.* X, 605, not, as Brinkgreve, to dizziness.

522f. laborat vitta. The hair stands up in the prophet's frenzy, and the fillet is in danger of falling. The description is applicable to the more frenzied type of Greek seer rather than to Roman divination (cf. Warde Fowler, *op. cit.* p. 297).

524 See n. on l. 493, and cf. *Th.* X, 609 *tandem exundanti permisit verba furori*; Lucan V, 165ff. *Mugitibus* abl. of separation.

525 'His voice won the struggle against the frenzy that opposed it'; cf. Gratt. 520 *eluctabitur iram*.

528f. meus iste, meus. *Silv.* V, 5, 69 *meus ille, meus*.

et me. There is no need to alter *et*, which can, as Klotz observes, mean *quoque* as in Virg. *Ecl.* III, 62 *et me Phoebus amat*; Petr. 57 *eques Romanus es: et ego* *regis filius*; but the sense is perhaps improved by having a question-mark after *profundi*: 'Are you a goddess of the deep? I too am inspired by a god, Apollo.' Cf. *Th.* III, 625 f. *sed me vester amor nimiusque arcana profari Phoebus agit.*

529 f. latebris quibus abdere. See n. on l. 199.

    eversorem Asiae. A reminiscence of Virg. *Aen.* XII, 545 *Priami regnorum eversor Achilles.*

    video: sc. *te.*

    Cycladas altas. See n. on l. 204.

531 turpi…furto. Dat. of purpose, as Delph. ('apta occultando turpiter filio') and Jannaccone, not abl.

532 occidimus. 'We are undone!' Calchas sees the whole scene in his trance and describes it stage by stage.

533 fluxae. Used also of clothes in Lucan II, 362; VIII, 367; of limbs *Ach.* II, 108.

534 timidae…parenti. Cf. l. 211. *Et…ne* for *neve*, as Val. Fl. VIII, 436.

535 Jannaccone punctuates *quaenam haec? procul improba virgo!* but this gives an unusual ellipse of the imperative.

    inproba. See n. on l. 41 above, and cf. Val. Fl. VI, 681 f. *imminet e celsis audentius improba muris virgo.*

536–552 DIOMEDE AND ULYSSES REPLY

538 haerentem. 'Hesitating', as *quid haeres?*, l. 867.

    Calydonius…heros. See n. on l. 500. The envoys to Scyros are variously named: St. and Philostratus give Ulysses and Diomede; Ovid mentions Ulysses and Ajax; the scholiast on Hom. *Il.* XIX, 326 has Phoenix and Nestor; ps.-Apollodorus and Hyginus have Ulysses alone.

539 neque enim comes ire recusem. Borrowed from Virg. *Aen.* II, 704 *nec, nate, tibi comes ire recuso*; cf. Hor. *Sat.* II, 5, 16 f.

540 si tua cura trahat. 'If your anxiety should induce you to go.'

540 ff. The passage is imitated by Claud. *Rapt. Pros.* III, 318 ff. *dum pignus ademptum inveniam, gremio quamvis mergatur Iberae Tethyos* (cf. *Th.* IV, 387 f. *claustra novissima rubrae Tethyos*).

    aversae. 'Distant', as *averso…sub Haemo, Th.* VII, 42; and in *Th.* V, 357 we should with PD read *averso…in Haemo.*

    aquosi. Ov. *Her.* III, 53 has *numina matris aquosae* of Thetis.

543 fecundum…erige pectus. Borrowed from Virg. *Aen.* VII, 338 *fecundum concute pectus*; cf. Cic. poet. *Div.* I, 22 *claras fecundi pectoris artes. Fecundus =* 'fertile'.

544 f. Forms a virtual apodosis to the previous line and a half. If Ulysses shows his cunning, no seer would dare to challenge him in foreseeing the outcome of their exploit.

    non…quis. The use of the indefinite *quis* with *non, neque* is uncommon: Cic. *Brut.* 151 *non enim facile quem dixerim plus studi quam illum…adhibuisse* is a rare example from Cicero.

mihi. Ethic dat.

545 subicit. The sense is 'adds' (to Diomede's words) rather than, as Mozley, 'makes answer'; first syllable short only post-Aug.

546f. illa. If acc. pl., *illa* and *sic* are somewhat tautologous, so that *illa* may be intended as agreeing with *virgo*; cf. II, 102 *sic dabat ille pater.*

virgo paterna. Athena is the guardian of Diomede in the *Iliad*; so also of Tydeus, his father, in St. (cf. *Th.* II, 684ff.). The explanation referring *paterna* to Athena's birth is less probable.

me spes lubrica tardat. 'The uncertainty of expectation makes me hesitate.'

548 castris inducere. See n. to ll. 124f.

552 verum. Noun: Brinkgreve (as Nisard) mistakes it for an adv.

553–559 ULYSSES SETS OUT

553 Agamemno. *Agamemnon* is the usual form, but *-o* twice in Cicero (*Tusc. Disp.* III, 62; IV, 17) and elsewhere; with short final syllable Sen. *Agam.* 514 (Gronovius' correction).

555f. Cf. Virg. *Georg.* I, 381f. *e pastu decedens agmine magno corvorum increpuit densis exercitus alis*; Sil. II, 215f. *sicut agit levibus per sera crepuscula pennis e pastu volucres ad nota cubilia vesper.*

556f. Both St. and Silius have the same pair of similes with comparable language; Sil. II, 217ff. continues from the passage quoted above with a four-line simile on bees, containing the phrase *mellis apes gravidae*; the gen. after *gravidus* is less common than the abl. used here. It is difficult to say which passage of the two is earlier. Silius has Hymettan, not Sicilian bees.

mitis. Of mild climate, as *Th.* I, 334; II, 382; *Silv.* I, 1, 102f.

558f. Ithacesia carbasus. 'The canvas of Ulysses' ship' (*carbasus* elsewhere pl. in St.). *Ithacesius* represents the Homeric name for the Ithacans, Ἰθακήσιοι, but is rare in Latin: here only in St.; Pliny, *N.H.* III, 85; Sil. VIII, 539. Other Greek examples of the termination -ησιος are given by Kühner-Blass, *Gk. Gram.*³, II, 292, Anm. 2; in Latin, apart from direct borrowings from the Greek, the suffix is not found (*Megalesia* is 3rd decl.; for *Melitesia*, Gratt. 404, we should read *Melitensia*).

auras poscit. Virg. *Aen.* IV, 417 *vocat iam carbasus auras.*

sedere. The collective noun takes pl. verb, as in l. 841 *solvuntur laudata cohors.* For the description cf. *Th.* IV, 807f. *nauticus in remis iuvenum.. fit sonus.*

560–591 ACHILLES AND DEIDAMIA FALL IN LOVE

560 imagine. Here 'guise'; cf. Ov. *Met.* III, 250, VII, 360 *falsi sub imagine cervi.*

561 furto. Also used of their clandestine love in ll. 641, 669, 903, 938.

564 namque. This introduces a narrative anterior in time to ll. 560–3, where *furto* and *culpae* indicate the full development of the love affair. From l. 564 onwards St. reverts to the much earlier period when the affair was perfectly innocent.

565 'And the departure of his mother cast off (lit. "released") his innocent shyness.' So Lucan v, 259f. *metus exsolverat audax turba suos.*

569 resumit. 'Went back to': see n. to l. 693.

571f. levibus sertis...ferit. 'Pelts her with light garlands' (Mozley). Line 571 must be taken with *ferit*, not, as Brinkgreve evidently takes it, with l. 570.

574f. digitosque sonanti infringit citharae. P has *sonantis*, no doubt by assimilation to *canentis* in the next line, and Brinkgreve and Jannaccone keep this, the former evidently understanding it as acc. pl.; but that gives a strained meaning to *sonantis*. K. Prinz in *Philol.* LXXIX, 199 objects to *infringo* with dat., and suggests *cithara*, interpreting 'and tires her fingers on the sounding cithara'; but it can, as he admits, be paralleled in a somewhat different sense by Ter. *Ad.* 199, and St. is fond of compounds with *in-* followed by dat. (e.g. ll. 548 *inducere*, 570 *inhaeret*). *Digitos*, like *manum*, refers to Deidamia's fingers; perhaps 'makes her fingers supple for (playing on) the lyre'.

576 ligat amplexus. Cf. *alliget amplexus*, *Anth. Lat.* XXII, 5, ed. Riese; similarly *iungere* Val. Fl. I, 163; *Th.* XII, 385f.

577 quo vertice. 'How high': abl. of description.

580ff. proferre...demonstrat. 'Shows how to move'; *demonstro* with inf. is not found before this passage, but *monstro* is so used in Hor. *Sat.* II, 8, 51f.

581 attrito pollice. Spinning, especially for one just learning, has the effect of wearing down the skin of the thumb; cf. Tib. I, 4, 48 *opera insuetas atteruisse manus.*

582 colos. See n. on l. 635, where *colus* is the form preferred by the MSS.

perdita. 'Spoiled', a weaker sense of the verb even than *Th.* x, 648, of Hercules serving Omphale, *perdere Sidonios umeris...amictus.*

583 pondusque tenentis. 'And his weight as he embraces her.' Mozley seems to take *pondus* with *vocis*, but even if *pondus* can mean this, *-que...-que* clearly connects two separate phrases.

584f. quodque fugit comites. 'And (a point which escapes her companions)....' This is understood by editors as a causal clause dependent on *miratur*, making Achilles subject of *fugit*; but such an ind. followed by two subjunctives would be very unusual. The gloss *latet* in Cod. Brux. points to the true interpretation, which is given by R. D. Williams in *Proc. Camb. Philol. Soc.* n.s. I (1950–1), 17.

nimio...anhelet. 'At his staring too eagerly and pausing for breath in the midst of his words.' This seems more natural than Mozley's 'hangs breathless on her words'. *Intempestivus* simply denotes an abrupt and unexpected break.

588f. The same picture is drawn from Juno's point of view in *Th.* x, 61–4.

590 medii. 'Intervening'; see Owen on Ov. *Trist.* II, 192, and cf. ἐν μέσῳ εἶναι.

591 versos...amores. Prop. II, 8, 7 *omnia vertuntur: certe vertuntur amores*; here, however, not of faithlessness but of a new kind of love.

592 G. P. Goold, *CR*, 1951, 71, would transpose this line to take the place of the existing l. 772. It is perhaps rather an interpolated summary based on l. 385 *timido commisimus astu.*

593–618 THE BACCHIC FESTIVAL

593 Agenorei. Semele, mother of Dionysus, was daughter of Cadmus, son of Agenor king of Phoenicia. St. also uses the adj. in the wider sense of 'Theban'.

sublimis. Not, as Brinkgreve, 'aptus ad orgia, quia sublimis', but simply 'lofty'; constr. *ad orgia* with *stabat*, 'stood ready for'.

594 admissum. 'Towering to.'

595. trieterida. *Trieteris* (τριετηρίς) is applied to any festival recurring every two years—this is the force of *alternam*—not every three, as translations and dictionaries give, for the Greek reckoning of years was inclusive; though St. may perhaps have thought of it as every three years, for the Romans misuse the reckoning; e.g. *Silv.* II, 6, 72 *cum tribus Eleis unam trieterida lustris* is a circumlocution for eighteen years (15+3). In reality the Olympic games were every four years. In *Th.* IV, 722; VII, 93 *trieteris* is used of the Nemean games, which took place every two years; but the usual meaning, as here, is of a festival of Bacchus, which occurred at night (ll. 619ff.) and, at least on Mt Cithaeron, in mid-winter. Cf. *Th.* II, 661ff.; IX, 480; Virg. *Aen.* IV, 301ff.

596 f. scissum...trabes. The rending (σπαραγμός) of animals and uprooting of saplings (Eur. *Bacch.* 734ff., 1103 f.) was part of the traditional Bacchic ritual. Brinkgreve completely misses the point and interprets the former as the skins worn by the Bacchants and the latter as thyrsi!

599 inaccessum. Normally 'that cannot be approached', here 'must not'.

antrum. The place where the rites are carried out is described in very varying language. In ll. 593ff. it is a grove; in l. 645 a grove on a mountain; but in ll. 658f. *haec...moenia* suggests that the city is close at hand. (The same ambiguity prevails over the question of visibility: see n. to ll. 643ff.) But St. may, as at *Th.* IX, 905, be following the usage of Propertius, who in several passages makes *antrum* a rocky hollow; e.g. in Prop. I, 2, 11 the *arbutus* grows in an *antrum*, which can hardly be a cave; and Prop. I, 1, 11, IV, 4, 3, IV, 9, 33 make better sense so taken. Housman on Manil. v, 311 quotes *C.G.L.* IV, p. 486, 11 *antrum, vallis*; and St. seems to know the Propertian meaning in *Silv.* I, 2, 253 *Umbro...Propertius antro.*

601 exploratque aditus. *Th.* II, 370; *Ach.* I, 736.

temerator. First in St., here and *Th.* XI, 12.

602 agmine. 'Among the troop' (see n. to l. 900); 'wander into the troop' would require the dat. after *oberro.*

604 solventem bracchia. St. has various verbs for conveying feminine motions of the arms: l. 634 *diffundere bracchia*; *Silv.* III, 5, 66 *molli diducit bracchia motu.*

605 sexus. 'His own sex', as opposed to *mendacia matris.*

607 admota. 'Compared with him.' This use of *admoveo* can perhaps only be paralleled by Juv. II, 147f. *his licet ipsum admoveas.* In the present passage there is no difficulty in the meaning, owing to the idea of physical proximity.

608 Aeacidae. Editors give *Aeacide* (abl. as Ov. *ex Pont.* II, 4, 22; Sil. XIII, 800) with EBkqR, but the abl. of agent without a prep. in St. is used very sparingly, and apparent examples of it in his works can often be explained in an instrumental

sense (e.g. *nimio possessa Hyperione*, *Silv.* IV, 4, 27 = 'nimio sole'; *toto Iove...*
adactum, *Th.* X, 927 = 'totis viribus'). In other poets too the normal constr. is dat.
of agent or prep.; see n. on l. 497, and cf. Wilkins on Hor. *Epist.* I, 19, 3. If as an
alternative we construct *superbo...Aeacidae* with *admota*, the dat. is compulsory.

premit. 'Eclipses', as *Silv.* I, 2, 115 f. *quantum Latonia nymphas virgo premit.*

609 nebrida. The νεβρίς, fawn-skin worn by the Bacchantes, appears in Latin
poetry first in Sen. *Oed.* 438; St. has it also in *Th.* II, 664; *Silv.* I, 2, 226; *Ach.* I, 716.

610 hedera. Elsewhere in St. pl. only. Ivy was also twined round the thyrsi.

611 flaventia tempora. Ov. *Am.* I, I, 29. The colour of Achilles' hair is
mentioned in Hom. *Il.* I, 197; XXIII, 141 ξανθὴν ἀπεκείρατο χαίτην: cf. Claud. IV
Cons. Hon. 557 *flavum...Achillem.*

612 redimitum missile. 'The wreathed thyrsus.'

613 attonito...metu. Lucan VIII, 591.

615 remisit. 'Has relaxed', used frequently with *animum* in prose.

617 mitram. See n. to l. 715.

618 armat. Bacchus is regarded as converting his thyrsus into a spear by fitting
it with an iron tip.

hostiles...Indos. Bacchus is represented as having conquered various
Indian chieftains and subsequently founded cities and civilised the country. Mozley
comments that this is a kind of inverted simile, the effeminate Bacchus going to
war being compared to the manly Achilles as a Bacchant; but St. is perhaps thinking
more of the similarities of dress, etc., than of any contrast. Cf. *Th.* VIII, 237 ff.;
XII, 787 f.

619-639 ACHILLES' SOLILOQUY

619 f. Scandebat. For *scando* of natural phenomena cf. Pliny, *N.H.* XVIII, 264
sol...ad aquilonem scandens; and *ascendo* is commonly found in this sense.

roseo...iugo. *Roseus* is used frequently of the sun or dawn; here of the
rising moon, which when just above the horizon sometimes appears red.

fastigia caeli. Manil. II, 795 (so edd.), 881; III, 506; Pliny, *N.H.* II, 212
(sing.).

620 totis...alis. *Silv.* V, 4, 15 f. (to Sleep) *nec te totas infundere pennas luminibus
compello meis.*

621 amplectitur orbem. Virg. *Aen.* VIII, 369 *nox ruit et fuscis tellurem
amplectitur alis.*

622 paulum. Constr. with *tacent.*

624 timidae commenta parentis. Ov. *Met.* XIII, 38 f. *timidi commenta...animi.*
Mozley wrongly renders *commenta* as 'precepts'.

625 imbelli. See n. to l. 207.

626 florem animi. The usual phrase for the prime of youth is *flos aetatis*;
Sen. *Ep.* XXVI, 2 says paradoxically that his mind claims old age as *florem suum.*

627 agitare. With *tela* 'brandish', with *feras* 'chase', cf. Virg. *Aen.* VII, 478.

627 f. Perhaps a reminiscence of Virg. *Georg.* II, 486 f. *o ubi campi Spercheusque....*

629 promissasque comas. In Hom. *Il.* XXIII, 141 ff. Achilles tells how Peleus vowed a lock of Achilles' hair and a hecatomb to Spercheus if his son returned safe from Troy. Cf. *Silv.* III, 4, 86.

desertoris alumni. *Desertor* in adjectival sense only here and Sen. *Phoen.* 45 *desertor anime.*

630 honos. See n. on l. 798.

Stygias...iam raptus ad umbras. *Silv.* III, 5, 37 *Stygias prope raptus ad umbras*; *Th.* XI, 85 *Stygiis...in umbris.*

632 dirigis. The MSS. have this form here, not *derigis*. *Derigo* is the earlier form of the two, and Isidore (*Diff.* I, 153) tells us that in the sense 'straighten' *de-* is correct, in the sense 'direct' *di-*; this distinction is not always observed, but can apply to this and the three other occurrences in St.: *Silv.* II, 2, 84 *de-* ('straighten'); *Th.* VIII, 524 *di-* ('direct'); IX, 773 *di-* Pω (perhaps the better orthography for 'direct'), *de-* BDN.

633 mihi. Probably dat. of advantage rather than dat. of agent.

iugales. Used, like *equi* and ἵπποι, to denote a chariot.

634 'To fling my arms about with vine-covered thyrsi': *diffundere* is commonly used of hair, etc., but there is no exact parallel for its use with limbs.

635 colus. Whereas at l. 582 the MSS. prefer *colos*, here the evidence is in favour of *colus*; in other places St. seems to vary between the two forms, and often the MSS. disagree. Evidently the 2nd decl. form was the commoner, for Serv. on *Aen.* VIII, 409 says '*huius coli*' dicimus, non ut Statius '*huius colus*'.

636 virginis. Objective gen. after *ignem*, as Ov. *Met.* X, 253 and elsewhere in Ovid.

637 aequaevam...facem. *Fax* = 'amor', as commonly, so that *aequaevus* means 'for one of the same age'. *Ignem, facem* are most easily understood as obj. of *dissimulas*, the abl. (*igne*, etc.) being supplied with *captus*.

638 dissimulas. Note the return, after *ego*, to 2nd pers.

premes. 'Suppress.'

639 pudet heu! See n. on l. 503.

nec. 'Not even' (=*ne...quidem*), a usage perhaps borrowed from οὐδέ: cf. Hor. *Sat.* II, 3, 262f. *nec nunc, cum me vocat ultro, accedam?* Virg. *Ecl.* III, 102; Prop. II, 29, 26; in prose, only in very rare Ciceronian examples before Livy (see Kühner, *Lat. Gram.*², II, ii, 44); common in Silver Latin.

640-660 ACHILLES FORCES HIS LOVE ON DEIDAMIA

641 torpere. So *torpentes...lacus*, *Th.* IX, 452; *amnis torpens*, IV, 172.

642 vi potitur votis. A direct borrowing from Ov. *Met.* XI, 264f. *confessam amplectitur heros et potitur votis ingentique implet Achille*; cf. also Virg. *Aen.* III, 56.

toto pectore. Evidently a proverbial expression, as shown by *toto pectore, ut dicitur*, Cic. *Leg.* I, 49; *Tusc. Disp.* II, 58. Serv. on *Aen.* IX, 276 paraphrases it *omni affectu*.

643 f. admovet amplexus. Cf. Ov. *Met.* VI, 631 f. *cur admovet...alter blanditias?*

vidit. *Risit* (EBqR) could be supported by Virg. *Ecl.* III, 9; Val. Fl. VI, 209f.; *Th.* V, 356f. *rubuit...Pallas, et averso risit Gradivus in Haemo*; but *vidit* is more suitable here, and St. may have been thinking of the Catullus passage quoted below.

chorus...astrorum. The same phrase in *Silv.* III, 3, 54, where Vollmer compares Soph. *Ant.* 1146 χοράγ' ἄστρων (of Dionysus); Tib. II, 1, 88; Manil. I, 670 f.; cf. also Varro, *Sat. Menip.* 269 Buecheler *caeli chorean astricen*, and for the interest of stars in the doings of men, Cat. VII, 7 f. *aut quam sidera multa, cum tacet nox, furtivos hominum vident amores.* Barth remarks that the darkness of the night mentioned in l. 640 is inconsistent with the moon and stars being said to witness the happenings; this is on a par with Statius' vagueness as to the exact locality (see n. on l. 599).

    rubuerunt. The maiden goddess blushes at the sight.

645 More vividly expressed in *Th.* V, 552 f. *longoque profundum incendit clamore nemus.*

646 discussa nube soporis. For *discussa nube* cf. *Th.* IX, 175; XII, 4. For *nubes* of a cloud of sleep cf. Val. Fl. III, 65 f. *iniqui nube meri*; VIII, 81 *primi percussus nube soporis*; similarly of death, *Th.* X, 281; *Silv.* IV, 6, 72 f.

649 verbis...amicis. See n. on l. 79 *dictis...amicis.*

650 Ille ego. A boastful phrase, familiar from the lines preceding *arma virumque...* at the beginning of the *Aeneid* (I, 1ᵃ–1ᵈ): many other examples are collected by Owen on Ov. *Trist.* II, 533. The present passage and *Th.* VIII, 666 refute Owen's theory that where *ille ego* means 'I am the man', *sum* is always expressed. Other Statian occurrences are *Th.* IX, 434; XI, 165; *Silv.* V, 5, 38, 40.

    caerula mater. Prop. II, 9, 15, Hor. *Epod.* XIII, 16 and Ov. *Met.* XIII, 288, all referring to Thetis.

651 paene Iovi. This slight correction by Gustafsson of P's *paene Iovis* is rightly accepted by nearly all modern editors. *Iovi* can easily have become *Iovis* owing to the following *s*. Achilles is almost Jupiter's son, i.e. would have been but for the warning given (see n. to l. 1). For this idea of quasi-relationship cf. Lucan VI, 363 f. *tuus, Oeneu, paene gener*; *Th.* IV, 289 f. *qui tibi, Pythie, Ladon paene socer.*

    inmisit alendum. *Th.* I, 581 *mandat alendum*; Virg. *Aen.* III, 49 ff.

652 f. foeda...tegmina. Cf. l. 142.

    ni...te visa. For *nisi* with abl. abs. after *nec* cf. II, 127 f.

655 defles. Usually a transitive verb, but used absolutely in *Th.* III, 204 also.

656 caelo paritura. Cf. l. 254 *magni...puerpera caeli.* The reference is probably still to Thetis rather than, as Mozley, to Peleus as being descended from Jupiter.

657 "Sed pater—." An aposiopesis spoken by Achilles as if it were an objection by Deidamia.

    igni. St. usually has the abl. *igne*; but *igni* also in *Th.* V, 194; XII, 275; *Silv.* II, 1, 216; III, 3, 104 (but *igne* 105); V, 3, 204. See Housman in *CQ*, 1933, 70.

658 f. haec...moenia. See n. on l. 599 *antrum.*

    versa. Cf. Virg. *Aen.* V, 810 f. *cuperem cum vertere ab imo...periurae moenia Troiae*; *Th.* I, 262 *verte solo Sparten.*

659 pendas. 'Pay for', usually with *poenas*, etc., in the metaphorical sense; but *culpam* in Val. Fl. IV, 477 f.

660 omnia. Internal acc.; cf. *Th.* X, 654 *consanguinei...atque omnia fratres*; *Ach.* II, 9.

662–674 DEIDAMIA CONFIDES ONLY IN HER NURSE

662 regina. King's daughter, as l. 823.

monstris. Emphasises the strangeness of the happenings; cf. l. 890.

663 f. These two lines are weak, and Garrod rejects them, but it is difficult to see why they should have been interpolated. Koch's *luminis ignem horruit* would improve the sense, but the corruption is unlikely.

666 premat. 'Crush.' The repetition of the verb in l. 668 ('suppresses') gives an ugly effect.

fortassis. This rarer form is found only here in St.: cf. Hor. *Sat.* I, 4, 131; Ov. *A.A.* I, 665 (precedes a vowel in these examples); Hor. *Sat.* II, 7, 40 (precedes a consonant).

667 hausurum poenas. Perhaps borrowed from Virg. *Aen.* IV, 382 f. *spero...supplicia hausurum*; Cicero uses the verb with *calamitates, dolorem* and *luctum* as objects. Similarly *exhaurio*: Virg. *Aen.* IX, 356 *poenarum exhaustum satis est.*

668 diu deceptus. The love which she had concealed from others and hardly liked to admit even to herself.

671 raptum...pudorem. Ov. *Met.* I, 600 *rapuit...pudorem; pudor=*'virginitas'. Ovid's *occuluit* in the same line may have suggested it in l. 673 below, although used in a different sense.

672 in pondere. The prep. denotes a physical state, as *in vulnere primo, Silv.* V, 1, 18.

673 occuluit. See n. on l. 671.

plenis...metis. See n. on l. 258.

674 index...resolvit, i.e. 'partu resolvendo rem indicavit'.

675–688 THE GODS FAVOUR ULYSSES' ENTERPRISE

675 Early editors, following the worse MSS., began the second book at this line; the scribes had perhaps wished to divide the first from the incomplete second book more equally. In support of the better MSS. there are quotations by Eutyches of l. 898 and by Priscian of l. 794, both as coming from Book I. The old numbering is given for comparison in the left margin.

676 The MSS. have *innumerae mutabant Cyclades auras*, and P. H. Damsté, in *Sertum Nabericum* (festschr. S. A. Naber, 1908), pp. 79 ff., gives a plausible defence of the MSS. reading, paraphrasing: 'Cyclades vim ventorum infringebant, mare vento minus expositum efficiebant.' But although his parallels show that St. uses *muto* in unusual senses, the phrase is still somewhat strained, and various emendations have been proposed. Both Garrod's and Köstlin's readings, the latter adopted by many modern editors, alter three words; and Garrod's involves using the sing. *Cyclas* for the pl. If we simply alter *auras* to *oras* (cf. Housman on Lucan I, 18; a similar corruption in *Th.* III, 1 *orae* P: *aulae* ω), the sense will be: 'The countless Cyclades were changing one prospect of their shores for another' (cf. *mutare faciem*). For *innumerae* cf. *Th.* v, 56.

677ff. The description of the Cyclades is very similar to Virg. *Aen.* III, 125ff., where Delos, Naxos, Olearos and Paros are appropriately mentioned in the voyage from Troy to Crete. Here on the other hand, given in reverse order, they are out of the direct route, which would lie between Euboea and Andros. But a far worse mistake is the inclusion of Lemnos in the group of islands almost two hundred miles south of it, as pointed out by Köstlin in *Philol.* XXXV, 532; cf. Klotz in *Philol.* LXI, 300; Kürschner, *op. cit.* p. 62; Legras in *REA* X, 57f., who quotes Ov. *A.A.* II, 79ff. for a similar example. Moreover Samos is far too easterly, and there is no logical sequence about the journey. We have no evidence that St. visited Greece, and other examples of his geographical vagueness have been shown in the notes to ll. 201, 410f.

raditur alta Lemnos. Val. Fl. v, 108f. *alta Carambis raditur.*

678 decrescit. Seems to diminish as the ship sails away from it; so Sen. *Tro.* 1047f. *ubi omnis terra decrescet pelagusque crescet*; imitated by Claud. *Rapt. Pros.* I, 189 *totaque decrescit refugo Trinacria visu.* See also n. to *Ach.* II, 22. The sense of *decrescere* in *Th.* VIII, 397 is somewhat different.

Bacchica Naxos. Virg. *Aen.* III, 125 *bacchatam...iugis Naxon*; according to one legend (Diod. v, 52) Dionysus was taken by Zeus to Naxos in his childhood. The island was also famous for its wines.

679 ante oculos crescente. Sil. XV, 216 *admoto crescebant culmina gressu.*

680 libant carchesia. Virg. *Aen.* v, 77 *libans carchesia Baccho*; *carchesia* in St. only here and *Th.* IV, 502.

681 responsi...fidem. 'The truthfulness of the oracle': Ulysses and his companions were *dubii* (l. 683).

682 Arquitenens. A somewhat archaic epithet of Apollo (used by Naevius and Accius, Virg. *Aen.* III, 75, etc.); also in *Th.* IV, 750; *Silv.* IV, 4, 95. Both *arquitenens* and *arci-* are found.

683 inpulit. Only St. uses *impello* in the exact sense of *immitto*, here and *Th.* III, 482; IV, 734.

pleno dedit omina velo. Cf. Prop. IV, 6, 23 *plenis Iovis omine velis.*

684 pelago. Although *pelagi (secura)* makes equally good sense, *pelago* has better MS. authority, and St. is perhaps still thinking (cf. n. on ll. 677ff.) of Virg. *Aen.* III, 124 *pelago...volamus.* See Klotz in *Philol.* LXI, 300; Damsté in *Mnem.* 2nd ser. XXXV, 131. *Pelago* is abl. of the way by which.

686 arcebant. *Arceo* with inf. is not uncommon in poetry from Ovid onwards: *Th.* I, 455f.; *Silv.* II, 1, 34f.

aegram lacrimis. Val. Fl. III, 283 *lacrimis ac mentibus aegri.*

689–708 ULYSSES AND DIOMEDE REACH SCYROS

689 frangebat radios. Cf. Lucan III, 521f. *ut matutinos spargens super aequora Phoebus fregit aquis radios.* To account for the lack of heat in the morning or, as here, evening, it is assumed that the sun-god cuts short his rays; Lucan, however, in the passage quoted above seems to be thinking rather of refraction.

690 penetrabile litus. *Litus* (see n. to ll. 75f.) here denotes the sea by the shore of the Ocean, and *penetrabile* visualises the horses of the sun plunging into it.

anhelis. Cf. ll. 180f.

693 resumere pontum. Amplified by l. 694. Both here and in l. 569 there is a slight extension of the normal meaning of *resumo*. Wernsdorf's *contum* is inappropriate: oars, not poles, are required.

694 Zephyros...cadentes. Ov. *Met.* VIII, 2 *cadit Eurus*.

supplere. 'Eke out.'

695 accedunt iuxta. Ov. *Met.* VIII, 809. Brinkgreve wrongly says that *iuxta* = *statim*. Baehrens' *accedunt iussa* (*et*), adopted by Kohlmann, is not Latin at all.

indubitata. Cf. l. 747; post-Aug. and mostly in prose.

697 Cf. Virg. *Aen.* III, 79 *egressi veneramur Apollinis urbem*.

698 providus heros. *Th.* IV, 197.

702 servator. Uncommon in the meaning 'watchman', 'guardian': Lucan VIII, 171; *Th.* III, 352. As Barth pointed out, the existence of a look-out for ships is an anachronism.

ignota. Construe with *carbasa*.

703 succedere terris. Virg. *Aen.* VII, 214.

704ff. Wolves are normally, in similes, described in packs; an example is *Th.* X, 42ff. (*agmine multo* P: *mixto* cett.; but perhaps *muto* may be conjectured; for the confusion see app. cr. to l. 747). Ov. *Met.* XIV, 778 has *tacitorum more luporum*. In Hom. *Il.* X, 297 the same two heroes are compared to two lions.

hiberna sub nocte. *Th.* IV, 85.

707 dissimulant. In *Th.* XII, 605, a simile from an old but still bellicose bull, St. has *dissimulat gemitus*.

708 vigilare = *ut vigilent*, a constr. which can cause ambiguity by confusion with indirect statement; cf. Hor. *Carm. Saec.* 5ff. *Sibyllini monuere versus virgines lectas puerosque castos dis...dicere carmen*.

709–717 DIOMEDE ADDRESSES ULYSSES

709 heroes. This is the only example in verse of *heroes* with -*es* remaining short (elsewhere found before a consonant); but the acc. in -*ăs* shows that it must normally have been so pronounced.

710 portus. Acc. pl.; *interiaceo* is found with acc. in prose also.

711 terunt. Perhaps 'while away' the road with conversation, an extension of *tempus terere*, rather than 'tread'.

715 terga. Probably drums made of ox-hide, as at l. 829.

mitras. Headgear wound round the head and normally having ear-flaps, worn by women, especially Bacchantes (*Th.* IX, 795), and by Bacchus (see l. 617); described by Serv. on *Aen.* IV, 216; Daremberg-Saglio s.v. mitra.

716 aspersas...auro. Pliny, *N.H.* XXXVII, 155 *ex iis aureis guttis adspersa*.

nebridas. See n. to l. 609.

718–725 ULYSSES' REPLY

718 illi subridens. A reminiscence of Virg. *Aen.* I, 254, XII, 829 *olli subridens*, but without the archaism.

ore remisso. The same phrase in *Th.* VII, 60; it suggests a relaxing of tension or an indulgent smile.

719 virginea. The order of words shows that this is to be taken with *aula*, not as Brinkgreve with *fraude*.

721 citus. Commonly used in poetry for the adv. For the movements of Diomede see n. to ll. 732 f.

723 f. asperrimus. *Asper* often of bas-relief or incised work; e.g. Ov. *Met.* XII, 235 f. *signis exstantibus asper antiquus crater*.

astat; nec sat erit. The text adopts Garrod's emendation *nec* for *haec* (E *hoc*), and the reading of ER, *astat*, rather than P's *hasta*. If the original reading had been *hasta*, it would be difficult to account for *ardet* in BKQ; and *hasta haec sat erit* is a weak sentence. Moreover P frequently inserts a gratuitous *h*; see app. cr. to ll. 73, 198 (*hastans!*), 255, 271, 885; and cf. *Silvae*, ed. Phillimore, introd. p. xx, on *Silv.* I, 2, 235. (This is also true of E; the places at which E inserts or omits *h* are too numerous to be mentioned in the app. cr.) On the other hand Garrod is wrong in saying (*CR*, 1914, 67) that to have a semicolon after *asperrimus* (reading *hasta*) is an 'impossible metrical break'; a break before the last word of the line, sometimes two-syllable, sometimes three-, occurs in *Silv.* I, 1, 57; II, 3, 47; III, 3, 12; III, 5, 106; *Th.* II, 452, 548; *Ach.* I, 735, and elsewhere. For *astat* cf. *Th.* VI, 291; for *nec sat erit*, which gives point to the remainder of ll. 724 f., cf. l. 600 *nec satis est*.

lituo bonus. *Bonus* is followed both by dat. (as *Silv.* IV, 3, 134) and instr. abl.; the latter is preferable here.

Agyrtes. St. uses this name, perhaps borrowed from Ov. *Met.* V, 148, also of a Theban in *Th.* IX, 281. In Greek ἀγύρτης, derived from ἀγείρω, is not one who gathers a crowd together but a begging priest, one who collects money.

726–749 ULYSSES AND DIOMEDE ARE RECEIVED BY LYCOMEDES

728 pridemque. The *-que* here co-ordinates adj. and adv., as Hor. *Sat.* I, 4, 18 *raro et perpauca loquentis*.

tuas pervenit ad aures. Virg. *Aen.* II, 81; Ov. *Met.* V, 256; VII, 694; IX, 8 f.

732 f. At ll. 721 ff. Ulysses instructs Diomede to remember to bring the gifts from the ship *ubi tempus erit*; but it is clear from ll. 732 f., 766, 815 that Diomede actually goes with him to the palace. At ll. 819 f. Diomede and Agyrtes arrive with the gifts the following morning; St. merely omits mention of Diomede's return journey before this.

tanta...stirpe. Abl. of comparison after *meliorem*. Cf. Hor. *Od.* I, 15, 28.

733 Ithaces ego ductor. *Ithacis* (EBKQR) can be paralleled by Sil. III, 317, 388; but P's *Ithacus* suggests that as at *Th.* IV, 56f. *tecta Mycenes impia* (*Mycenis* codd., corr. Gronovius) the correct reading may be *Ithaces*. Cf. *Th.* VIII, 482 *pilenis* †b for *Pylenes*; IX, 255 *thebis* P for *Thebes*. The form *Ithace* is found in Hor. *Epist.* I, 7, 41; Ov. *Trist.* I, 5, 67; *Paneg. Mess.* [Tib. III, 7] 48. St. has neither *Ithaca* nor *Ithace*, but is very fond of Greek forms: see n. to l. 415. For *ductor* with gen. of place cf. *Th.* III, 348f. *optime Lernae ductor*; V, 733 *ductor Nemeae*.

734 metuam...fateri. *Th.* V, 623 *quid enim timeam moritura fateri?* It is characteristic of Ulysses' cunning that he tells a lie while pretending to let the king into a military secret.

735f. imus. Constructed with inf. of purpose, as *Silv.* IV, 4, 61; V, 3, 10f.; *Ach.* I, 821f.

  explorare aditus. Cf. l. 601.

738f. Adnuerit. Perf. subj. of wish for pres. subj., perhaps with the idea of predestination. For the rare parallels to this see S. A. Handford, *The Latin Subjunctive*, p. 88.

  secundent...dei. Virg. *Aen.* VII, 259.

740 inlustrate. 'Honour.'

741 famularis turba. Sen. *Thy.* 901.

743f. magnae virginis. A 'girl' conspicuous by her size.

745f. vagis. Cannot perhaps be paralleled as applied to immovable objects, but the idea is 'labyrinthine'.

  obit. 'Wanders through.' Heinsius' correction for *adit* is certainly an improvement; *adeo* in the sense of visiting can hardly apply to Ulysses, who is already in the palace; for *obeo* cf. Cic. *Fam.* VII, 1, 5 *ut nostras villas obire...possis*.

746f. ille. St. is perhaps thinking of some particular painting or sculpture; even if he is not, the effect of *ille* is vividly pictorial.

  tenens. 'Holding on to', as Livy XXIX, 32, 5 *tenuit...vestigia Bucar*.

  muto...Molosso. The Molossian hound, a species of wolf-dog, was more commonly employed as a watch-dog (Virg. *Georg.* III, 404ff.) than for hunting; but Lucan IV, 440 *venator tenet ora levis clamosa Molossi* shows that they were among the hounds trained not to bark on discovering their quarry—hence *muto*. Cf. also the simile in Sil. X, 77ff.

  legit. 'Threads his way through', as in *Th.* I, 376; II, 497; III, 325.

750–771 ACHILLES AND DEIDAMIA MEET THE NEWCOMERS AT A BANQUET

751 fida. See n. to l. 171, and cf. Ov. *Trist.* I, 3, 64 *et domus et fidae dulcia membra domus*.

753 iure. Mostly a prose adv., but used also in *Th.* II, 439; here '(were alarmed) as they had a right to be'. Garrod conjectures *aure*, comparing *Th.* I, 366, but the original reading of E, on which his conjecture relies, is not correctly given in his app. cr.

nova. The *nova* in 753 and *novos* in 754 are admittedly somewhat jarring, but *sua* (K) looks like a scribe's attempt to avoid this. In *Th.* IX, 209, 211 *nova* occurs twice in the same position in the line; cf. E. Laughton, *Class. Philol.* XLV, 83 for some examples of subconscious repetition in Cat. LXIV; A. B. Cook, 'Unconscious Iterations', *CR*, 1902, 146, 256; R. G. Austin on Quint. XII, 1, 41. In *Silv.* II, 7 *arduus* occurs four times in thirty-three lines.

755 vel talis. Even in his girl's clothes.

vidisse. St. often uses perf. inf. for pres., e.g. *Th.* I, 86, 321, etc.

fervent. Here of bustle, as *Th.* I, 525; II, 52; III, 120; V, 144; *Silv.* IV, 3, 61.

756 picto discumbitur auro. So P (Garrod in *CR*, 1914, 67 is wrong in implying otherwise; the first hand in P clearly intended to write *auro*); the reading of the other MSS., *ostro*, may have arisen from Virg. *Aen.* I, 700 *stratoque super discumbitur ostro.* The reference is probably to gold-embroidered covers on the couches; cf. Suet. *Jul.* LXXXIV, 1 *lectus eburneus auro ac purpura stratus*; Cic. *Tusc. Disp.* V, 61 *textili stragulo magnificis operibus picto.* See Klotz in *Philol.* LXI, 302.

758 The *palus Maeotis*, one of the traditional dwelling-places of the Amazons, is the Sea of Azov. In *Th.* XII, 526 St. refers to its being frozen over.

760 sepositis...armis. Schrader's emendation (MSS. *suppositis*) avoids making the Amazons recline with their weapons actually underneath them; there seems no foundation for Jannaccone's note 'cenano giacendo sulle armi all' uso militare'.

761 intentus. Cf. Virg. *Aen.* II, 1 *conticuere omnes intentique ora tenebant.*

762 perlibrat. Lit. 'weighs carefully', i.e. ponders or sums up; there is no parallel for this metaphorical use of *perlibro*, but we have the same idea with the uncompounded verb in *Th.* IX, 165f. *paulum stetit anxius heros librabatque metus*; and *delibero* is probably derived from *libra* (see Ernout & Meillet, *Dict. Etym. de la Langue Latine*).

763 lumina. 'Lamps.'

extemplo. F. Hand, *Tursellinus*, II, 672 (whence Lewis & Short) and Garrod in *CR*, 1914, 67 translate 'at first', comparing Livy XXII, 12, 6 *et prudentiam quidem novi* (Gronovius: *non vim* P) *dictatoris extemplo timuit*; but the normal meaning 'immediately', taken with *latuit*, not with *iacentum*, suits the context better: Lactantius interprets as *ilico, mox*.

764 erectum...genas. 'With head uplifted'; so *Th.* II, 506; V, 95; but in *Th.* II, 470 *erectus saetis*, abl.

766 defigit. See n. on l. 367.

obliquo lumine. 'With a side-glance'; cf. *Th.* X, 887.

767f. quid nisi. This is the reading of P, and can be retained whether or not we omit the doubtful verse 772. There seems no need, with Klotz and others, to punctuate *quid? nisi...*: *quid si* is a standard phrase for 'how would it be if...?' as in l. 912; and *quid nisi*, though not common, occurs twice in Ov. *Trist.* I, 8, 29ff.

blando...sinu. 'With kind embrace', not, as Mozley, 'to her soft bosom'; cf. *Silv.* II, 7, 38; V, 5, 84.

768 pectora. Klotz in *Philol.* LXI, 303 argues for the possible retention of *tempora*, and Brinkgreve reads it; but the Roman women's *rica* (veil), which Klotz thought St. might be alluding to by an anachronism, was actually worn only at sacrifices. *Tempora* may have arisen from attraction of the scribe's eye to the neighbouring *semper*.

771 crinale...aurum. Virg. *Aen.* XI, 576.

772 See notes to ll. 592, 767 f.

773–818 SPEECHES OF LYCOMEDES AND ULYSSES

774 paterisque, i.e. as he makes a libation; an unusual instrumental abl.

775 fateor. Often used in parenthesis, as *Silv.* II, 1, 67; III, 4, 39.

decora. The sing. is commoner as applied to pl. nouns in this sense, but cf. Virg. *Aen.* I, 428 f. *columnas..., scenis decora alta futuris.*

776 ff. Lycomedes speaks as Nestor in the *Iliad* (VII, 132 ff.; XXIII, 629 ff.) and Evander in Virg. *Aen.* VIII, 560 ff.; cf. *Aen.* V, 397 ff.; Val. Fl. I, 336 ff.

778 quae. Attracted from *quas*; not for *cuius*, as Brinkgreve. It is normal usage, where, as here, the relative clause forms a kind of parenthesis, for the relative pron. to agree with the attribute (O. Riemann, *Syntaxe Lat.*[7], p. 58).

779 carinas. The trophies would properly speaking consist of the beaks (*rostra*) of ships, as in Virg. *Aen.* VII, 186. But *carinas* (= 'ships') serves also as obj. of *fregi*.

780 The apodosis is suppressed by aposiopesis, as may also be the verb *esset* in protasis and relative clause.

782 vires...meas. So Venus addresses Cupid in Virg. *Aen.* I, 664 as *nate, meae vires.*

783 novos...nepotes. 'Young grandsons.'

784 arrepto...tempore. Cf. l. 318; *abrepto* (P) is not appropriate. Housman in *CQ*, 1933, 13 prefers *adrepto* to account for the two readings; but they can have arisen from the incorrect form *arepto.*

788 meritos...iuravit in enses. 'Hath sworn...allegiance to our righteous arms' (Mozley); cf. *Th.* VII, 377 f. *nam liber in arma impetus, et meritas ultro iurastis in iras,* and note the personification.

790 velorum obtexitur umbra. Borrowed from Virg. *Aen.* XI, 611, of a shower of darts, *caelum...obtexitur umbra.*

791 inrevocata. Whereas *irrevocabilis* is common, *irrevocatus* in this sense (*in-...-tus* for *in-...-bilis,* as *invictus*) is very rare: *Th.* VII, 773 *Mors inrevocata.*

792 tantae data copia famae. Cf. *Silv.* I, 2, 31 f. *quamvis data copia tantae noctis.*

793 campo. A favourite metaphor of Cicero's; e.g. Cic. *Mur.* 18 *nullum...vobis sors campum dedit in quo excurrere virtus...posset.*

794 vigili...aure. *Silv.* III, 5, 35.

trahentem. An extension from the use of *trahere* with *ore, naribus,* etc.; cf. Hor. *Od.* II, 13, 32 *bibit aure.*

795 demissa...lumina. So in the sing. Virg. *Aen.* XII, 220.

flectant. Commonly used of the eyes, e.g. Virg. *Aen.* IV, 369 *num lumina flexit?*—similarly Lucan III, 4; Mart. XIV, 173, 1.

798 omnis honos. Not, as Mozley, 'all honour there awaits him', but in a concrete sense, as *Silv.* I, 2, 233, IV, 1, 27, of Roman magistrates, 'every great rank is there'. Although Quint. I, 4, 13 remarks that *-os* for *-or* is antiquated, *honos* is used far more frequently than *honor* by St., even where metre does not require it.

799 cessant. 'Stay back' from the war.

800 steriles damnatus in annos. Cf. *Th.* IV, 183 *mutos Thamyris damnatus in annos*; V, 108 *longis steriles in luctibus annos*; *Silv.* IV, 2, 12. The constr. is a Silver Latin one, first in Lucan II, 307 *caput in cunctas damnatum...poenas.*

803 cunctas...sorores. This phrase is applied in l. 46 to the fifty Nereids; but we do not know the number of Lycomedes' daughters. In l. 783 the king calls them *haec turba*. According to Barth one alleged scholiast hazards that Deidamia had four sisters, another says the number is unknown.

805 novissimus. 'Last'; cf. Ov. *Met.* II, 115; *Th.* VI, 191f. *tunc piget ire domum, maestoque novissima campo exit.*

806 ille quoque. Garrod reads *ille quidem* with BKQ, objecting that *remittit* does not apply to Achilles. But we should imagine *exisset stratis* as implying that Achilles was on the point of speaking, when Deidamia's action forced him to restrain himself; and that Ulysses likewise checks himself. *Remittit*='puts aside' rather than 'tones down', as shown by *tamen* following.

809 sidereis...voltibus. Cf. *Th.* V, 613 *heu ubi siderei vultus?* Similarly *Silv.* III, 4, 26 *puerum egregiae praeclarum sidere formae.* More often of gods, as *sidereos artus* of Venus in *Silv.* I, 2, 141; and so of Domitian I, 1, 103.

voltibus aequas. Comparatio compendiaria, but not the usual form of it, which would be *vultus divis aequos.*

810 olim. See n. on l. 16 above.

811 virili. Krohn's *virilis*, agreeing with *species*, is very plausible, but there is perhaps no need to alter *virili*; for *species* is commonly used in the sense of 'beauty'. With either reading the adj. is unexpected, since elsewhere Lycomedes' daughters have no manly attributes whatever.

812 occurrit. 'Replies.'

813 Palladias...aras. Kürschner notes that Sen. *Herc. Oet.* 586f. mentions both *Palladias ire per aras* and Bacchic *orgia* in a similar context.

814 novus...auster. Brinkgreve comments: 'Auster eos advexit, alter auster eos quos nempe Troiam ituros esse Lycomedes putat, avehet.' This may explain the general sense of the line, but it was a *Zephyrus*, not a south wind, which brought them to Scyros (ll. 682, 694); St. is far from exact in these descriptions. For the destination of the party on leaving Scyros see n. to II, 18f.

816 depositis...curis. Cf. Virg. *Georg.* IV, 531 *tristes animo deponere curas.*

817 tranquilla sub pace. Taking up ll. 807f. *tranquillus in alta pace mane.* For *sub* cf. *sub somno* in medical language.

818 gravatur. Deponent, 'grudges', as *Silv.* III, 1, 69; IV, 3, 20; *Th.* VIII, 317.

819–840 ULYSSES AND DIOMEDE WATCH THE DANCING

820 praedicta. The gifts mentioned in ll. 721 ff.

821 nec minus. 'Likewise.'

egressae thalamo. *Th.* I, 534.

Scyreides. This form occurs here only, and there is no corresponding form in Greek.

822 ostentare. For the inf. see Introd. p. 16.

verendis. 'Revered.'

823 ff. nitet...lucebat. Sing. nouns joined by *et* or -*que* often take sing. verbs in St.; cf. ll. 239 f., etc.

regina. See n. to l. 662.

824 ff. Very much the same picture, also in a simile, in Val. Fl. v, 345 f. *aut Sicula sub rupe choros, hinc gressibus haerens Pallados, hinc carae Proserpina iuncta Dianae.* Note that the point of Statius' simile is not the comparison of Deidamia and Achilles with individual goddesses, but the fact that both shine out among the surrounding crowd; hence there is no need for Damsté's *feroxve* (*Mnem.* 2nd ser. xxxv, 140) or Brinkgreve's 'chiasmus' of names.

Hennaeas. The MS. reading *Aetneas* is impossible after *Aetnae*, and Henna was the scene of the rape of Proserpine; it is actually a fair distance from Etna.

ferox. Likewise of Minerva Mart. xiv, 179, 1 *virgo ferox*; *Th.* ii, 715 *diva ferox*; Sil. ix, 457; *Octavia* 558 (Sen., etc., ed. Teubner).

827 Ismenia buxus. 'The Theban flute', lit. box-wood, called Theban on account of its connection with Bacchic rites.

828 f. aera Rheae. 'Cymbals of Rhea', i.e. of Cybele, whose worship became merged with that of Bacchus: *aera* are also associated directly with Bacchus, as in *Th.* ii, 78; iv, 668, etc.

enthea...terga. 'Drums that inspire frenzy.' *Entheus* is used several times by St.; not found before post-Aug. poetry.

recursus. Applied by Virg. *Aen.* v, 583 to those taking part in the 'game of Troy'.

831 f. multiplicant. 'Complicate' (Mozley), or perhaps 'accelerate'. A similar usage of the verb in *Th.* vi, 790 f., where *geminatque rotatas multiplicatque manus* is said of Capaneus alone.

Curetes...Samothraces. The Curetes, early inhabitants of Crete, worshipped Zeus with dancing and clashing of spears (Call. *Hymn* 1, 52 ff.); in Samothrace dances were associated with the mysteries of the Cabiri.

actu. Paul. ex Fest. p. 17 Müller: (*actus*) *modo* (*significant*) *motum corporis, ut histrionum et saltatorum, qui etiam ex hoc ipso actuosi dicuntur.* There is no parallel other than the above for this use of *actus* with dancers, but it is so applied to actors elsewhere.

832 f. obvia versae. In two rows opposite each other.

pectine Amazonio. *Pecten* is not found elsewhere as a dance, but was evidently one in which the two rows interlaced (cf. *iungere bracchia* l. 836) like the teeth of two combs. Call. *Hymn* III, 240 ff. mentions dances of Amazons, first one with shields, then a cyclic dance in honour of Artemis, like the cyclic dances of the Spartan women in ll. 833 f.

834 plaudentes. Mozley translates 'shouting her praises'; but the meaning seems rather 'beating time', either with hands or feet, as Virg. *Aen.* VI, 644 *pars pedibus plaudunt choreas.* Dances by Diana and the Oreads are described in a simile in Virg. *Aen.* I, 498 ff.

intorquet. 'Whirls round in' (*Amyclis* abl.) rather than, as Mozley, 'whirls into'.

838 plurima. Internal acc., as *multa*, l. 686, a constr. found as early as Ennius (*Ann.* 49 Vahlen[3]).

839 indignantem. 'Disdaining.'

841–885 ACHILLES SEIZES THE WEAPONS AND BECOMES A WARRIOR

841 solvuntur. Pl. verb with *cohors* as *Th.* II, 524; VI, 262; X, 9; Claud. *Rapt. Pros.* II, 118, 124; cf. *iuventus*, l. 559 above.

842 in mediae...sedibus aulae. The same phrase in *Th.* XII, 695; but *mediis in sedibus aulae*, II, 148; III, 396.

843 tractura. 'Which would attract.'

844 pretium. 'A recompense', as frequently in Livy.

845 arcet. Used absolutely, as in *Th.* VI, 37 *arcet et ipse pater.*

846f. callida dona. The proverbial Greek gifts (Virg. *Aen.* II, 49).

varium. There is no need to emend to *vafrum: varium* = πολύτροπον: cf. Sall. *Cat.* V, 4 *animus audax, subdolus, varius.*

849f. respondentia. Sounding in answer to one another; W. R. Smyth in *CQ*, 1951, 79 gives parallels for this absolute use of *respondeo*. Note the alliteration of *t*, both initial and medial, in these two lines.

limbis. 'Headbands', a different meaning from l. 330.

852 orbem. 'Shield.'

853f. caelatum pugnas. Retained acc. after pass. part.: see Roby, §§ 1126–7, and cf. *Th.* II, 277; IV, 267f.

rubebat bellorum maculis. Brinkgreve takes this as merely meaning that the shield, as it depicted men being wounded, appeared to be stained with blood. Not only is such an interpretation unnatural, but *et forte* shows that real stains are being spoken of, which contrast with the gleam implied in *radiantem*. Gifts of hospitality were not necessarily unused.

855 genas. 'Eyes' (see n. to l. 516).

856 nusquam. 'Of no account.'

858ff. Similes of trained animals also in *Th.* VIII, 124ff. (there too the lion is angered *cum lux stetit obvia ferri*) and Lucan IV, 237ff., where the end of the simile, *a trepido vix abstinet ira magistro*, is akin to l. 863. Cf. also *Silv.* II, 5, the poem on a lion fallen in the amphitheatre.

mores accepit. 'Has submitted to rules'; so *mores* of iron, Pliny, *N.H.* XXXVI, 126; *accipiunt...disciplinam*, of sea-lions, *N.H.* IX, 41; *moribus* (so MU) *...receptis*, of the Nile, Lucan X, 329.

iubas. Acc. of the part affected: see Introd. p. 17.

nisi iussus. This would be in the amphitheatre, when confronted with other animals.

861 Cf. *Th.* VIII, 124, quoted in n. to ll. 858 ff.: the gleam of the sword in the simile corresponds to that of the shield in l. 852.

862 eiurata. A technical term used mostly in political and legal language, rare in poetry: 'is repudiated.'

863 timido...magistro. See n. to ll. 858 ff., and cf. *Silv.* II, 5, 3 *domino parere minori.*

864 lux aemula. 'The rivalling gleam', i.e. vividly reflected light.

865 simili...auro. The same phrase in *Silv.* II, 7, 129 of a statue.

talem. Refers back to the simile of ll. 858–63.

867 haeres. Cf. l. 538, and for ll. 867–8 Adrastus in *Th.* I, 682 f. '*quid nota recondis? scimus' ait.*

868 semiferi Chironis. *Silv.* II, 1, 89; Ov. *Met.* II, 633.

869 caeli...nepos. Achilles' grandfather Aeacus was son of Jupiter.

870 suspensis...signis. This clearly does not mean that the standards were hung up. It may mean 'raised' (ready for the expedition), but 'hesitating', 'in suspense' is better: cf. *Th.* I, 195; *Ach.* II, 37, etc. The *-is* endings in ll. 870–1 provide a strong assonance, as in ll. 138 f. and elsewhere. For the sense cf. Ulysses' words to Achilles in Ov. *Met.* XIII, 168 f. *tibi se peritura reservant Pergama: quid dubites ingentem evertere Troiam?*

871 dubiis. In danger of falling; cf. l. 884 *trepidante domo*; Lucr. V, 1237 *concussaeque cadunt urbes dubiaeque minantur.*

872 abrumpe moras. *Th.* XI, 201; commoner is *rumpe moras.*

874 amictu. Abl. of separation.

875 grande. Adv., as *Th.* XI, 237; XII, 684; *Silv.* III, 1, 50, 130; only in post-Aug. poetry. Lewis & Short give the quantity wrongly as *grandē.*

878 intactae. The suggestion is that, although Achilles had only partly loosened the garments (ll. 874 f.), they miraculously fell of their own accord. This is perhaps associated with the miraculous sudden growth mentioned below; cf. also next note.

879 consumitur. Not simply 'is seized' (Brinkgreve) or 'sumitur simul' (Jannaccone), as shown by the parenthesis *mira fides.* The spear is too short (*brevior*) for Achilles, who in Hom. *Il.* XVI, 140 ff. possesses a gigantic spear given to Peleus by Chiron; the spear, and even surprisingly enough the shield, are 'swallowed up' by his hand. Similarly by a rather gruesome metaphor Menoeceus' self-sacrifice is described by his mother in the words *viden' ut iugulo consumpserit ensem?* (*Th.* X, 813). See also n. to l. 446.

880 mira fides. *Silv.* IV, 4, 81; V, 1, 33: 'marvellous to believe'; cf. *Silv.* III, 1, 8 *vix oculis animoque fides.*

umeris excedere. Achilles' shoulders seem to tower above the other two; cf. l. 294. *Excedere* in this sense with personal obj. is first used here.

881 Aetolum. See n. to l. 500.

calor. So too in Lucan II, 324 of zeal for war. *Tantum...penates* is added to explain how Achilles seemed to the onlookers so much taller than Ulysses and Diomede.

883 gradu. A technical term for the stance taken by a combatant; cf. Ov. *Met.* IX, 43 *inque gradu stetimus certi non cedere.*

884 f. Pelea. This form of the adj. is given by PE, while at l. 551 St. has the usual form *Peleius*; similarly he has *Capanēus* and *Capaneius*, *Penthēus* and *Pentheius*, *Thesēus* and *Theseius*, corresponding to the Greek forms ει and ηι respectively.

quaeritur. 'Is looked for in vain'; cf. *Th.* IV, 704 *amnes quaerunt armenta natatos* (*amnis...natatus* Garrod with better MS. support but less naturally); XI, 278 *hi quaerunt artus.*

885–920 LYCOMEDES AGREES TO THE MARRIAGE

886 grandia. Cf. Cic. *Brut.* 289 *subsellia grandiorem et pleniorem vocem desiderant*, and the similar sense of *grande* adv. (see n. to l. 875).

887 accepit pectore. The phrase implies not only that Achilles hears her voice but that it touches his inmost feelings.

888 The same struggle between *virtus* and passion (there *occultus...ardor*) recurs at II, 29 f. For *infracta* see Owen on Ov. *Trist.* II, 412.

889 limina. This is evidently the reading of all good MSS., and there is no need to retain the reading of older editors, *lumina.* We have been told that Achilles is inside the palace (l. 884), so that *limina* must refer to the king's own apartment.

890 monstra. See n. to l. 662.

891 For the acc. of Greek proper nouns of the 3rd decl. in Latin poetry see Housman in *Journ. Philol.* XXXI, 258. Examples of the use of *in* with weapons are given by Heuvel on *Th.* I, 712.

895 fas dixisse. See n. to ll. 73 ff. (*timuisse*).

896 f. corda. 'Mind.' For the use of *adverte* cf. *Silv.* III, 2, 3 f., of sea deities, *placidum...advertite votis concilium.*

bonus. 'Graciously', much the same as *libens.*

898 nato. Dat. after *iungunt.*

899 The line has a distinctly legal sound: Achilles is descended from gods on both sides, and his parents are imagined as reciting their illustrious ancestry to the prospective father-in-law, and basing their claims (l. 900) on this list. *Allēgo* (lit. to commission on private business; here to bring forward names) is very rare in poetry. For *utroque a sanguine* cf. *Th.* I, 392 *utroque Iovem de sanguine ducens.*

900 agmine. Likewise of women, *Th.* V, 652; VI, 132; VII, 240; XII, 125; *Ach.* I, 301, 555, 602, 623, 799; *Silv.* III, 2, 13.

901 degeneres. Similarly in Virg. *Aen.* IV, 13 *degeneres animos* follows Dido's conviction that Aeneas is of divine descent.

902 concipe foedus. A phrase borrowed from Virg. *Aen.* XII, 13, where Turnus asks Latinus for the hand of Lavinia.

903 tuis. Emphatic: Achilles insists that he is now related to Lycomedes.

906 f. The sense seems to be: Lycomedes is entitled to ask for atonement from Achilles but not from Deidamia; if he insists on some punishment, Achilles would even be willing to forego the expedition against Troy.

907 triste. 'Sullenly'; see n. to ll. 908 ff.

quid lumina mutas? Cf. ll. 271 f.

908 ff. Lycomedes is hardly given a chance to speak, while events are telescoped in such a manner that the birth of Pyrrhus is assumed to have taken place. The following sentence may be punctuated in three ways: (1) with commas after *inmitis* and *ensis*, as some old editors; this, connecting *inmitis* with *turba*, is an unnatural order; (2) with exclamation mark after *ensis*, as Krohn and most modern editors, 'how often shall the pitiless sword be plied! We are a multitude!' Mozley, following most old commentators, interprets this as meaning that Lycomedes, if he is so angry, will now have not only Achilles and Deidamia to kill but Pyrrhus too (cf. ll. 659 f.). But (*a*) *immitis*, when applied by St. to weapons (*Silv.* III, 1, 34 and probably *Th.* IX, 19), does not seem to have its full strength 'unnatural'; (*b*) Achilles has called the king *care pater* (l. 892), even *gratior et magno...parente* (l. 895); and Mozley is going too far in rendering *quid triste fremis?* as 'why these angry cries?' (3) With comma after *ensis*, as some old editors and Brinkgreve. This seems the best punctuation, *quotiens* being 'as often as'. Achilles is alluding to Lycomedes' words at ll. 780–3, where he longs for male offspring which could take up arms: Lycomedes is now not the only male of the royal family, there are Achilles and Pyrrhus also to uphold its honour in battle (*ensis* in this wider sense, as at l. 788).

turba. Applied to three people also in Prop. IV, 11, 76.

911 blandus...precum. This gen., of Greek origin, is sometimes called 'sphere in which'; it is not used elsewhere with *blandus* (for the abl. cf. Hor. *Epist.* II, 1, 135 *docta prece blandus*), but at *Th.* VII, 26 St. has *lenis belli*.

conpellit. 'Urges': cf. Klotz in *Philol.* LXI, 306 f.

914 depositum. See n. to l. 385.

915 fatis. 'Oracles' or 'divine utterances', as *Th.* X, 592 *fata deum*.

916 Although this line is contained in all MSS., it may be suspected for the following reasons: (1) *fac velit* is not found elsewhere, the normal phrase (as *Th.* II, 449, Virg. *Aen.* IV, 540, etc.) being *fac velle*, and the sequence of tenses *velit...sprevisset* is unusual; (2) Barth, objecting to *tamen*, suspected l. 917, which certainly follows awkwardly on l. 916 but is sound enough in itself (*nec tamen abnuerit*=*et tamen non-abnuerit*); (3) as Brinkgreve remarks, l. 917 looks back to l. 912, forming with the intervening lines a chiasmus of ideas, and the effect of this is increased by omitting l. 916; (4) for a similar dubious line cf. l. 772. If genuine, the line is parenthetical and represents an additional point in Lycomedes' mind as he weighs pros and cons.

917 Cf. *Th.* II, 189 f. *anne aliquis soceros accedere tales abnuat?*

918f. effert...gradum. Sen. *Med.* 891.

919f. Deidamia, in her worried state of mind, does not at first trust the forgiveness, and tries to conciliate her father. *Opposito...Achille* signifies that Achilles is, both literally and metaphorically, the bulwark behind which she takes refuge; alternatively a financial metaphor, 'pledging', may be intended.

921–926 ALLIANCE AND MARRIAGE CELEBRATIONS

921 Haemoniam. See n. to l. 98. Brinkgreve reads *Haemoniae* with P (we may compare *Silv.* III, 4, 17 *misisti Latio*), but the acc. is more natural with a place-name. For the omission of the prep. cf. II, 62; other examples are quoted by J. Ae. Nauke, *Observationes criticae*, etc., p. 16; S. Blomgren, *De Sil. Ital. Punicis quaestiones*, etc. (Uppsala, 1938), pp. 6f.

922 impleat. Cf. Virg. *Aen.* XI, 896f.

924 vires...excusat. 'Pleads his (lack of) strength as excuse.' Cf. Ov. *Met.* XIV, 461f. *vires Aetolius heros excusat*, where the context shows that Diomede refuses aid altogether.

925 retectum. 'Disclosed' to the general public. With this reading we should supply *est*, and not, with Wilamowitz, *De tribus carminibus Latinis*, p. 10, make *foedus* and *nox* joint subjects of *iungit*.

926 nox conscia. Ov. *Met.* VI, 588 *nox conscia sacris*; XIII, 15; Val. Fl. III, 211; Sil. IX, 180; cf. *conscia sidera*, Virg. *Aen.* IX, 429; *Th.* VI, 240f.; XII, 393.

927–960 DEIDAMIA'S LAMENT AT ACHILLES' DEPARTURE

927 Illius. Deidamia (so the scholiast of R), as she lies in bed and prepares to say farewell to Achilles the following day; though before reaching l. 929 one would expect it to refer to Achilles. But there is no need, with Baehrens, to postulate a lacuna after l. 928, for the preceding lines apply more aptly to Deidamia than to Achilles.

928 ipsas cogitat undas. She pictures to herself the very waves which the ships may have to grapple with.

930 fusa. Cf. Prop. II, 16, 24.

solvit. 'Lets fall': so Claud. *Rufin.* II, 258f. *solutis...lacrimis*.

932 tuos dignabere portus. Although PEBKQR read *portus*, all editors give *partus* with the inferior MSS., explaining either, with early commentators, as 'deign to look once more upon your child', or, as Brinkgreve, that the phrase asks if Achilles will again consider Deidamia worthy of becoming the mother of his children. But *portus*, in the metaphorical sense of 'refuge', is almost certainly right, for it is paralleled in the alternative question (l. 934) by *virgineae...latebrae*. The metaphor is common in Cicero, and likewise found in Virgil and Ovid; cf. also *Silv.* II, 1, 70 *tu domino requies portusque senectae*. With this reading, mention of the child is effectively left till the end of the speech (ll. 952ff.). For *dignor* see n. to l. 260.

933f. tumidus. 'Haughtily.'

capta...Pergama. 'The spoils of Troy'; cf. II, 65 *captos ad Pergama devehit Argos.*

937 invidit. The constr. is as in Virg. *Georg.* I, 503 f. *nobis caeli te regia, Caesar, invidet.*

939 permissus. Explains *o dulcia furta dolique*: Deidamia longs for her secret love, as marriage is only bringing about separation.

940ff. Note the threefold *i* followed by *redi*, an effect found, for example, in Cat. LXIV, 39–41, 63–5, 258–60.

paratus. See n. to l. 97.

942 nimis improba posco. We could construct *nimis* with *posco*, making *improba* fem. sing., but the parallel from *Th.* XI, 505f., *non improba posco vota*, suggests that it is neut. pl.; cf. Mart. IX, 67, 5 *improbius quiddam...rogavi.* For *inproba* see n. to l. 41.

945f. patriam pensare toris. To recoup the loss of Troy by marrying Achilles.

ipsa...Tyndaris. See the quotation from Martial given below.

947f. primae...culpae. *Th.* II, 233.

fabula...narrabor. There is a close parallel to ll. 945–8 in Mart. XII, 52, 4f. *dulcis in Elysio narraris fabula campo, et stupet ad raptus Tyndaris ipsa tuos.*

famulis. Mozley renders 'henchmen' (*famulus*); but the sense is rather that Achilles will tell stories of Deidamia to the Trojan women who become his slaves (*famulae*).

950 thyrsa. This, the reading of P, gives a heteroclitic neut. pl. of *thyrsus*, not found elsewhere in Latin, but examples from later Greek poetry are mentioned by Klotz in *Archiv für Lat. Lex.* XII, 130.

954 quid. Somewhat contemptuous.

955 Thetidi. See n. to ll. 285f.

958f. ingentis. Oriental slaves were noted for their height.

captum...Ilion. Rhetorical exaggeration; cf. ll. 933f.

reversus. The participle is attached as nom. to the main verb, to which it does not logically belong; cf. such phrases as *puer memini.*

Phrygiae...gazae. Cf. *Troïa gaza*, Virg. *Aen.* I, 119; II, 763.

960 Damsté thought this line spurious, but all the MSS. have it, and there are other examples, e.g. *Th.* II, 743, of a book ending with a single line of this type. For the wording cf. Cat. LXIV, 59 *irrita ventosae linquens promissa procellae*, which St. no doubt had in mind; *Th.* V, 419 *praecipites vocem involvere procellae.*

BOOK II

1-22 ACHILLES LEAVES SCYROS

1 ff. Night enfolds the earth with darkness like a garment, and Day, which comes forth out of the Ocean (*dies*, as often, virtually identified with the sun), strips this off (for *exuit* cf. Val. Fl. III, 2). The sun, evidently obscured by mist, is said to be still dull (*hebetem*) from the proximity of Night and still watery from its immersion. Cf. *nondum pura dies* Claud. *Rapt. Pros.* II, 2, and for *rorantem Ach.* I, 243. *Hebes* is used of dull colour in Ov. *Fast.* V, 365; of precious stones Pliny, *N.H.* XXXVII, 98, 134; and of light Avien. *Arat.* 252, 455.

5 nudatum pectora palla. Achilles has either partly or completely discarded the woman's robe (cf. n. on I, 262) which he had been wearing.

7 cognata. Connected with Thetis.

10 passus, sc. *sit.*

11 escendat. Kohlmann's correction of P's *excendat*, governing *rates*; in *Th.* XII, 172 (*quos...in armos*) we should perhaps read *descendat* (ω) rather than *escendat* (P).

13 litat. 'Offers acceptable sacrifices.'

sub. 'On the edge of': St. frequently uses *sub* in a somewhat unusual way, as at I, 223, 476, 953; not, as Mozley, 'venerates with a bull the cerulean king below the waves'.

16 spumante salo. For the abl. cf. I, 43, and see R. D. Williams, *CQ*, 1951, 143, n. 4.

17 iuberes. The force of the subjunc. (as read by ER²) after *quamquam* here is 'although I felt that...'; for *quamquam* in St. see n. to l. 467. The reading of P is not as reported by Klotz and Garrod, but seems originally to have been *iuberis* (*-ris* above the line), then *iube* was altered, probably by the same hand, to *pube*.

18f. bella...ratesque. This phrase is similar to I, 927f., but neither tells us clearly whether the ship was making for Greece or the Troad. There seems hardly time for the Greek fleet to have sailed yet; on the other hand the winds mentioned are south (II, 20) and west (II, 46), which would tend to take the ship towards the Troad.

19 alno. Not abl., as Brinkgreve, but dat., a common poetic constr., cf. Ov. *Trist.* I, 4, 7f. *prorae puppique recurvae insilit; Th.* IX, 230; but the acc. is also used, as Lucan III, 626 *insiluit...puppim; Th.* II, 208f.

21 ardua. Constr. with *Scyros.*

ducere. 'To take on'; so *ducere colorem, pallorem*, Virg. *Ecl.* IX, 49; Ov. *Met.* III, 485; VIII, 760; Lucan VI, 828; also Lucan I, 544 *noctem duxere Mycenae;* Val. Fl. I, 307 *si nubila duxerit aether.*

22 discedere. There is perhaps no parallel for this use of *discedo* for apparent recession; but cf. *decrescere* I, 462, and *ubi terra recessit longius*, Ov. *Met.* XI, 466f. (similarly Virg. *Aen.* III, 72; *Th.* I, 549).

23–48 ACHILLES REGRETS LEAVING SCYROS, BUT IS INDUCED BY ULYSSES TO TURN HIS THOUGHTS TOWARDS THE WAR

23 Turre procul summa. Cf. *Th.* VII, 243, of Antigone, *turre procul sola.*

24 commissum. EBKQR have *confessum*, which Brinkgreve, following earlier editors, reads with the pass. sense 'acknowledged': this is a possible reading, but *confessus* is not found elsewhere in St. in this sense.

Pyrrhum. In other writers Achilles' son is more often called Neoptolemus. The name (*nomina* poetic pl. for sing.) Pyrrhus, which St. has not mentioned before, is said to have been given either (*a*) because he had red hair (πυρρός), or (*b*) because Achilles himself was called Pyrrha when disguised as a girl (Paus. x, 26, 1; Hyg. XCVI, 1; XCVII, 15; Eustath. on *Il.*, p. 1187, 22; Serv. on *Aen.* II, 469). But it seems more likely that the name Pyrrha was a later invention, itself based on Pyrrhus.

25 pendebat. Either 'was leaning out' (cf. *Th.* x, 457, of troops straining forward to watch from the top of a rampart) or 'was perched', as of goats, Virg. *Ecl.* I, 77; cf. *Th.* I, 332.

26 Deidamia watches so intensely that she seems to feel the motion of the waves herself, and can see the ship after her sisters have lost sight of it; cf. *Silv.* v, 2, 6 f.; Lucan VIII, 47 f., of Cornelia watching for Pompey's ship, *prospiciens fluctus nutantia longe semper prima vides venientis vela carinae.*

27 obliquos...vultus. *Silv.* II, 6, 102.

28 viduam. See n. to l. 82 below.

31 Cf. *Th.* I, 75 *non regere aut dictis maerentem flectere adorti*; both this parallel and the agreement of the other MSS. argue against E's *haerentem.*

34 erectum. See n. to I, 412.

reserato in limine. A reference to the temple of Janus; cf. Virg. *Aen.* VII, 613 *reserat stridentia limina consul*; *Th.* x, 652 *immensae reserato limine portae.*

35 violavit. Cf. I, 511.

36 f. furta, i.e. Achilles himself.

fidem. Here of the accomplishment of Thetis' wishes; cf. I, 681.

37 f. nimisque mater. Cf. *Th.* XI, 611 *crudeles nimiumque mei!* This attachment of the adverb is more pointed than taking *nimis...nimisque* together, as I, 695 *magis...magisque.*

38 umbra. 'Obscurity.'

39 clangore. Cf. *Th.* x, 552 *tuba luctificis pulsat clangoribus.*

41 nostrum. 'Our doing.'

42 dixit. So PER; Brinkgreve, claiming (in *Mnem.* 2nd ser. XLII, 109) that *dixit* is unsuitable as the speech is unfinished, reads *ultro* with BKQ, joining it to *quem...occupat*; but this is hardly suitable as applied to the second speaker. It seems more likely, since *dixit* has better MS. support, that *ultro* was inserted by a scribe to amplify *venisses.*

43 Longum. See n. to I, 140.

resides. Two explanations have been offered: (1) 'e longinquo repetendas', (2) 'inertiae meae'. Of these the former introduces an entirely new meaning of *reses*, while the latter, while less objectionable, creates an unusual transference of epithet.

45 Perhaps inspired by Ov. *Met.* VI, 131 *pictas, caelestia crimina, vestes*; *crimina* = 'a charge against'. See Enk on Prop. I, 11, 30.

46 fruuntur. There seems to be no parallel for this use of *fruor* in connection with ships, etc., nor does St. have it elsewhere with an inanimate subject. But the alternative reading *feruntur* has poor MS. support; for the confusion cf. *Th.* XII, 45, 388.

49–85 ULYSSES SPEAKS OF THE CAUSES
OF THE TROJAN WAR

50 si talia credimus. St. similarly expresses scepticism at traditional mythology in *Th.* II, 269 *ut prisca fides*, 595 *si fas est credere*.

51 electus...solvere. *Eligo* followed by inf. is found only in St., the other examples being *Th.* X, 635; *Silv.* III, 4, 62.

53 f. amico lumine. Cf. Virg. *Aen.* VII, 265 *vultus...amicos*; *Th.* VII, 361 f. *amicum pectus*.

54 Dionen. According to Homer, Zeus and Dione were the parents of Aphrodite. Dione as a synonym for Aphrodite is first found in Theocr. VII, 116; see *RE* s.v. Dione, and Heuvel on *Th.* I, 288.

56 f. dum Pelea dulce maritat Pelion. 'While pleasant Pelion gave Peleus in marriage to Thetis.' Later writers tell us that Eris (Discordia), the only one of the gods not invited to the wedding, threw her golden apple 'for the fairest' among the guests at the banquet: see H. J. Rose, *Handbook of Greek Mythology*, p. 128, n. 17.

59 faciles...Amyclae. Cf. I, 21; *faciles* has a predicative sense, 'an easy conquest'.

61 turrigerae. An Ovidian epithet of Cybele, who was sometimes portrayed with a turret, representing the cities of the world, upon her head: as, for example, in the Vatican seated statue illustrated in Daremberg-Saglio, fig. 2244; cf. Lucr. II, 606 ff.

veritas. Both *veritas* (P) and *vetitas* (EBKQR) are possible readings. Klotz in *Philol.* LXI, 309 asks who forbade the trees to be cut down: it is sufficient answer that they were sacred. *Vetitas* also adds to the wickedness of Paris. On the other hand *veritas* is perhaps more poetical, and may have been changed by a scribe (though the two are easily interchangeable) as being thought too bold. It is also supported by *Silv.* II, 6, 27 f. *Paris...invitas deiecit in aequora pinus*. As against this, P wrongly has *ver-* for *vet-* in *Th.* XII, 380; *Ach.* I, 81.

solo. Dat., as *Th.* VI, 89; VII, 92 (cf. J. Ae. Nauke, *Observationes criticae*, etc., pp. 18 f.), rather than abl., as Brinkgreve and Jannaccone: see Kühner, *Lat. Gr.²*, II, 1, 320. Examples cited by Nauke with *figo, defigo* (*Th.* V, 574; VII, 801 f.) are more probably abl.; though Livy VII, 3, 5 has (*lex*) *fixa fuit dextro lateri aedis*.

62 terras. For the acc. see n. to I, 921.

delatus. *Defero* is commonly used of sailing: cf. *Silv.* II, 2, 10; similarly *devehit*, l. 65 below.

63 pudet heu miseretque. *Th.* IX, 389.

64 f. Cf. I, 66 ff., and for *Helena...superbus*, Ov. *Met.* I, 752, IX, 443 *Phoebo...parente superbus*.

65 Cf. Virg. *Aen.* I, 68 *Ilium in Italiam portans*.

67 inexciti. Used in the sense of 'untroubled' by Virg. *Aen.* VII, 623 (wrongly given as ἅπαξ εἰρ. by Lewis & Short); here 'not urged on by others', amplified by *sponte*.

68 f. genialia...pacta. 'The marriage contract.' So *sacri...pacti religio*, Val. Fl. VIII, 401 f. The *lectus genialis*, dedicated to the *genius* of the house, was placed in the atrium; thus the adj. *genialis* comes to denote things connected with a marriage: cf. *Silv.* I, 2, 224; II, 7, 82 (*genitalibus* LM).

conubia. Here denoting wives, as Virg. *Aen.* IX, 597; *Th.* VIII, 62 *Siculo rapui conubia campo*, and elsewhere in St.; *amor, pignus* are likewise used in a concrete sense.

70 The comparison is perhaps, as suggested by Brinkgreve, inspired by Hom. *Il.* I, 154 ff., where Achilles says that he is not fighting the Trojans because they have plundered any oxen or horses of his or ravaged any of his crops.

72 ff. non tulit. *Th.* IX, 801; Ov. *Met.* I, 753, etc.

Agenor. In Hom. *Il.* XIV, 321 (so too a fragment of Antimachus, *Theb.* I), Europa's father is called simply Φοῖνιξ, i.e. the Phoenician; but later writers call him Agenor (*imperiosus* is perhaps intended as a translation of ἀγήνωρ). When she was carried off by Jupiter disguised as a bull, her father is said to have sent out his sons to search for her.

Europen. The Greek decl. serves to differentiate Agenor's daughter from the geographical term used just above (l. 64), which in St., except at *Ach.* I, 410, means the lands of the Greeks fighting against Troy rather than the continent of Europe.

74 f. aspernatusque...generum. Cf. *Th.* VII, 317 f., of Aegina.

est. Similarly separated from its verb at the end of the line in *Th.* III, 105, 686.

ut. The Greek ὡς is commonly used in this sense, 'as' introducing a predicate, but *ut* is rarely so found except in the restrictive sense (Lewis & Short s.v. ut, I, B, 4, *b*).

75 ff. Aeetes, king of Colchis and father of Medea, is said, according to ps.-Apollod. I, 9, 24, to have pursued the Argonauts in two successive expeditions: one immediately after the escape of Jason and Medea, which was checked by Medea killing her brother Apsyrtus and throwing his limbs into the sea; the other in which the king sent out a large number of Colchians to hunt for the Argonauts. Ap. Rh. IV, 212 f. has a different account, according to which Apsyrtus leads a band of Colchians against the Argonauts, and is killed by Jason on an island in the Danube.

semideos reges. *Th.* III, 518 (ἡμίθεοι, Pind. *Pyth.* IV, 12).

ituram in sidera. After its voyage the Argo was transformed into a constellation (Arat. 342 ff.).

78 f. Phryga semivirum. Virg. *Aen.* XII, 99.

litora circum...volitantem. Virg. *Aen.* VI, 329 says of the unburied *centum errant annos volitantque haec litora circum.*

80 Barth remarks that the hurried and angry speech is represented in the versification, with four elisions in one line. The construction is awkward, the negative being limited to the first half; a comma is needed after *equi* to make this clear.

82 vidua...sede. Cf. l. 28 *viduam...domum*; *Silv.* V, 1, 198 *viduos...penates.*

84 Cf. *Th.* II, 426 *propior capulo manus.*

85 inpulit. See n. to I, 306.

86–93 DIOMEDE ASKS ACHILLES FOR AN ACCOUNT OF HIS CHILDHOOD

86 Excipit. *Th.* X, 360; XI, 75.

87 ritus. Much the same as *mores*; there is no religious connection here. Barth expresses surprise at St. implying that the Greeks have never heard of Achilles' upbringing in Chiron's cave; on the contrary, they have, but are pressing him for details. Thus St. brings about the inverted chronology customary at the beginning of epics.

elementa. Cf. l. 166; *Th.* VI, 140 and Lact. on that line.

88 mox. H. J. Rose in *CQ*, 1927, 57 contends that in class. Latin *mox* means not 'soon' but 'not now', 'after a while'; cf. Tac. *Agr.* XI, 5, where *mox segnitia cum otio intravit* refers to a wholly different era from what precedes. In St. it can have these last meanings, but it can also mean 'soon'; otherwise, for example, Thetis' promise at I, 266 has no point.

89 laudum...semina. See n. on I, 188 f.

90 virtutisque aditus. Mozley translates 'how thy valour grew', apparently taking the phrase after *edis*, but from its position it is more natural to take it after *pandere*; the comma which all editors have at the end of l. 89 is better omitted. Chiron reveals to Achilles the steps to perfection, and *virtus* is more embracing than 'valour'.

91 multumque faventibus. A very weak amplification.

edis. Klotz in *Philol.* LXI, 309 shows that P's reading is preferable to *ede* after *quin*; but as regards metrical usage Jannaccone (n. to II, 86) is incorrect in saying that St. avoids a short open syllable at the end of the line where there is a break in punctuation, as shown by *Th.* VI, 810; XI, 417, etc.

93 The reading of P, *et his primum arma ostendisse lacertis*, is upheld by Brinkgreve and Klotz with hiatus at the caesura, the former comparing *Th.* VIII, 36; X, 441. But at *Th.* VIII, 36 the break in punctuation would in any case make a hiatus easier, though Baehrens may have been right in conjecturing *minas*, since P has *mina*; while X, 441 is a difficult line, where we certainly cannot be sure that the unsupported reading of P is correct. On the variant readings at *Th.* III, 710, where the question involved is the lengthening of a syllable before the caesura, see Housman in *CQ*, 1933, 6. Since St. clearly avoids even an ordinary hiatus, it is unlikely that he would have tolerated one with a word ending in -*um*, for which very few parallels exist in any poet (see L. Müller, *De re metrica*, pp. 376f. and Postgate in *CQ*, 1912, 40; such examples as Tib. I, 5, 33 are made easier by a slight break in punctuation). As E omits the line and the other MSS. do not help, we can only conjecture; and Schenkl's *primum me*, which gives a harsh but possible scansion (cf. II, 146), seems preferable to other emendations. For the corruption cf. I, 196, where, after a final *s*, EBKQR omit *se*.

94-167 ACHILLES' ACCOUNT OF HIS EARLY YEARS UNDER CHIRON

96 in teneris...annis. *Silv.* II, 7, 54 *primum teneris adhuc in annis*; Ov. *A.A.* I, 61 *primis et adhuc crescentibus annis* (whence perhaps the reading here *crescentibus* of the *codd. dett.*).

reptantibus. See n. on I, 477.

98ff. ex more. Cf. Virg. *Aen.* VIII, 185f. *non haec sollemnia nobis, has ex more dapes....* For the food of Achilles see D. S. Robertson in *CR*, 1940, 177, where parallels from vases are given and Pind. *Nem.* III, 48f. fully discussed (if in that passage we read σώματα...ἀσθμαίνοντα, there is a good parallel to *semianimis*); also Kürschner, *op. cit.* pp. 32f. The animals mentioned, which also include boars and bears, were supposed to pass on to Achilles their qualities of strength, fierceness and swiftness. Among the ancient derivations of the name Achilles, probably none of which is correct, we find α-χιλός and α-χεῖλος (see *RE* s.v. Achilleus), the former being supposed to mean 'unnourished by vegetables', the latter 'weil seine Lippen die Mutterbrust nicht kannten'. As there is no early reference to these derivations, they probably owed their origins to the legends about Achilles' food, which may go back to the *Cypria* (Robert, *Heldensagen*, I, 80 n. 3), rather than vice versa.

hausisse. *Th.* VIII, 246 *hausisse dapes*.

Ceres. The Thesaurus states that this is the only example in St. of *Ceres*= 'bread'; but we have also *Th.* I, 524.

105 We should (although *trepido* is found with acc. in poetry) construct *ad* also with *saxa*; for this type of constr. cf. Val. Fl. I, 716; *Th.* V, 189; VIII, 384; *Silv.* I, 1, 57; I, 2, 56; I, 3, 50; V, 2, 132.

108 fluxa. 'Loose', conveying to the Romans the sense of effeminate; see n. to I, 533.

110 torserat. Cf. *Silv.* V, 1, 17 *altera cum volucris Phoebi rota torqueat annum.*

111 A reminiscence of Cat. LXIV, 342, also of Achilles, *flammea praevertet celeris vestigia cervae*; cf. *Th.* IV, 271. Pind. *Nem.* III, 51f. recounts how the young Achilles, through his swiftness, slew deer without hounds or nets.

114 admissus. 'At a gallop', as in the phrase *admisso equo*.

115 vago. Not 'incerto, titubante' (Brinkgreve), but 'wide-ranging' (Ellis on Cat. LXIV, 340 *vago victor certamine cursus*).

120 murmure. A favourite word of Statius' (used fifty times), not always of a gentle sound: e.g. *Th.* XII, 170 of a tiger, IV, 801 and *Silv.* I, 3, 22 of rushing waters. Here it probably applies to wild animals rather than, as Mozley, to Achilles' shouts.

121 f. inbelles...dammas. Mart. IV, 74, 1; XIII, 94, 2.

sectari. Understand *me passus est.*

timidas...lyncas. Cf. Hor. *Od.* II, 13, 40 *timidos agitare lyncas*; the gender is always fem. in St.

123 f. tristes. 'Sullen'—a personification as applied to animals.

fulmineos...sues. *Th.* VI, 868 *fulmineo...dente sues*; XI, 530 f.

127 nigro. Cf. *Th.* X, 298 f. *nigrantia tabo gramina.*

127 f. See n. to I, 652 f.

129 vicina pube. The rendering 'cum pubertas appropinquaret', in the Delphin ed. and Brinkgreve, is incorrect, since *pubes* cannot signify *pubertas*: see Garrod in *CR*, 1914, 67. The phrase means rather 'among the neighbouring youth', a type of local abl.

130 Mavortis imago. *Th.* XII, 523 *duri Mavortis imago*; VII, 808 *talis erat...belli fluitantis imago*: 'appearance', 'form'.

131 ff. The description of various types of weapon is similar to *Th.* IV, 64–7, though there the different races are not mentioned. The tribes given here are all except *Balearicus* northern: the Paeones from Macedonia, the Sauromatae (Sarmatae) from east of the Don until the third century B.C., then moving westwards, the Getae from the Danube, the Geloni from the Dnieper.

rotatu. Only here in classical Latin.

quo turbine. A reminiscence of Virg. *Aen.* XI, 284 *quo turbine torqueat hastam*. For the form of the indirect questions cf. I, 190 f.

contum Sauromates. Cf. Val. Fl. VI, 162 *ingentis frenator Sarmata conti.* Poles were also used for pushing the enemy off walls, Virg. *Aen.* IX, 510; Lucan VI, 174.

falcem. 'Falchion' (Mozley), a short sword curved like a scythe: schol. Juv. VIII, 201 *per 'falcem supinam' armatura Thracum intellegenda est.*

134 f. habenae. Literally, as in Livy XXXVIII, 29, 6, the thong of a sling; here, as Lucan III, 710 *Balearis tortor habenae* and elsewhere, virtually for the sling itself.

suspensa...vulnera. A bold substitution of effect for cause, the real obj. being the weapon which produces the wounds.

136 inclusum...aëra. So Pliny, *N.H.* X, 112, of the flight of birds. In *Th.* IV, 67 *vacuo...diem praecingere gyro*, the invisible circle forms a belt round the air it encloses; here it cuts off, or parts, the air it encloses.

distingueret. 'Parted', as Manil. I, 580 *(Phoebus) cum medium aequali distinguit limite caelum.*

137 A very weak line.

138 iungere often denotes the bridging of rivers, etc.; here the jumping across is a metaphorical bridging.

139 aërii...montis. Cat. LXVIII, 57; Virg. *Ecl.* VIII, 59.

140 quo...gradu. Mozley wrongly translates 'with what stride to run upon the level': this would require the subjunctive. Achilles is taught to climb mountains with as big a stride as on level ground.

simulacra. In apposition to *molares*.

141 curvato umbone. All modern editors give *scutato umbone*, with P, but this implies *umbone* to be understood as 'elbow', whereas after *scut-* the normal meaning 'shield' or 'boss' would naturally spring to mind. *Scutato* may have arisen from a gloss *scuto* to explain *umbone*.

142 intrare. W. Morel in *CR*, 1941, 75 gives sound arguments for dismissing P's reading *errare*. There seems little advantage in *ardentes penetrare*, conjectured by D. S. Robertson in *CR*, 1942, 117, and the phrase is less easy with asyndeton. Cf. *Th.* IX, 797f. *didici...horrendas...domus magnarum intrare ferarum* (Parthenopaeus recounting his similarly Spartan upbringing).

143 memini. Followed by *oratio recta*, as in *Th.* II, 350; Livy II, 2, 7 *meminimus, fatemur, eiecisti reges.*

144 pastus. Perhaps nowhere else of swollen rivers, though used of stars, winds, rainbow, etc., 'refreshing themselves' (*Th.* VII, 8f.; IX, 405f.; XI, 115; *Ach.* I, 220).

145 vivas...trabes. Trees just uprooted (*vulsas* is probably a gloss); cf. *Th.* VIII, 298ff. *aras arboribus vivis...texi imperat*; *Silv.* II, 3, 41 *vivam...harenam* ('fresh').

147 stare...contra. 'Stand fast against the current.'

148 gradu totiens obstante. A typically exaggerated description of Chiron's greater resisting power with four feet: note the alliterative effect in the second half of the line.

149f. stabam. 'Tried to stand fast': *nec* (EB²KQ) is evidently due to a misunderstanding of the force of this imperf.; but *sed* and *nec* are frequently confused in MSS.

latae caligo fugae. The word *caligo* is used by St. in the following senses: (*a*) gloom, *Th.* I, 380; V, 154; (*b*) the mist surrounding a deity, *Th.* IX, 727; X, 146; (*c*) a mist on the river Ismenus exuding from the spirits of dead bodies, *Th.* IX, 433 (cf. *umentes nebulas*, IX, 454); (*d*) a distant haze, *Th.* III, 498 *immensi fruitur caligine mundi* (where St. is perhaps also thinking of the rotation of the universe); IV, 28 *magni caligo maris*; (*e*) the 'vapours' of divination, *Ach.* I, 521; (*f*) metaphorically of death and war, *Th.* V, 197; VIII, 502; (*g*) physical dizziness, *Th.* VI, 510; (*h*) mental dizziness, *Th.* X, 735; *Silv.* II, 2, 138; V, 5, 52. Here the sense is not quite clear: there is surely, with a swift river, no question of a distant haze, as the Thesaurus renders; so that physical dizziness caused by the current (*fuga* somewhat as in I, 236, cf. Val. Fl. IV, 656f. *fuga ponti obvia*) may be meant.

150 minari. Historic inf.

152 abi. This contraction (for *abii*) is not found elsewhere in the 1st pers. sing.

agebat. 'Drove me on.'

154 Oebalios. 'Spartan' (see n. to I, 20), as in *Silv.* V, 3, 53; there is probably no reference to Hyacinthus (in Mozley's note to *Silv.* V, 3, 53 wrongly called

Narcissus), killed accidentally with a discus by Apollo. Pind. *Isthm.* I, 25 mentions Castor and Pollux as having excelled at discus-throwing.

in nubila condere. The same phrase in *Th.* VI, 681, a passage useful for our knowledge of the sport. By an exaggeration the athlete is said to bury the discus deep into the midst of the clouds; cf. the use of *condo* with weapons plunged into the body (Virg. *Aen.* IX, 347f., etc.). Elsewhere St. speaks of the discus splitting the clouds: *Silv.* III, 1, 155f.; V, 3, 53.

155 liquidam...palen. Referring to the oiled bodies of wrestlers (*liquidam* = 'sleek'), as *Th.* VI, 830 *uncta pale*: these two occurrences only in St., who is the first to use the word. His innovations in vocabulary are listed by M. Schamberger, *De P.P.S. verborum novatore*, ch. I; cf. n. to I, 357f.

nodare. *Nodus* is a firm hold or lock in wrestling: Virg. *Aen.* VIII, 260 (*Cacum*) *corripit in nodum complexus*; *Th.* VI, 890f. *evadere nodos...parantem*, of Agylleus wrestling against Tydeus. From this St. has the verb *nodare* transitive here and in *Silv.* III, 1, 157 *manu Libycas nodare palaestras*, meaning to turn one's wrestling into a series of *nodi*. We may compare also *Th.* IX, 277 (*Capetum*) *sorbebat rapidus nodato gurgite vertex*, where the reading of QN, *nodato*, is rightly accepted by editors.

spargere caestus. So *bracchia...spargat*, Val. Fl. I, 421f.

157f. Achilles' musical skill has already been referred to in I, 118, 187ff.; cf. Hom. *Il.* IX, 185-9.

priscos...virum...honores. The epithet is transferred (=*priscorum*), as in Cat. LXIV, 50 *priscis hominum variata figuris.*

159 auxiliantia morbis. *Silv.* V, 1, 159f. *ars operosa medentum auxiliata malis.* For Chiron's medical skill see n. to I, 117.

160ff. Note the change of sequence in the verbs dependent upon *edocuit*; cf. Virg. *Aen.* I, 297ff. (after a historic pres.).

hiantia vulnera. *Silv.* II, 1, 4 *vulnus hiat*; used several times in the medical writings of Celsus, as is also *cohibeo* (l. 162).

claudat. C. Brakman in *Mnemosyne*, 2nd ser. LVII, 256 states that St. prefers *cludo* to *claudo*. The MS. figures, however, are: *claudo* (*clausus*), 27; *cludo*, 10 (in several places a few MSS. have *claudo*); form doubtful, 7; reading doubtful, 1 (*Silv.* V, 3, 140).

163 sub pectore fixit. Sil. VII, 554. For Chiron as a lawgiver see Kürschner, *op. cit.* p. 31.

165 biformes. *Th.* I, 457f. *bimembres Centauros.*

166 elementa. See n. on l. 87 above.

167 meminisse iuvat. Virg. *Aen.* I, 203.

scit cetera mater. This ending to Achilles' narrative seems somewhat inappropriate, since Ulysses and Diomede would hardly be helped by being referred to Thetis; perhaps Achilles is preferring to keep silence about his stay in Scyros, for which his mother was responsible. It is also abrupt, but in this respect similar to Parthenopaeus' account in *Th.* IX, 799f. *et—quid plura loquar? ferrum mea semper et arcus mater habet....*

INDEX

References other than numbers in brackets are to pages. Numbers in brackets refer to notes on lines of the text.
The orthography is not necessarily the same as that of the text, which is based mainly on the orthography of the Puteaneus.
I and *J* are treated as one letter.

INDEX